D0706090

For the City & the World
CONVERSATIONS IN CATHOLIC STUDIES AND SOCIAL THOUGHT

Joan and Ralph Lane Center for Catholic Studies
and Social Thought Lectures 2005-2010
University of San Francisco
Association of Jesuit University Presses
San Francisco, CA
2010

Table of Contents

Conversations in Catholic Social Thought

Lectures by the Anna and Joseph Lo Schiavo Chairs in Catholic Studies and Social Thought

To Joan and Ralph
for their vision,
and their dedication to
the Catholic intellectual tradition.

Acknowledgments

This volume has been brought together to mark the 5th anniversary of the founding of the Joan and Ralph Lane Center for Catholic Studies and Social Thought at the University of San Francisco (USF). This selection represents a sampling of some of the many fine programs the Lane Center at USF has produced during the last five years.

Many thanks are due to the speakers who have joined us here at USF and who have shared their thoughts, insights, wisdom and research with the Lane Center. In particular we thank those authors who have given us permission to use their work for this collection.

We would also like to thank Rev. Stephen Privett, S.J., president of the University of San Francisco, for his support of the Lane Center from its initial development. Special thanks to Jennifer Turpin, former Dean of the College of Arts and Sciences and now the Provost and Academic Vice President at USF, for her vision and encouragement.

Additionally, other important contributions to this collection have been made by Eugene Vinluan-Pagal of the USF Office of Publications for his design work, Keith Powell, a student in the Master's of Fine Arts in Creative Writing program at USF, for his assistance. And, Teresa Walsh, a childhood neighbor of the Lanes in San Francisco, who worked as copyeditor for this project.

Above all we would like to acknowledge Joan and Ralph Lane, dedicated Catholics committed to the intersection of Catholic social thought and contemporary social issues, whose vision sparked the creation of the Lane Center. The Lane Center now celebrates five years of dialog between contemporary culture and the Catholic tradition because of their generous support.

Foreword
Dr. Jennifer E. Turpin

Ralph Lane was a thinking man, a lifelong teacher and student, who cared profoundly about the real exchange of ideas and fearlessly confronted what it means to be fully human in a complex and conflicted world. Ralph and his wife Joan dedicated their lives to justice and peace, and to the mission of the University of San Francisco. We have been fortunate benefactors of their passion and commitment to these ideals.

Ralph was one of those few teachers who became a legend. Generations of students were exposed to social theory and practice through their classes with Ralph, who pioneered community engagement as a teaching method. Ralph recognized early on that San Francisco was an ideal social laboratory, which students could not only study but also one they could affect for the good. Ralph's Catholic faith and his dedication to Catholic social teachings informed not just how he taught and what he wrote about, but who he was in relation to others and to the community. He always strove to achieve the common good and to serve those with the least social power. He and Joan supported others in their endeavors to do the same, and over the years they sponsored conferences on important social issues, supported the journal *Peace Review: A Journal of Social Justice*, and helped to found the Leo T. McCarthy Center for Public Service and the Common Good.

Five years ago, shortly before Ralph passed away, Joan and Ralph established the Joan and Ralph Lane Center for Catholic Studies and Social Thought at USF. The Center is dedicated to advancing the Catholic intellectual tradition with a focus on Catholic social thought throughout the Church and the world. Since its inception, Director Mike Duffy, Associate Director Julia Dowd and our distinguished Lo Schiavo Chairs, Rev. Stephen Schloesser, S.J. Most Rev. Robert McElroy, and currently Rev. James Stormes, S.J. have worked tirelessly to continue Ralph's legacy, promoting serious engagement with the pressing issues of our times through a host of events, publications, and academic programs.

This volume brings together some of the best lectures the Center has sponsored over the years. Ralph would have been proud to see this impressive collection, a manifestation of his lifelong vision and passion.

Dr. Jennifer E. Turpin Provost and Vice President of Academic Affairs, University of San Francisco

Introduction
Rev. John A. Coleman, S.J.

Sustaining a Noble Tradition, Encountering Cultural Change, Engendering Social Activists to Change the World

I t is a high honor and pleasure for me to pen the introduction to this splendid and very illuminating (several even ground-breaking) set of essays for the book, *Conversations in Catholic Studies and Social Thought,* published by the Joan and Ralph Lane Center for Catholic Studies and Social Thought at the University of San Francisco. I was privileged, on October 12, 2004, to deliver the inaugural lecture for the Lane Center, which was subsequently published as "Globalization as a Challenge to Catholic Social Thought."[1] I assumed, in that introductory lecture for the Lane Center, that Catholic Social Thought, as the title of this chapter suggests, is both a noble tradition to be sustained but also one that needs to address wide-spread cultural shifts (always the case but, in that lecture's instance, by reason of major changes due to new conditions of globalization) and find ways to foster and form social activists who could change the world to a new, more humane, configuration (more respectful of human dignity, solidarity, the common good, care for creation). I take it that a similar goal lies behind the Lane Center.

I am also grateful to write this introduction as a partial tribute to Joan and Ralph Lane Jr., both of whom I first met almost fifty years ago, in 1961. I was a fledgling high school teacher, teaching sociology to high school seniors at the Jesuit Saint Ignatius High School and sought the advice of the senior and more experienced Ralph Lane Jr. who was a professor of sociology at the University of San Francisco. During those early years of the 1960s, I became aware that Ralph had done his doctoral studies under the distinguished Jesuit sociologist, Joseph Fitzpatrick S.J., at Fordham University. Fitzpatrick was not only a first-rate sociologist but, himself, a staunch advocate of Catholic social thought, a devotee of the labor priests in Catholicism and a champion of the newly immigrant Puerto Ricans.[2] Like Fitzpatrick, Ralph Lane Jr. combined careful scholarship with social advocacy. In the early 1960s he was a member of an incipient Catholic Inter-Racial Council in San Francisco, which combated the still regnant restrictive covenants in house buying. He also, of course, pioneered the Student Western Addition Project at the University of San Francisco, which involved student placements to enhance learning by social experience and to further justice for African Americans living in the, then, Western Addition. Later, in the 1960s, Ralph and I collaborated with

Professor Jack Curtis on a textbook in sociology, *Sociology: An Introduction.*[3] Ralph contributed the chapters on the political system and the economic system. My close friendship with Ralph and Joan dated especially from that time. They attended my ordination to the priesthood in 1967.

Over the years, in lovely dinners either at the Lanes or in the Jesuit Community, I came to see and appreciate Ralph and Joan's deep commitment to issues of justice. When they came into a substantial inheritance and founded the Lane Family Foundation, they helped to fund *Peace Review* at the University of San Francisco and a "Ralph Lane Jr. Peace and Justice" essay contest. They gave money to church-based community organizations helping ordinary people take control over their neighborhoods to rid them of crime or to obtain needed police support, charter schools or clinics. They also funded university scholarships for Hispanic young women at Watsonville High School, which Joan Lane had attended.

In 1990, Ralph approached me to help organize, with him and Sister Margaret Cafferty, a truly exciting national conference, held in San Francisco under the aegis of the University of San Francisco, to celebrate, bring forward and correct, where necessary, Catholic Social Teaching. The hundredth anniversary of the issuance of *Rerum Novarum*—the great labor encyclical of Pope Leo XIII—approached, in 1991. We all agreed that it was important, in that conference, to bring together a cast of actors who represented the whole church: bishops (not just as outside magisterial teachers but listeners as well), acclaimed academics in theology, economics and related social science fields, and activist practitioners. We included Ernie Cortes, from The Industrial Area Foundation and the main organizer of San Antonio C.O.P.S. (Communities Organized for Public Service), which had turned around the police and the civil society in San Antonio, Texas. We also included Caryl Coston, O.P., one of the founders of Network, a national advocacy group in Washington, D.C. lobbying for legislative change for the poor, and Mary Evelyn Jegen, S.N.D, a vice-president of Pax Christi U.S.A., a peace group. We included, as well, thoughtful executives of large for-profit companies, known for their ethics and responsibility and, also, prominent labor leaders. The idea was a dialogue to further a tradition, confront any of its weak spots and to engender new imagination about how to bring forward the tradition of Catholic social thought.

Ralph and Joan Lane Jr., who funded this large conference of some 100 participants, sought total anonymity about their funding role. When I edited the essays from this conference in a book, *One Hundred Years of Catholic Social Thought: Celebration and Challenge,* I may have blown Ralph and Joan's desire for anonymity by dedicating the book to " Ralph Lane Jr., colleague and friend, without whose generosity this book could never have appeared."[4] The conference and book looked for ways to bring forward, in changed cultural, political and economic circumstances, the richness of Catholic social thought. It included sections on work, family and peace. One essay dealt with and was titled, *"Women's Ways of Working;"* a correlative essay by the distinguished economist, Robert Kuttner, treated the issues of worker rights and responsibilities in a changed competitive context. Six essays dealt, in some depth, with the issues of war and peace, pluralism, pacifism and the conditions for peace in the new international system. The essays on family and sexuality broached, gingerly but forthrightly, the way Catholic social teaching was inductive, empirically oriented (using social science data), tentative, open to change and collaborative. Sexual ethics, on the contrary, was all too often deductive, non-tentative, authoritarian, non-collaborative, heavily reliant on past statements.[5]

When Ralph retired as a distinguished Professor and good citizen at the University of San Francisco in 1988, he summoned me to pick any of his sociology books I might want to take away. From that time on, Ralph and I would meet, minimally monthly, for lunch at a small restaurant at Fourth and Market in San Francisco. He liked to joke that, when he retired, Joan told him that she had married him for life but not necessarily for lunch, so he needed to find some new outlet. He did so by enrolling in creative writing courses at San Mateo Community College. Over time, Ralph published two books of poetry. In one of them, entitled *Do I Grow Old: First Poems,* Ralph lingers mightily over that verb "grow"—it is not the being older but the growing that counts.

In our monthly luncheons, Ralph would often read one of his most recent poems or discuss possible projects for the Lane Foundation (including, eventually, the Joan and Ralph Lane Jr. Center for Catholic Studies and Social Thought). Ralph and Joan provided financial support for the Leo T. McCarthy Center for Public Service and the Common Good. The last term in that Center's title, lifted from Catholic social thought but, alas, rather passé really, at present, in American parlance, caught Ralph's attention. Being a long-time pal of Leo McCarthy, former Lieutenant Governor of California and Speaker of the Assembly, did not hurt. For a while, Ralph continued the earlier pattern of the "One Hundred Years of Catholic Social Thought" conference. Joan and Ralph sponsored a one-off conference on "Re-discovering Justice: Awakening World Faiths to Address World Issues," a celebration of the fiftieth Anniversary of the founding of the United Nations in San Francisco, which brought to the city the Nobel Peace Laureate Bishop Desmond Tutu— and also eventuated in a book.[6] Another notable conference sponsored by the Lanes in the late 1990's focused on issues of women's work and challenges in a changed economy and family situation.

But as Ralph and I met monthly and talked about his plans, it became clear that he envisioned a more permanent, institutional home for his concerns for addressing social justice issues, Catholic social thought, the animation of new activists and cultural shifts on the horizon. At the end of our luncheon sessions, Ralph would often go to confession to me at the corner of Fifth and Market Streets. I used to kid him that, one day, I would actually wear a stole and alb while absolving him of his peccadilloes. He laughed and said: "It is San Francisco. Who would take any notice?" I am actually referenced in one poem in Ralph's volume, "Do I Grow Old?" *Ankling up Market Street to the corner of 4th with my Jesuit friend after my block long recital of petty faults, he reassures me all was forgiven before confessed. God knows and loves the manner we were made.* In the beginning lines of that poem, entitled "Seeking," Ralph claims: *I'm not seeking God's grandeur in dappled things nor gaping at glaciers, canyons deep down nor awed by spewing volcanoes nor seeing predator swans float gracefully by realizing underneath jackals prevail. Turning instead to fellow humans fighting frailties, … encouraging others to feel beloved.*[7]

In another poem (my favorite in that volume), Ralph grouses: *I'll never be a mystic—I know that is not for me because I'm stuck here working with those I love.*[8] In one, addressed to me I presume, called "Prayer: Are You listening John C?" Ralph ends with a prayer: *O God, come into this mess!*[9] That pregnant and poignant prayer, so akin to the incarnation and to Ignatian concerns about finding God in all things, even in the mess of politics, shaky peace, economic downturns, and ecological threats, can serve as a veritable leitmotif for the Lane Center's future work. Ralph, the poet, was always also Ralph the seeker, working for a more humane, just world of dignity and flourishing. He knew that addressing societal injustices was often a messy, if God-blessed, activity.

Turning to this splendid collection of essays, I asked myself how Ralph might see and read those which were delivered after his death in 2007. I remember his vivid enthusiasm about Stephen Schloesser's essay on Jesuit hybrids. Ralph knew that confronting cultural change took imagination, depended on literature and art and inculturation as much as on high thought. Ralph had not sat, during a sabbatical in Cuernavaca, Mexico, under the feet of the renowned social philosopher Ivan Illich in vain. Illich called for a deep renewal of traditional roots and an equal turn to respect for cultural wisdom, as found in stories, relationships and a humane technology.[10]

What strikes me in this volume is how it touches many of the earlier themes found in *One Hundred Years of Catholic Social Thought.* It includes in its dialogue the voice of bishops: Archbishop George Niederauer's essay on the fiction of Flannery O'Connor and Bishop Robert McElroy's application of just-war theory to the Iraq War. It confronts Catholic Social Thought with an appraisal that takes a feminist critique into account. It draws upon the social-activist work of Kurt Denk in working with prisoners and for restorative justice. It addresses the justice in Catholic thinking about sexuality (James Alison's essay on Queer Perspectives) and brings forth, drawing on theologians and social scientists, new perspectives on how culture shifts demand attention from Catholic social thought (the essays of James Stormes and Thomas Massaro). It tries to link Catholic social thought to bio-ethics (the chapters by Albert Jonson and Maura Ryan).

Reading this volume, I was reminded of the words of the United States' Catholic bishops, in a pastoral written to commemorate the hundredth anniversary of *Rerum Novarum,* which can also serve as an on-going challenge to the Lane Center's future:

Across this country and around the world, the church's social ministry is a story of growing vitality and strength, of remarkable compassion, courage and creativity. It is the everyday reality of providing homeless and hungry people decent shelter and needed help, of giving pregnant women and their unborn children life-giving alternatives, of offering refugees welcome and so much more. It is believers advocating in the public arena for human life wherever it is threatened, for the rights of workers and for economic justice, for peace and freedom around the world and for "liberty and justice" for all here at home. It is empowering and helping poor and vulnerable people realize their dignity in inner cities, rural communities and in lands far away. It is the everyday commitment and tradition of countless people, parishes and programs and of local networks and national structures—a tradition of caring service, effective advocacy and creative action. At the heart of this commitment is a set of principles, a body of thought and a call to action called Catholic social teaching.[11]

As the Lane Center celebrates its first half-decade of achievements and looks to the future, it could do worse than make its own that verb in Ralph Lane's title for his first book of poems. As the Lane Center matures, it can continually ask itself "do I grow" as I get older? My last lunch with Ralph Lane Jr. was in September 2007, just weeks before I left to go teach for a semester at Fu-Jen University in Taipei and also just weeks before Ralph died. Re-reading this fine collection of essays made me mindful that barely a month goes by without my, wistfully, wishing I could once again connect with wry and ever-witty Ralph over some new poem and his eager plans for the flourishing of the Lane Center.

Rev. John A. Coleman, S.J. Associate Pastor of St. Ignatius Chuch, San Francisco

Notes:

1. The lecture was published as " Globalization as a Challenge to Catholic Social Thought" in *Origins*, vol. 34, no. 20, October 28, 2004, pp. 322-328. It was republished (with footnote references) in John A. Coleman S.J., ed., *Christian Political Ethics* (Princeton, New Jersey: Princeton University Press, 2007, pp. 170-188.

2. Joseph Fitzpatrick, *Puerto Rican Americans* (Englewood Cliffs, New Jersey: Prentice-Hall, 1987).

3. Jack Curtis, John A. Coleman and Ralph Lane, *Sociology: An Introduction* (Milwaukee, Wisconsin, Bruce Publishing Company, 1967.)

4. John A. Coleman S.J., ed., *One Hundred Years of Catholic Social Thought: Celebration and Challenge* (Maryknoll, New York: Orbis Press, 1991). The book ran through two editions and was in print for well over a decade. The title chosen, rather self-consciously, talked (because of its changeable nature due to changed circumstances, even given fixed core principles) of Catholic social "thought" rather than "teaching." The book also insisted that practitioners, and not just magisterial teachers, contributed mightily to the development of Catholic social thought.

5. See Richard McCormick S.J., " Human Sexuality: Toward a Consistent Ethical Method" in Coleman, *One Hundred Years of Catholic Social Thought* pp. 189-197.

6. Joseph Angilella and Alan Ziaka, *Re-Discovering Justice: Awakening World Faiths to Address World Issues* (San Francisco: University of San Francisco Press, 1999).

7. Ralph Lane Jr., *Do I Grow Old? First Poems*, 2003 p. 40.

8. Lane, *Do I Grow Old?* p.37

9. Lane, *Do I Grow Old?* p. 36

10. Ivan Illich, *Tools for Conviviality* (New York: Harper and Row, 1973).

11. United States Catholic Bishops, *A Century of Social Teaching: A Common Heritage, a Continuing Challenge* (Washington, D.C.: United States Catholic Conference, 1990).

A Feminist Appraisal of Catholic Social Thought

Dr. Kristin A. Heyer

Assistant Professor of Religious Studies, Santa Clara University.
Dr. Heyer taught at the Department of Theological Studies at Loyola Marymount University from 2003-2009.

CATHOLIC SOCIAL CONCERNS LECTURE SERIES I November 9, 2007

One year ago Bob Herbert wrote a chilling op-ed in the *New York Times*. He began by drawing our attention to the shootings at the Amish schoolhouse in Nickel Mines, Pennsylvania[1] and the way in which girls were singled out by the shooter. Herbert pondered the lack of outrage at that fact, concluding that we have become so accustomed to living in a society saturated with misogyny that violence against females is more or less to be expected. He went on, providing examples ranging from the fact that a girl or woman is sexually assaulted every few minutes in the U.S, to the media's relentless ten-year replay of Jon Benet Ramsey footage, to gangsta rap, and charged that "the disrespectful, degrading, contemptuous treatment of women is so pervasive and so mainstream that it has just about lost its ability to shock."[2] We are similarly horrified by recent characterizations of the widespread and brutal sexual violence in the Congo as *almost normal*, a violence that is accomplished with utter impunity and that is escalating. Other global examples of women's dehumanization abound: half of all women live on less than $2 a day, illiteracy rates among women are nearly 50% higher than among men in many countries, and inheritance laws and criminal statutes make it easy for men to take advantage of women.[3]

Meanwhile, the term "feminism" has become a dirty word. A recent *Newsweek* poll indicates 29% of American women identify themselves as feminists. My own experience over recent decades, although anecdotal, bears out a backlash against the women's movement: I witnessed as Rush Limbaugh's "feminazi" epithet took hold among my high school peers. When my husband was in college at a Jesuit university about 15 years ago, he was the sole student to raise his hand in his honors seminar when the students were asked who would consider themselves feminists. Today, I can only characterize my own students as hesitant to embrace the label (at best), and one women's studies student confessed that her friends frequently ask why she minored in men hating. Even while Hillary Clinton advances as the first female front-runner for a presidential nomination in history, a consumer-driven culture has shifted feminist discussion from talk of liberation to talk of self-improvement, as Susan Faludi's latest book argues, where purchasing replaces protests, an "ersatz feminism where you're free to buy whatever push-up bra you want."[4] The signs of the time are grim for women on a host of levels.

Grounded in the Genesis' account of all humans' creation in *imago Dei* and Jesus' prophetic praxis in relationship to women,[5] Catholic teaching

promotes the role of women in the family but also has increasingly emphasized their valuable contributions in public life. While feminists have rightly
critiqued the inadequacy of some traditional documents on the nature and
role of women, several Episcopal and papal statements have been prophetic in
their protest against whatever offends the dignity of women. Whereas many
inside and outside the church cast feminism and Catholicism as incompatible
ideologies,[6] both approaches affirm equal human dignity, seek justice for the
vulnerable and liberation for the oppressed. A feminist concern for women's
experience *as disadvantaged* and for their *equal social power* both reflects and
challenges Catholic social thought. That said, Catholic feminism per se entails
neither masculinization nor heresy. Catholic feminism takes up the meaning
of the Gospel and God's action in human lives in light of women's lived experience, asking what the tradition does to and for women.[7] This question helps
orient my appraisal today.

   While we encounter significant consonance between Catholic social
thought and feminism, we also encounter an inadequate response that
downplays support for women in public and domestic spheres alike and
that focuses on behaviors devoid of a social context. Rather than historically
assessing the documentary heritage, I would like to focus on the scope and
mode of contemporary Catholic social witness in light of three concerns:
1) the substance of women's issues remains too narrowly construed; 2) a
methodology that shortchanges integration of issues and consultation is inadequate; and 3) a *separate but equal* complementarity hinders women's ability to
flourish in social roles. While my accent here is on a feminist critique, I will
also highlight global, national and local initiatives embodying Catholic social
thought that offer hope for women's well being.

Danger Posed by Narrowly Construing "Women's Issues"

In its emphasis and public witness, Catholic social thought narrowly construes
women's issues, limiting them to what is referred to as *beltway issues*. This
narrow construal is incomplete and impedes the development of an adequate
answer to the wide-scale suffering women face. This constricted focus on
reproductive matters misses the other experiences by women that constitute
violations of dignity and justice. Conversely, a generic construal of justice issues
without attention to gendered elements is also dangerously inadequate. In
contrast to the church's public voice on issues like abortion or same-sex marriage,
we seldom find the magisterium emphasizing physical or sexual violence
against women or the dehumanizing conditions limiting women in many parts
of the world. Given these realities, a Catholic witness that remains blind to the
full experience of women not only risks inattentiveness to the *anawim*, but also
risks complicity.

Women cultivate 60-80% of food in developing countries yet own less than 1% of the land.[8] Recent reports also indicate that, as of 2005, approximately 80% of lay ecclesial ministers in the U.S. were women, a rapid feminization of pastoral leadership in the Catholic Church.[9] We might say that in the fields, as in the church, women perform the majority of work yet do not enjoy equal power or rights. John Allen recently compared this trend to an AFL-CIO (2007) study that documents the decline in average wages and social prestige attached to job categories that come to be dominated by women. The study indicated that employment categories in which women occupy 70% or more of the jobs pay one third less than comparable jobs more likely to be held by men. In the U.S., this amounts to a $114 billion loss for men and women in predominantly female jobs. Allen rightly warns, "For a church that supports a *just wage* in broader society, making sure its own employees are not the object of gender-based discrimination in wages will be an on-going challenge."[10] Generic calls for just wages without adequate incorporation of gendered analyses do not challenge either glass or stained-glass ceilings.

HIV/AIDS is a particularly urgent and deadly issue for women, and it's a matter that reaches beyond typical women's issues. In July of this year UNAIDS' Director, Undersecretary General of the United Nations, Peter Piot, identified the most significant development in the AIDS epidemic as "its growing feminization." A brief overview of this trend exemplifies the dangers inherent in a narrow construal of women's issues as well as an inattention to the social contexts that impact women's lives. A feminist emphasis on the social context of ethics reminds us that AIDS is a sexual and a social issue and that these two dimensions are inseparable.[11]

Nigerian theologian, Teresa Okure, has argued that two viruses more dangerous than HIV enable its rapid spread among societies' most vulnerable: sexism and global poverty. Together they help explain the alarming reality that, in many countries of the developing world, the most important risk factor for HIV infection is being a married woman.[12] In late 2006 UNAIDS reported that 39.5 million adults and children were living with AIDS, with 15-24 year-old married women in Sub-Saharan Africa at greatest risk for HIV. These are women who practice abstinence and fidelity but whose husbands do not. A growing number of medical and moral experts, including soon-to-be Lane Center scholar-in-residence, James Keenan, join Okure in underscoring how gender inequality and poverty become breeding grounds for HIV and AIDS.

In the United States, women also account for a growing share of new HIV and AIDS cases: in 1985 women represented 8% of AIDS diagnoses, by 2005 they accounted for 27%. Women of color are disproportionately affected: African American women comprise 12% of the population but account for 66% of estimated AIDS cases among women (or 23 times the rate for white women), and they account for the highest number of HIV-related deaths. Studies indicate women with HIV/AIDS are disproportionately low-income (nearly two-thirds had annual incomes below $10,000 compared to 41% of men) and are more likely to postpone care than men.[13] Whether in South African villages, the streets of New Delhi or dorm rooms in San Francisco, women commonly experience a subordination and lack of autonomy that diminishes control of their own bodies, and this increases the threat of behavior that leads to infection. In the U.S. about half of new HIV infections occur in individuals aged twenty-five or younger, and, while young women on college campuses are often educated about risk prevention, they remain unlikely to say "no" to their partners or insist their partners use a reliable barrier. In a study across Catholic campuses, medical practitioners reported that the root cause of young women's particular vulnerability lay in "an inability to put legitimate concerns for the health and well being of both self and partner before the physical or emotional needs of the partner."[14] These young women's culturally conditioned desire to please threatens their lives.

Around the world, the grip of sexual double standards, harmful concepts of masculinity and patriarchal religions combine to jeopardize women's health and well being. In addition to a lack of genuine autonomy, women's vulnerability to HIV is directly linked to contexts marked by poverty and violence. Catholic social thought has prophetically addressed social sin in recent decades, but too rarely offers sustained critiques of sexism and how it intersects with other unjust structures to facilitate the spread of HIV/AIDS. Medical anthropologist Paul Farmer argues that AIDS has remained a "disease of men" in the minds of most because "the majority of women with AIDS had been robbed of their voices long before HIV appeared to further complicate their lives. In settings of entrenched elitism, they have been poor. In settings of entrenched racism, they have been women of color. In settings of entrenched sexism, they have been, of course, women." He is convinced that economic, political and cultural forces significantly shape the dynamics of HIV transmission.[15]

An individualistic paradigm, which places undue emphasis on personal behavior, is an inadequate response to HIV/AIDS as it affects women. Most women with AIDS do not have multiple sexual partners or use IV drugs, and, since the majority of married women infected with HIV had no other partner other than their husbands, exhorting fidelity and monogamy does not protect women from infection. In fact, as Margaret Farley aptly suggests, a simple reiteration of moral rules for sexual behavior sometimes serves to heighten the shame and stigma associated with AIDS and to promote mistaken moral judgments of individuals and groups, while ignoring the genuine requirements of justice and truth in sexual relationships.[16] Punitive images of women as purveyors of infection (mothers who contaminate offspring or prostitutes) remain far more common than images of the social contexts—the homelessness, barriers to health care, absence of jobs or child care—that conspire to increase HIV/AIDS among women. Alongside the negative images of women, it is the significance given to personal choice alone that holds sway.[17] As Farmer points out, the examples of young Haitian women driven into nonvoluntary sexual unions by abject poverty, or the fact that half of Bombay's sex workers are recruited through trickery or abduction, "call[s] into question facile notions of 'consensual sex.'"[18] He rightly laments, "There is something unfair about using personal agency as a basis for assigning blame while simultaneously denying those blamed the opportunity to exert agency in their lives."[19]

The U.S. Catholic Conference of Bishops (USCCB) issued *Called to Compassion and Responsibility* in 1989 (which is their most recent response to the HIV/AIDS crisis). In it, personal vices like self-abusive behavior (drug use) and sexual promiscuity top their list of obstacles to HIV prevention. The bishops discuss gender complementarity to underscore *Humanae Vitae's* teaching and highlight the virtues of sexual integrity and chastity, but the only social sin they address is the influence of a culture of self-gratification. By contrast, Piot has called for combating AIDS by embracing gender equality, allocating more seats for women at decision-making tables, accepting zero tolerance for gender-based violence, and improving female-specific HIV prevention methods and gender equality in treatment access. The bishops' statement was written in the late 1980s, but to this day it is difficult to locate information about AIDS on the USCCB website. HIV/AIDS is not listed as a priority issue with regard to life or social justice under domestic or international topics; instead, HIV/AIDS materials are found under Hispanic Affairs and the Secretariat for African American Catholics. This fall the National Catholic AIDS Network, the only national organization devoted exclusively to helping the Catholic Church respond to the pandemic, shut down.

I want to acknowledge significant signs of hope regarding AIDS and Catholic social action; for one, the Catholic Church remains one of the largest providers of services to those affected by HIV/AIDS. Catholic Relief Services' AIDS programming reaches 50 countries across Africa and the hardest-hit regions of Asia and Latin America. Other examples include several collaborative projects that focus on women in particular, such as Yale Divinity School's *Women's Initiative*, which partners African women theologians with scholars at Yale to address intersections of gender, faith and HIV/AIDS in the service of women's empowerment. Collaborating with the Circle of Concerned African Women Theologians, the group focuses the theological resources of international faith communities on transforming traditional attitudes about sexuality and the status of women, as well as effective responses by women to HIV/AIDS in Africa.

Methodology: Feminist Critiques Reflect Catholic Social Values

Just as a narrow construal of women's issues and the isolation of sexual issues from social analysis impedes Catholic witness, a methodology that shortchanges integration across issues and consultation remains inadequate for addressing complex issues. Moreover, a feminist approach that enables wide participation and models just embodiment, reflects the very values espoused by Catholic social tradition itself. As Maria Riley and Nancy Sylvester put it, "The feminist insight, 'all is connected,' reveals the integral nature of the human experience, and therefore, of justice and peace."[20] While the Catholic tradition addresses a wide range of social issues in light of the reach of its communitarian personalism, too often it proceeds in a way that isolates issues from each other and their social context, rather than holistically attending to relational patterns and social contexts. The regrettable opposition of life and dignity issues in Catholic social witness sheds light upon this methodological shortcoming.

Next week, when the U.S. bishops convene in Baltimore, they will vote on a new version of the conference's political responsibility document, which attempts to address the relationships among social issues more pointedly. The draft document says, "A consistent ethic of life neither treats all issues as morally equivalent nor reduces Catholic teaching to one or two issues." The highly publicized *wafer watch* and the proliferation of voter guides during the last election encouraged narrow litmus tests, in contrast to an approach steeped in the interrelatedness of a range of issues. Certainly the relative moral weight of fundamental life issues, or *which bricks are indispensable to a building's foundation*, as Archbishop Chaput of Denver recently put it, will remain a point of contention in the bishops' meeting and the election year to follow.

The seamless garment heritage and the Congregation for the Doctrine of the Faith affirm the integral unity of the faith; nonetheless, the U.S. church, through its relative silence in the face of certain bishops' communion sanctions or narrow-shaming rhetoric, has de facto isolated issues and made them non-negotiable. Emphasizing the interrelatedness of life and justice issues would enhance Catholic integrity and credibility. For example, more explicitly linking opposition to abortion to concrete policy issues, such as prenatal care, infant feeding programs, health care and education would help Catholics guard against partisanship and attend to the full range of issues on which the tradition touches. Likewise a Catholic commitment to the oft-cited *culture of life*, challenges American values, not only with respect to abortion or euthanasia, but also with respect to the Iraq war, torture and immigration.[21]

The Catholic tradition's underdevelopment with regard to issues facing women and families, in concert with its antiabortion advocacy, fails to do justice to its rich moral vision. We can see this particularly with regard to abortion. Many have drawn attention to the strong correlation of abortion rates with poverty, and this underscores the urgency of connecting life with social justice. Lisa Sowle Cahill convincingly argues, "The greatest obstacle to wider appreciation of the Catholic Church's 'pro-life' message on abortion is its too-frequent silence on women's economic and political rights, as well as women's rights in the family, marriage, and maternity." All of these rights are affirmed in recent Catholic social teaching—Pope John Paul II linked relevant social sins to abortion in his 1995 *Letter to Women*—yet the church's pro-life advocacy is typically characterized by a one-sided emphasis on the rights of the unborn. Cahill also points to the recent call by the Vatican urging Catholics to cease support for Amnesty International (AI) (because of recent AI policy changes) as indicative of the church's tendency to "downplay its ecclesial, social and political support for women, and the full equality of women," thereby undermining "its own message that the welfare of women and children is important."[22] She rightly points out that, given "realities such as gang-rape of women in war and frequent ostracization of women who have been sexually violated," the Vatican's response that abortion is murder, that it kills an innocent child and that it cannot be justified even in cases of rape was "hardly an effective way to communicate the fullness of the 'gospel of life.'"[23]

By contrast, several prophetic Catholic politicians, who find themselves in an unenviable position on both sides of the aisle, have pushed their parties to comprehensively address this volatile issue. Bob Casey Jr., from Pennsylvania, recently took both parties to task for their inadequate positions,

> We can't realistically expect to tackle the difficult question of abortion without embracing the *radical solidarity* with women who face a pregnancy that Pope John Paul II spoke of many years ago. If we are going to be pro-life, we cannot say we are against abortion of unborn children and then let our children suffer in degraded inner-city schools and broken homes. We can't claim to be pro-life at the same time as we are cutting support for Medicaid, Head Start, and the WIC program. I believe we need policies that provide maximum feasible protection for the unborn and maximum feasible care and support for pregnant women, mothers and children. The right to life means the right to a life with dignity.[24]

Several recent essays by Nancy Dallavalle and Dan Finn expose the ways in which a rhetorically antiabortion posture frequently serves to further partisan political ends.[25]

In Gregory Kalscheur's article in *America*, where he addresses John Courtney Murray's legacy with regard to morality politics during the last election, he aptly asks, "Have we listened to the voices of women who have felt compelled to make the choice for abortion, and are we working to establish a set of social policies that might provide women with the support needed to make the decision to carry their baby to term?"[26] This key step in building a culture of life brings us to a second feminist methodological critique of Catholic social thought, that of the need to foster broad consultation and participation in the development of this thought.

The U.S. bishops have been praised for the consultation they undertook while drafting the economic and peace pastorals of the 1980s. At that time, they widely and substantially engaged ethicists and public policy experts, laity, priests and religious and then revised subsequent versions in light of comments received from ordinary Catholics. Feminists and others have pointed out how the collegial consultation of a listening hierarchy puts into practice key Catholic social principles, such as human dignity, participation and subsidiarity. Broad consultation has not been the norm, however. As Kathleen Kennedy Townsend reminds us in her recent book *Failing America's Faithful*, the U.S. bishops' unsuccessful women's pastoral in the 1980s and early 90s did not fail due to simple disagreements over which women's issues to address, with American women favoring the need for equal pay and child care, and the Vatican insisting upon contraception, abortion and priesthood; rather, at issue was the consultative nature of the process itself: "The bishops refused to believe they had anything to learn from listening to women." In the words of Bishop Francis P. Murphy, "Bishops are teachers, not learners; truth cannot emerge through consultation." The exclusion of women's voices (or married persons' voices in the case of *Humanae Vitae*) from the development of church teaching fails to attend to the promptings of the Holy Spirit among the people of God and fails to embody the conciliar emphasis on inductively engaging humanity's joys, hopes, fears and anxieties. A top-down method overlooks the context of women's experience at the peril of a truncated analysis, and thereby undermining effectiveness, credibility and even fidelity to the fullness of God's reign. In Rosemary Radford Ruether's words, "Whatever diminishes or denies the full humanity of women must be presumed not to reflect the divine or an authentic relation to the divine, or to reflect the authentic nature of things, or to be the message or work of an authentic redeemer or a community of redemption."[27]

A sign of hope in this regard is how NETWORK, a Catholic social justice lobby, models more consultative processes. Founded in 1971 by religious sisters from a variety of orders, it is the first registered Catholic social justice lobby in the U.S. NETWORK uses Catholic social teaching, the life experience of people who are poor and a feminist perspective as lenses for policy analysis. Its embodiment of Catholic feminism is evidenced in NETWORK's participative decision making and its collaborative management style guided by "power sharing rather than domination." The uniformity of staff salaries (regardless of position, time served or education level) emphasizes the fact that the work that *everyone* does enhances the achievement of the mission. Reminiscent of *Justitia in Mundo's* maxim that those who speak about justice must first be just, NETWORK's efforts to institutionally model its values stands in contrast to the internal challenges sexism, clericalism and authoritarianism can pose to Catholic social witness.

In terms of its inductive approach, every presidential election season NET-

WORK presents priority issues and then polls its membership to determine on which issues they would like to see NETWORK focus its energies. This consultation/affirmation process is important both to ensure NETWORK represents the concerns of its members as well as to live out its commitment to collaboration and participation. The organization also works hard to get input from people who are poor, especially when they draft statements, e.g., in 2000, NETWORK gathered economists, ethicists, and social workers, along with staff and participant representatives from four direct service agencies to generate their *Economic Equity Statement*. Finally, NETWORK values its coalition work, not just strategically but theologically, for they see God at work in other human rights movements. Veteran NETWORK lobbyist Catherine Pinkerton, CSJ, notes NETWORK staffers continually ask themselves how they can find God at work amid pluralism and open themselves up to what may appear as strange or *other* but often resonates with Catholic beliefs. As she puts it, "How do we find God at work and cooperate with that work of God dancing across the world?"[28] Thus theirs is not a triumphalistic imposition of Catholic beliefs, but rather a mutual engagement with an active openness to the presence of God outside of the Church and to learning from the other.

Embodying Support for Women's Social Equality: The Role of the Catholic University

Post John XXIII, the vision of woman in official Catholic social thought has evolved from Pope Leo's portrait of women as a weak creature in need of shelter and control through obedience to her natural master,[29] to an affirmation of her full equality in public spheres; however, an ambivalence toward women's social roles persists. A tension (if not contradiction) exists between Catholic teachings on equal human dignity and affirmations of women's contributions in social and political life, on the one hand, and an emphasis on women's maternal function, familial vocation and gender complementarity, on the other. Even as the self-declared *papa feminista*, John Paul II, supported women's equal access to social, economic and political goods, he emphasized the *feminine genius* of motherhood as women's primary vocation and a dualistic complementarity of the sexes. This anthropological dualism underlies the ways in which women are treated or not treated, and a separate-but-equal status continues to hinder women from flourishing in their work inside and outside the household. What might be the role of Catholic universities in researching, thinking and discussing these issues?

Catholic social thought emphasizes the fact that social involvement is indispensable for full personalization, but the separate spheres ideology has helped sustain not only inequities in the workplace, but also a lack of mutual accountability in household and parenting responsibilities.[30] Feminists have rightly raised the issue of the *second shift*, which disproportionately burdens women who work outside of the home. It has been well documented that in academia, women who have small children face many more obstacles to tenure and promotion than men with small children. While we academics constitute a privileged sector of working women, the example is helpful in seeing ways in which Catholic universities are well positioned to support women by fostering policies and practices that help professors balance work-life demands.

Many women with small children face a time bind and fail to thrive professionally because of intense competition, long hours and on-going demands to publish. Because of these difficulties, many women postpone having children until post-tenure or do not have them at all. The average assistant professor is at least forty years old at the time of tenure, so fertility is an issue, yet having a baby sooner can harm one's chances of earning tenure.[31]

Given the Catholic social tradition's affirmation of women's equal dignity, the significant role of the family in society and the need for institutions to protect both, Catholic universities are particularly obligated to support mothers, as a matter of justice.[32] As the U.S. bishops urged in *Economic Justice for All*, "Efficiency and competition in the marketplace must be moderated by greater concern for the way work schedules and compensation support or threaten the bonds between spouses and between parents and children." To begin with, universities should at least institute transparent and family-friendly leave policies. The lack of clear procedures in many universities generates uncertainty and fear, pits women against women and undermines trust. My own experiences of trying to publish especially quickly so I did not have to choose between starting a family and keeping a tenure-track position, which meant, absent a policy, negotiating one-on-one with my Jesuit dean, and then, given the situation, meeting secretly with other women throughout the college to draft a mission-based rationale and leave policy. All of this took significant time and energy. I am pleased to report I was offered a generous leave, which I have encouraged other women to use as precedent. I am equally pleased to report that different coalitions' work on leave procedures recently culminated in a just policy. Loyola Marymount University's (LMU) leave policy now provides new mothers the option to take one semester off from teaching at full pay or an academic year off at half pay, with no penalty for stopping their tenure clock for one year. I understand Santa Clara extends a paternity leave alongside its maternity leave for one full quarter with pay. Catholic universities also have a good deal to learn from non-Catholic institutions' support for women and families. I recently heard about Stanford's policy that grants employees $10,000 to help cover adoption costs. Beyond just leave policies, offering quality and affordable childcare (for staff, faculty and students alike), considerately scheduling meetings and fostering a supportive environment can dramatically improve women's experience. Absent this ethos, when women do take maternity leave and/or stop the clock, other colleagues may express resentment or demand higher output. Backlash can range from subjective discussions of *fit* in personnel decisions (citing inadequate commitment to the department if family obligations are visible), or implicit understandings that, if women have *extra time*, additional publications should be expected.

Last year my college initiated a working-parent group to help meet various needs, from support and resource sharing to advocacy. Regardless of family status, extra service work and informal advising disproportionately impact women and faculty of color on campuses in ways that remain relatively invisible and detrimental. My own institution recently synthesized the results of multiple listening sessions, anonymous surveys and exit interviews to produce a campus climate report that identified both concerns common to women faculty and faculty of color and strategies for creating positive change. The final report offered proposals geared toward creating a climate in which *all* faculty can thrive, but its recommendations make clear the particular challenges women face in the academy with respect to workload disparities, respectful recognition of work and the need to increase the sense of inclusion, voice and community. It remains to be seen whether the ambitious and promising list of proposals will lead to concrete change, but the overwhelming sense that women were heard and their experiences not taken for granted, is itself a significant step. LMU Dean of Communication and Fine Arts, Barbara Busse, has noted that Catholic universities "must put our own privileged houses in order," since "mutuality is a false promise if we do not ... model in our universities the conditions we wish to create beyond our campuses."[33]

The Jesuits gathered at the 34th General Congregation in 1995 issued a specific decree on *Jesuits and the Situation of Women in Church and Civil Society*, in which they confess a complicity in a form of clericalism that reinforces male domination "with an ostensibly divine sanction." They then identify the first step to conversion as the need to "listen carefully and courageously to the experience of women ... in a spirit of partnership and equality." They add, "There is no substitute for such listening ... lest any action bypass the real concerns of women and ... confirm male condescension and reinforce male dominance."[34] Genuine listening is no simple undertaking, given the reality of women's experiences we have visited briefly here, from global violence to domestic scapegoating to local inequities. As Mary Garvin reflected, in light of the potential role the *Vagina Monologues* might play in realizing this goal of courageous listening (this means listening to all of women's experience, "not sanitized, edited, controlled and conforming to church teaching, not pleasant, not comfortable. But the truth."[35] Heeding the call to be open to women, their issues and experiences comprehensively construed and fully engaged with, Catholic universities can continue to better embody just practices that support women. If a Catholic university is where the church does its thinking, perhaps humane praxis in areas touching on women and families' well being will help author the next wave of Catholic social thought, a wave of thought more adequately reflecting norms of justice and mutuality.

I would like to conclude with the idea that Catholic social thought does not consist merely of what gets authored by popes or emphasized by bishops, but also by what is lived by communities of hope and faith. This year the women-led community empowerment organization from my East Los Angeles parish won the Catholic Campaign for Human Development's prestigious *Sister Margaret Cafferty Development of People Award* for its efforts to secure basic human rights for the people of Boyle Heights. The mothers and grandmothers of *Comunidad en Movimiento* (*Community in Movement*) have courageously and tirelessly taken to the streets and visited council members' offices to secure the safety of their children. Likewise, from one congressional session to the next, NETWORK doesn't just critique the church from a feminist perspective; it enacts Catholic social teaching in its political ministry of justice. Just as our tradition should not narrowly construe women's issues as merely sexual, justice for women, in the fullest sense discussed in this talk, must not be marginalized as the concern of a few, much less as incompatible with the Catholic social mission to safeguard dignity and promote genuine solidarity.

Notes:

1. I wish to express gratitude to Isabel Arrastia for research assistance with this talk

2. Bob Herbert, "Why Aren't We Shocked?" *New York Times* October 16, 2006.

3. Peter Piot, "Message on the Occasion of World AIDS Day," December 2004.

4. Jennie Yabroff, "From Barricades to Blogs," *Newsweek* (October 22, 2007) 44. SUSAN FALUDI

5. Decree 14, Documents of the Thirty-Fourth General Congregation of the Society of Jesus, (St. Louis: Institute of Jesuit Sources, 1995) no. 364 (p. 172-3). Decree 14, no. 366.

6. John Paul II's concern in *Mulieris Dignitatem* that "women's pursuit of their rights not end in their 'masculinization'" or then-Cardinal Ratzinger's accusation that Christian feminists are "seeking power" or making themselves "adversaries of men" or trying to "dominate men" (Ratzinger authored *On the Collaboration of Men and Women in the Church and World* released by Vatican July 31, 2004) come to mind.

7. Georgia Masters Keightley, "Catholic Feminism's Contribution to the Church's Social Justice Tradition," in Francis P. McHugh and Samuel M. Natale, *Things Old and New: Catholic Social Teaching Revisited* (Lanham, MD: University Press of America, 1993) 333-363 at 334, 336-37 and Andrea Lee, I.H.M. and Amata Miller, I.H.M., "Feminist Themes in Laborem Exercens" in Charles E. Curran and Richard A. McCormick, S.J., *Readings in Moral Theology No. 5: Official Catholic Social Teaching* (New York: Paulist Press, 1986) 418.

8. Reports from 2006 show that in sub-Saharan Africa and the Caribbean, they produce up to 80 percent of basic foodstuffs. In Asia, they account for around 50 percent of food production. In Latin America, they are mainly engaged in subsistence farming, horticulture, poultry and raising small livestock." (http://www.globalissues.org/HumanRights/WomensRights.asp and http://www.actionaid.org/actionaid/food_rights.aspx)

9. John L. Allen, Jr., "Lay Ecclesial Ministry and the Feminization of the Church," All Things Catholic column in *National Catholic Reporter* (June 29, 2007) accessed at http://ncrcafe.org/node/1201.

10. Ibid.

11. Lisa Sowle Cahill makes this point more generally about issues of sexuality in "Feminism and Christian Ethics: Moral Theology" in Catherine Mowry LaCugna, ed., *Freeing Theology: The Essentials of Theology in Feminist Perspective* (New York: HarperSanFrancisco, 1993) 211-234 at 212.

12. Kevin Kelly, "Conclusion: A Moral Theologian Faces the New Millennium in a Time of AIDS," in James Keenan, S.J., ed., with John D. Fuller, S.J., M.D., Lisa Sowle Cahill, and Kevin Kelly, *Catholic Ethicists on HIV/AIDS Prevention* (Continuum, 2000) 324-332 at 325.

13. HIV/AIDS Policy Fact Sheet from The Henry J. Kaiser Family Foundation (July 2007) online. Women postpone care disproportionately because of their caretaking roles, lack of transportation, or because they become too sick.

14. Regina Wolfe, "Establishing U.S. Campus-Based HIV/AIDS Awareness and Prevention Programs," in Keenan et. al., 170-71.

15. Paul Farmer, "Women, Poverty, and AIDS," in Farmer, Margaret Connors and Janie Simmons, *Women, Poverty, and AIDS: Sex, Drugs, and Structural Violence* (Monroe, ME: Common Courage Press, 1996) 3¬37 at 5-6, 23.

16. Margaret A. Farley, *Compassionate Respect: A Feminist Approach to Medical Ethics and Other Questions* (Paulist Press, 2002) 10-11.

17. Farmer, 33.

18. Ibid., 22.

19. Ibid., 28-9.

20. Maria Riley, O.P. and Nancy Sylvester, I.H.M., *Trouble & Beauty: Women Encounter Catholic Social Teaching* (Washington, DC: Center of Concern, Leadership Conference of Women Religious, and NETWORK, 1991) 48.

21. Paul Lauritzen, "Holy Alliance? The Danger of Mixing Politics and Religion," *Commonweal* (March 24, 2006) 14-17 at 16-17.

22. Cahill, "Protection of Life: Priorities and Politics" in Richard Miller, ed., *We Hold These Truths: Catholicism and American Public Life, Catholic Church in the 21st Century Series*, (Liguori, MO: Liguori Press) forthcoming.

23. Ibid.

24. Bob Casey, Jr. (D-PA), Pope John XXIII Lecture "Restoring America's Moral Compass: Leadership and the Common Good" available at http://inquirer.philly.com/rss/news/091406caseyremarks.pdf (accessed February 7, 2007).

25. See Nancy A. Dallavalle, "Resilient Citizens: The Public (and Gendered) Face of American Catholicism," in T. Frank Kennedy, ed., *Inculturation and the Church in North America* (New York: Crossroad, 2006) at 23-43 and Daniel Finn, "Hello, Catholics: Republicans & the Targeting of Religious Voters," *Commonweal* (November 4, 2005) 14-17.

26. Gregory A. Kalsheur, "American Catholics and the State: John Courtney Murray on Catholics in a pluralistic democratic society," *America* (August 2-9, 2004) 15-18 at 18.

27. Rosemary Radford Ruether, *Sexism and God Talk: Toward a Feminist Theology* (Boston: Beacon Press, 1983) 19.

28. Personal interview with Catherine Pinkerton, C.S.J., 7/23/02.

29. Christine E. Gudorf, *Catholic Social Teaching on Liberation Themes* (Lanham, MD: University Press of America) 1980, 259.

30. See Christine Firer Hinze, "U.S. Catholic Social Thought, Gender, and Economic Livelihood," Theological Studies 66 (2005) 568-591 for a lucid assessment of these intersecting issues.

31. Robert Wilson, "How Babies Alter Careers for Academics," *The Chronicle of Higher Education*, December 5, 2003.

32. Bridget Burke Ravizza and Karen Peterson-Iyers, "The Price of Motherhood: Are Catholic Universities Willing to Pay It?" *Catholic Education: A Journal of Inquiry and Practice.*

33. Barbara Busse, "Just Listen: Jesuit Higher Education and the Situation of Women," *Conversations in Jesuit Higher Education, Listening to Women: Equity and Impact 29* (Spring 2006) 19-21 at 21.

34. Decree 14, no. 369, 372.

35. Mary Garvin, S.N.J.M., "Dusting Off a Document," *Conversations in Jesuit Higher Education: Listening to Women: Equity and Impact 29* (Spring 2006) 38.

Restorative Justice and Catholic Social Thought: Challenges as Opportunities for Society, Church, and Academy

Rev. Kurt M. Denk, S.J.

Jesuit priest, Maryland Province of the Society of Jesus. Fr. Denk, S.J. served from 2004-10 as a chaplain at San Quentin State Prison while completing an M.Div. at the Jesuit School of Theology, and a J.D. at the Univ. of California, Berkeley (Boalt Hall).

CATHOLIC SOCIAL CONCERNS LECTURE SERIES I February 29, 2008

G ood afternoon. It is a privilege to be here with you this afternoon to speak about the restorative justice movement and Catholic social thought. By way of overview, I begin with an introductory theological reflection on our theme of restoration and healing. I then survey the restorative justice alternative to the problem of crime and violence; address connections between themes in restorative justice and Catholic social thought; and conclude with some reflections on how the *challenges* of restorative justice are, as well, *opportunities* for society, church, and academy.

I would like to begin by recounting a story, which is, to my mind, one of the best depictions of restorative justice from the broad New Testament imagination. And that is Luke's account of Jesus' pardon of the sinful woman from Luke 7:36-50:

> A Pharisee invited [Jesus] to dine with him, and he entered the Pharisee's house and reclined at table. Now there was a sinful woman in the city who learned that he was at table in the house of the Pharisee. Bringing an alabaster flask of ointment, she stood behind him at his feet weeping and began to bathe his feet with her tears. Then she wiped them with her hair, kissed them, and anointed them with the ointment. When the Pharisee who had invited him saw this he said to himself, "If this man were a prophet, he would know who and what sort of woman this is who is touching him, that she is a sinner." Jesus said to him in reply, "Simon, I have something to say to you." "Tell me, teacher," he said. "Two people were in debt to a certain creditor; one owed five hundred days' wages and the other owed fifty. Since they were unable to repay the debt, he forgave it for both. Which of them will love him more?" Simon said in reply, "The one, I suppose, whose larger debt was forgiven." He said to him, "You have judged rightly." Then he turned to the woman and said to Simon, "Do you see this woman? When I entered your house, you did not give me water for my feet, but she has bathed them with her tears and wiped them with her hair. You did not give me a kiss, but she has not ceased kissing my feet since the time I entered. You did not anoint my head with oil, but she anointed my feet with ointment. So I tell you, her many sins have been forgiven; hence, she has shown great love. But the one to

whom little is forgiven, loves little." He said to her, "Your sins are forgiven." The others at table said to themselves, "Who is this who even forgives sins?" But he said to the woman, "Your faith has saved you; go in peace."[1]

Now, please indulge me, I've always regretted that the woman is nameless, and so, about seven years ago, I began calling her Cynthia. I propose Jesus' pardon of Cynthia as a frame for our conversation because this Gospel episode centers on Cynthia's *restoration* to God, to her community, and indeed to her very self through a *justice* of Jesus that is relational, that knows and sees Cynthia's root dignity and faith.

In particular, I want to distill two images, and two consequent lessons, from this scene. The first image is Jesus' passionate interrogation of Simon: "then [Jesus] turned to the woman [thus seeing her] *and said to Simon*, 'do *you see* this woman?'" (emphasis added.) Obviously, no, Simon did not, or could not, or would not see this offender whom Jesus saw, and proclaimed restored to the community. Lesson one: a Christian vision of justice for those who commit wrongs requires that we see, that we look upon, others first as persons (who have committed offenses), as persons with whom we have a mutual relational claim. That we not, that is, look at them simply as objects, as offenders, thereby, rather, overlooking them. Just as we look inside our own hearts during the penitential rite of every liturgy, to see and offer up our own offenses, so too our ecclesial duty is to *see* the root dignity and personhood of every *other* offender in our midst.

The second image is Jesus' adjudication of Cynthia, if you will: "'so I tell you, her many sins have been forgiven; hence, she has shown great love' … [and Jesus] said to her, 'your sins are forgiven … your faith has saved you; go in peace.'" The logical construction of Jesus' adjudication is worth paying attention to: her many sins have been forgiven, hence she has shown great love, hence she is saved by her faith and returned to her community, sent forth in peace. Thus, lesson two: our duty, indeed our very ability to fulfill the Greatest Commandment, the love commandment (cf. Matthew 22:34-40; Mark 12:28-34; Luke 10:25-28; John 13:34), stems from our being restored, and our restoration of others, to social and ecclesial communion.

Combine the lessons: the Christian vision of justice is restorative, and requires that we first see, and search for if we don't see, the root dignity of every person who has offended through crime or violence. This seeing of the offender as a Christian responsibility finds support elsewhere in the Gospels: the Prodigal Son (Luke 15:11-32), the Woman at the Well (John 4:1-42), and Jesus' pardon of the good thief at his crucifixion (Luke 23:39-43). We see it especially in Matthew 25: "for I was … in prison and you visited me" (Mt 25: 35, 36). Matthew's image of Jesus as prisoner, and the prisoner as Jesus, offers a fitting segue to the main focus of my reflections this afternoon, since, of course, prison is the context where many an offender in our society lives.

The Restorative Justice Alternative to the Problem of Crime and Violence

I turn now to the problem of crime and violence and the restorative justice alternative. Today's newspaper highlights a study from the Pew Center announcing that our incarceration rate has reached 1 of every 100 adults in the United States.[2] To many among us, such vast incarceration reflects innumerable individuals' moral ills, but it also reflects social injustices. This is the position of the United States Catholic Bishops in a remarkable document published in November 2000 entitled *Responsibility, Rehabilitation, and Restoration: A Catholic Perspective on Crime and Criminal Justice*.[3] I will return to that document throughout my presentation. In any case, both restorative justice and Catholic social thought would appear to agree that our society witnesses too much incarceration, and too little healing of victims, of offenders, and of social consciousness. Consider the following statistics:

- As of December 31, 2006, the most recent date for which the U.S. Department of Justice has published figures, there were over 2.2 million federal and state prison inmates.[4] When we add in those on probation and parole, the total number of citizens under the supervision of corrections departments reaches 7.2 million nationwide: a 290% increase since 1980, and a six-fold increase since 1970.[5]

- Our nation's incarceration rate in 2006, 751 inmates per 100,000 population, is the highest reported rate in the world.[6] The U.S. has 5% of the world's population and 22% of the world's prisoners.[7]

- From a family and social justice perspective, consider the following: compared to the national 2.9% increase in incarceration from 2005 to 2006, the number of women under corrections authorities' jurisdictions rose 4.5% in that period.[8] More and more, incarceration is a family affair, and consider the staggering impact on families when, now, *both* mothers and fathers are missing from their families and communities.

    1. Particularly alarming are the racial disparities attendant to incarceration in the U.S.:[9] At the end of 2006, 3,042 per 100,000 black males were sentenced prisoners, compared to 1,261 per 100,000 Hispanic males and 487 per 100,000 white males.[10] That means a black male has a 32% chance of serving time in prison during his life, a Hispanic male a 17% chance, a white male a 6% chance.[11]

    2. One analyst calculated that in 2004, the ratio of incarcerated men per 100,000 black males in the U.S. was over five times the ratio of incarcerated men per

100,000 black males in apartheid South Africa some eleven years earlier.[12]

3. Racism is particularly prevalent with respect to the death penalty: of those executed since 1976, 35% have been black, yet African-Americans are about 12% of the U.S. population.[13] Notably, about 80% of murder victims in cases resulting in execution were white, while only 50% of murder victims overall are white.[14]

Now, an obvious question or retort in response to this raft of statistics would be whether our high rate of incarceration is an unfortunate, but necessary, response to the plague of crime. Statistics suggest, rather strongly, this is not the case.

- While the U.S. leads the world in its incarceration rate, our rate of crime victimization equals the rate of crime victimization among 17 of our peer, industrialized nations.[15] Research demonstrates little or even no correlation between crime and incarceration rates: for example, North and South Dakota, with virtually identical demographic characteristics, have had consistently similar crime rates for decades, and yet South Dakota incarcerates at a rate more than twice that of North Dakota.[16]

- Public perception of crime, and actual crime, simply do not match. While there is a widespread reported sense that crime remains as much if not more pernicious than in the past, violent crime was relatively stable from 1970-1994, after which it declined significantly.[17]

- Furthermore, 82% of those sentenced to state prison in 2004 were convicted of nonviolent offenses; and beginning in the early 1980s and continuing over the course of 20 years, those in prison for drug offenses rose from 1 in 10 to 1 in 4, so that over half of today's federal inmates are incarcerated for drug offenses.[18] This is not to say that drugs are not a problem, but it begs the question whether incarceration is the answer.

The point of all of this? As one advocacy group concludes, in light of such statistics, "we can not incarcerate away the crime problem."[19] There must be some alternative.

And here we begin to examine the restorative justice alternative. The renowned Mennonite restorative-justice theorist and practitioner, Howard Zehr, offers a good working definition: "restorative justice is a process to involve, to the extent possible, those who have a stake in harms, needs, and obligations, in order to heal and put things as right as possible."[20] Zehr's definition already hints at an important aspect of restorative justice: it is a theory, but, fundamentally, it is a praxis, a dialectic of thought and action,[21] as are key tenets of Catholic social thought, such as subsidiarity, solidarity, and the preferential option for the poor.[22]

Thus, from the outset it is important to see that restorative justice is a *process approach* to dealing with crime and violence. Restorative justice ultimately is meant to be lived out, to be incarnated, as we would say in a Christian context, in the real-world praxis of criminal justice and peacemaking in general. My aim here is to compare the restorative justice model to the traditional criminal justice model, the system that is responsible for the move to mass incarceration that I outlined minutes ago. Restorative justice is not limited to any one particular definition or practice. It is rather a set of principles intended to make amends, insofar as possible, after a violent event or other crime.[23] I will outline four guiding principles of restorative justice as I have synthesized them from a broad review of the literature on the subject.[24]

First Guiding Principle: *Relationships precede rules.* At present, our criminal justice model entails six components: 1.) Crime is lawbreaking, a breaking of rules; 2.) When a rule is broken, justice entails assigning and establishing guilt; 3.) Guilt is established "so that *just* desserts can be meted out;" 4.) Just desserts equal imposing punishment by "inflicting *pain;*" 5.) All of this occurs, procedurally, through more conflict,[25] namely in the form of the adversarial process of American common law jurisprudence. 6.) *This is an important point:* In the traditional system of criminal law the offense or crime is formalized as an offense against the state, even when the victim is very clearly a discrete other; therefore, in formal terms, the offender's offendee is the state, against which he must defend himself.[26] Crime victims, then, occupy this rather strange position outside the adjudicatory process, even though typically, it is they who have suffered the greatest felt harm. In brief: The traditional criminal justice system formalizes criminal offense in terms of an offender's violation of the positive law laid down by the state, which in turn requires state action to deter future offenses (by that offender and by others), and to punish the offender, remove him from society (for a time), and (at least ideally) rehabilitate his offending behavior. On the other hand, restorative justice comprehends crime as more than rule breaking; restorative justice sees crime as a violation or rupture of relationships, which require repair: relationships of offenders and victims, their families, and the community as a whole. First and foremost, crime ruptures relationships, and justice entails repairing them, insofar as possible.

Second Guiding Principle: Justice by participation rather than by proxy. The traditional criminal justice regime adjudicates by proxy: David assaults Peter, and upon arrest and indictment, David is represented by public defender, Donna, at a trial featuring prosecutor, Paula, and presided over by Judge Jane. Aside, perhaps, from being called as witnesses to what directly involved them in the first place, the original parties are rather passive; the prosecutor takes over in the name of the offended state. There are good reasons for this process, a careful consideration of which would take us too far afield today. Still, a basic, common sense, critical review is possible. Think of it this way: You, Pat, are a parent, and your child Charlie hits your neighbor, Nancy's, son, Sam, and takes Sam's toy. Basic human justice in this situation, probably across many if not most cultures, would involve the parents, Pat and Nancy, sitting down with the kids, Charlie and Sam, talking through the dispute, getting an apology from Charlie, an acceptance from Sam, and securing some kind of restitution from Charlie to Sam. In this hypothetical, a real injury has occurred, not simply to property and person, but to the relationship between the kids and, if it escalates, between their families. The response, and the process used to address the dispute, is a process of participation, not by proxies, by the parties involved. From the first premise, that wrongs involve relationships as much as, if not more, than rules, restorative justice concludes that responding to wrongs must involve a process of participation, not proxy.

Third Guiding Principle: Restoration of wounded communities, not just adjudication of offending individuals. Building on the first premise of relationality and the second premise of participation, the third principle emphasizes the broader community's role in all of this. Again, beneath the offense of any given crime, are the wounds that are inflicted, the relationships that are ruptured. Beyond the necessary adjudication of an individual offender, restorative justice aims at addressing the deeper wounds and, insofar as possible, restoring the balance to the relationships that have been ruptured. This restoration extends to the communities, the webs of relationships, impacted by a given offense. One noted theorist, John Braithwaite, uses the term "communities of interest" to describe the networks of individuals impacted by an offense.[27] Restorative justice certainly attends to what must happen to, and often for, an offending individual and his offended victim. But restorative justice ultimately aims at a broader, holistic restoration to right relationship of all individuals and communities of interest connected to a given offense. Various models of restorative justice encompass this perspective; whether through victim-offender mediation, family group conferencing, healing circles, or other modalities, restorative justice in practice emphasizes encounter, reparative process, and transformation of offenders, survivors, and their respective communities.

The Fourth Guiding Principle: The restorative justice continuum: from order, to rehabilitation, to shalom. At a basic level, the state's responsibility with respect to criminal justice is to maintain order. Two of the big four classical purposes of the criminal justice system, namely, deterrence of crime and isolation of the offending individuals from the community, instantiate this formal responsibility.[28] The third, punishment or retribution, acknowledges that, in the realm of criminal justice, the state has a responsibility to treat offenders in a manner that reflects the community's sense that the offenders' behavior violates the community's established sense of morality. The fourth, rehabilitation, speaks to a longstanding tradition dating (in this country) to the 18th century when the *penitentiary* came about,[29] that, with the exception of the most grievous offenses, neither punishment nor isolation of the offender from society are ends in themselves. Rather, punishment and isolation are part and parcel of an incarceration that entails a broader program aimed at treating an offender so that he may be rehabilitated.

Historically, we have seen in this country, and especially in California, a give and take with respect to the extent to which rehabilitation should, or even can be, part of the criminal justice system's responsibility. In the late 1970s, the California Legislature passed measures explicitly declaring that the Corrections Department's mission was to isolate and punish, *not* to rehabilitate.[30] In 2005, Governor Schwarzenegger renamed the California Department of Corrections, adding the word "Rehabilitation" (Now it is the CA Dept. of Corrections and Rehabilitation.); however, to what extent this renewed emphasis will take root remains to be seen.

In any case, traditional criminal justice aims, minimally, at order, and maximally, at rehabilitation. Where restorative justice differs is in its conviction that communities ideally desire not simply order, not just the rehabilitation or treatment of its ill members, but a deeper and more constitutive peace, that is, a fundamental at-rightness and well-being of relationships, which actually feeds the growth of relationships. Biblically, this is the concept of *shalom*. Obviously, while not all restorative justice theorists advance a biblical view, there is a common current in restorative justice theory that articulates how restorative justice aims at more than fixing the effects of an offense but puts forward a transformative social vision.[31]

So we have four guiding principles of restorative justice: relationships precede rules; justice by participation rather than by proxy; restoration of wounded communities, not just adjudication of offending individuals; and the restorative justice continuum from order, to rehabilitation, to shalom. Before moving on to a closer analysis of connections between restorative justice and Catholic social thought, we need to address an obvious question: Does any of this work in the real world? The answer is *yes*.[32] Consider the following:

1.) Internationally: Perhaps one of the most significant international examples of restorative justice at work would be the truth and reconciliation commissions of South Africa and other nations.[33] Even for ordinary justice, many countries have begun to adopt restorative practices, with New Zealand perhaps the most cited. In the 1980s New Zealand, a country with very similar crime demographics as the U.S.,[34] embarked on a reform of its criminal justice system.[35] Eventually it switched from a top-down to a grassroots model, incorporated ancient justice practices of its indigenous Maori population, and then amended its constitution to mandate Maori-inspired restorative justice practices as the norm for its juvenile justice system. Ninety percent of cases following this model yield a consensus decision, which in most cases is formally ratified by a judge. Not only have New Zealand's recidivism rates for juvenile offenders plummeted, but the offense rate as a whole has dropped significantly.[36] The system is based on what has become one of the dominant methodologies of the restorative justice movement, the family group conference. Family group conferences bring in a wide circle of people connected with both an offender and a victim, to collaboratively devise a resolution to the offense at issue.[37] Looking at models across jurisdictions and cultures, the resolution that restorative justice methodologies yield depends on the crime and the context but may involve any one, or a combination, of: a formal apology, restitution, community service, substance abuse treatment or other counseling, or, as necessary, incarceration.[38]

2.) Domestically: restorative justice-oriented programs have been successfully implemented for both nonviolent and violent juvenile and adult proceedings in a number of jurisdictions, such as Alaska and Minnesota.[39] And we have an example right here in our own back yard. For the past eleven years the San Francisco Sheriff's Department has successfully implemented *Resolve to Stop the Violence Program* (RSVP). In its first year alone, and the success has continued, even amidst funding cuts, RSVP participants in an 8-week program had a recidivism rate 46% lower than non-participants; 12-week program participants had a recidivism rate 53% lower than non-participants; and 16-week program participants had a recidivism rate just shy of 83% lower than non-participants.[40] It costs California $35,000 to jail an inmate for one year; RSVP costs just $7 a day.[41]

Connections Between Restorative Justice and Catholic Social Thought

We now turn to the connections between the principles of restorative justice and of Catholic social thought. Here is a simple listing of the top-ten tenets of Catholic social thought. The following schematic is my own, though it borrows from the work of others. (Those familiar with Catholic social thought should be able to recognize the usual buzzwords.)[42]

1. Human dignity and respect for human life

2. The link between the religious and social dimensions of life

3. The link between love, *caritas*, and justice

4. Social and economic justice, with justice as "fidelity to the demands of relationship" (John Donahue, S.J.: see note 52.)

5. The value of and right to equality and to political participation

6. The balancing of rights and responsibilities

7.   Solidarity and the preferential option for the poor and vulnerable

8.   Stewardship and promotion of the common good

9.   The value of association and subsidiarity

10. Promotion of peace and liberation from structural sin

Let me begin with a three-word quote from Howard Zehr, the restorative justice theorist and practitioner, whose definition of restorative justice I quoted earlier: "Violations create obligations."[43] One of the fundamental ethical premises of Catholic social thought is that rights and responsibilities co-exist in a dialectical relationship.[44] The restorative justice principle, then, that violations of others' rights implicates an obligation or responsibility to restore what has become unbalanced, fits well with this principle of Catholic ethical tradition. Moreover, as should be clear from the Scriptural exegesis with which we began, and the study of restorative justice that we have just completed, both restorative justice and the biblical tradition that serves as a basis for Catholic social thought, are concerned to read such principles in light of a primary concern for healing persons and relationships. The principles only make sense if they are grounded in the more fundamental, the more radical, that is *root*, value of honoring and redeeming human life, human relationality, and human dignity.

As a way of schematizing the nexus between restorative justice and Catholic social thought, I propose four groupings of Catholic social thought's traditional tenets that parallel the four broad restorative justice themes I outlined earlier, creating a nexus.

The first nexus, foundations, compares Catholic theological anthropology with the first thematic category of restorative justice, relationships precede rules. As noted, restorative justice presumes that human relationality is our starting point, and that when offenses or crimes occur, they are an upsetting of a relational order, which requires restoration or balancing. As I hope is clear, this is not that far from Judeo-Christian creation theology and theological anthropology, itself a starting point for Catholic social thought.

Catholic social thought begins with the fundamental dignity of the human person, created *in imago Dei*, as a free, responsible, hopeful, and social-relational being.[45] Both the Old and New Testaments present an anthropology that conceives the human person to be relational, as regards God and as regards others, in terms of covenant. The story of creation, sin, grace, and redemption is one of relationship and of covenant, which, when broken, calls for healing and restoration.[46] There are key law texts in Scripture: In the Old Testament we have the Decalogue (Exodus 20:1-17), (Deuteronomy 5:6-21), the Exodus Covenant code (Exodus 20:22—23:33), the Holiness Code in Leviticus (Lev 17—26), and the Deuteronomic code (Dt 12—26). These law texts devote particular attention to the community's responsibility to the poor, the widow, the orphan, and the outcast. In the New Testament we have the Beatitudes (Matthew 5:3-12; Luke 6:20-22), the Greatest Commandment (Matthew 22:34-40; Mark 12:28-34; Luke 10:25-28; John 13:34) and Jesus' startling commandment to love one's enemies (Matthew 5:43-48; Luke 6:27-36).[47] But all of these law texts spring from and are rationalized by the fundamental anthropology of the human person created *in imago Dei* and destined for covenanted relationship with God and with others. Beyond these Scriptural law texts, we note the Catholic embrace of natural law as the foundation for ethical praxis, the premise being that, as created *in imago Dei*, humans possess an intellectual capacity to perceive the fundamental norms of moral life.[48] A key aspect of natural law is helping the person to intuit and apply moral truths communicated via relationship with God into the rest of human relationships.[49] So in terms of foundations, whether biblical or philosophical, the resonance should be clear between the anthropological themes in Catholic social thought and restorative justice's emphasis on human relationality preceding rules. As the U.S. bishops' document *Responsibility, Rehabilitation, and Restoration* states, "our society seems to prefer punishment to rehabilitation and retribution to restoration, thereby indicating a failure to recognize prisoners as human."[50] The restorative justice movement does not give up on human relationality premised on respect for others' lives, rights, and cultural meanings. Catholic social thought rests on a foundational anthropology premised on human dignity and respect for human life, and on the link of the religious and social dimensions of life.[51]

The second nexus is the *orientation of justice*, justice by participation rather than by proxy. From any ethical foundation, justice as fidelity to the demands of a relationship, initiates praxis, lived practice informed by reflection on those foundations. In restorative justice, as I have outlined previously, justice is sought thru direct participation by stakeholders, or, whereas our criminal justice system turns the process of justice over to professionals (more or less exclusively) restorative justice aims at including those communities of interest that are affected by the rupture of a relationship.

I would suggest that the orientation of participation rather than proxy has a close analogue in Catholic social thought's conception of justice as fidelity to the demands of relationship. This definition comes from Rev. John R. Donahue, S.J.'s work on the biblical foundations of justice as developed by Catholic social teaching.[52] I have explored, in other areas of my own research, how his definition also resonates with the Catholic philosophical tradition, and particularly with Catholic social thought's core concept of solidarity as "a learned habit, cultivated over time, that sees 'the other' as a neighbor called to share equally with us in the goods of creation and toward whom we have certain mutual obligations."[53] Justice as fidelity to the demands of relationship also coheres well with the personalist philosophy that orients the great social encyclicals of Pope John Paul II's pontificate.[54] The core insight here, similar to that of restorative justice's participation rather than proxy rule, is that true justice, true righting of wrongs, always inheres in a social context of mutual obligations, with all the demands and joys and challenges a mutual obligation implies. The key question centers on *who* is responsible for mediating that process of justice. The justice orientation of both restorative justice and Catholic social thought expands the circle of those who make justice happen, but also, in a *restorative* focus, each participating individual needs to be invested in the process, and allow herself or himself to be confronted, to be converted, by the expressed needs and experiences of the *other*. And, indeed, most restorative justice models place an emphasis on the encounter of an offender, if not with the particular person he has offended, then with some representative.[55] Encounter facilitates restoration, and this is the very phenomenon that, earlier, I suggested Jesus' pardon of Cynthia depicts. Encounter facilitates restoration.[56]

This second nexus between restorative justice and Catholic social thought accords with several of the ten tenets of Catholic social thought: the link between love and justice, the balancing of rights and responsibilities, and the value of association and subsidiarity. In other words, Catholic social thought's linking of love and justice corresponds with restorative justice's vision of restoration. As the U.S. bishops' document enunciates, "crime and corrections are at the intersection of rights and responsibilities," and the test of our social fabric "is whether we will exercise our responsibility to hold the offender accountable without violating his or her basic rights."[57] But how does such responsibility occur? Here the principles of association and subsidiarity resonate strongly. Rev William Byron, S.J. defines subsidiarity in terms that, I believe, are apt to the restorative justice vision of direct participation by stakeholders in a situation of offense. Fr. Byron writes:

> The principle of subsidiarity puts a proper limit on government by insisting that no higher level of organization should perform any function that can be handled efficiently and effectively at a lower level of organization by human persons who, individually or in groups, are closer to the problems and closer to the ground.[58]

Fr. Byron's words might as well be a description of the restorative justice principle of justice by participation rather than by proxy. Notably, that grassroots response by an immediate-level community to the harm done by crime or violence is not just the hope, but is the outcome, of restorative justice conferencing models.[59] Restorative justice practitioners Gordon Bazemore, Lori Ellis, Hennessey Hayes, and Mark Umbreit are among those who have documented these kinds of outcomes by comparing various restorative justice models and analyzing what types of methodologies are appropriate for assessing restorative justice outcomes.[60]

The third nexus has to do with a restorative orientation: in restorative justice the restoration of wounded communities, not just an adjudication of offending individuals and in Catholic social thought, the covenantal social ethics linking the religious and social.

If a justice orientation pertains to the specifics of addressing a given offense, this third area of nexus examines the broader social or community
approach to justice. The Restorative Justice Online website offers a definition
of restorative justice that emphasizes how I want to focus this aspect: "restorative justice *is a theory of justice* that emphasizes repairing the harm caused
or revealed by criminal behavior."[61] Violence and criminality are arguably as
much, if not more, a manifestation of broader social ills, as they are the outcome of particular individuals' choices.[62] As Catholic social teaching emphasizes, we need to challenge the broader culture of violence in which we live
and opt for a culture of life.[63] The core social relationships responsible for the
justice orientation of the second nexus—namely, victims and survivors, their
families and networks—inhere in the broader sphere of education, work, civic
and religious associations, and so forth. These broader associational spheres
need to contribute to restoring wounded relationships, and they also need to
understand themselves as a necessary, fertile ground for a restorative orientation to crime and violence in a broader, social context. The third restorative
justice theme, the restoration of wounded communities, not just the adjudication of offending individuals, recognizes this restorative social orientation.[64]
Although this orientation is not explicitly spiritual in all restorative justice
models, it is in many. And even in those that are not explicitly spiritual, there
is reference to values commonly associated with spirituality.[65]

Catholic social thought recognizes a similar principle, one of a covenantal
social ethics that links the religious and social dimensions of life.[66] If justice
is fidelity to the demands of relationship, and our relationships inhere in a
broader social context, then a Catholic perspective (like a restorative justice perspective) on crime and violence likewise, and necessarily, involves
a broader, covenantal social ethics. Justice touches not just on traditional
moral questions of right and wrong, rights and responsibilities, but also on
social and economic justice.[67] A covenantal social ethics emphasizes human
equality, political participation, subsidiarity, stewardship and promotion of
the common good, as well as solidarity and the preferential option for the
poor and vulnerable, which are all themes that lie at the root of Catholic
social thought, and these themes find explicit expression in the U.S. bishops'
Responsibility, Rehabilitation, and Restoration.[68] A Catholic-Christian response
to crime and violence, once again imaged by Jesus' pardon and restoration of
Cynthia, ultimately boils down to solidarity. In his 1987 encyclical *Sollicitudo
Rei Socialis* (On Social Concern), Pope John Paul II declared that solidarity recognizes that "we are all really responsible for all."[69] As the restorative
justice movement envisions a restorative-oriented response to crime and
violence, Catholic social thought premises a Catholic-Christian response
to crime and violence on similar grounds. To quote from the U.S. bishops'
Responsibility, Rehabilitation, and Restoration:

> Solidarity recognizes that "we are all really responsible for all."
> [Citation to *Sollicitudo Rei Socialis* § 38.] Not only are we respon-

sible for the safety and well being of our family and our next-door neighbor, but Christian solidarity demands that we work for justice beyond our boundaries. Christians are asked to see Jesus in the face of everyone, including both victims and offenders. Through the lens of solidarity, those who commit crimes and are hurt by crime are not issues or problems; they are sisters and brothers, members of one human family. Solidarity calls us to insist on responsibility and seek alternatives that do not simply punish, but rehabilitate, heal, and restore.[70]

The fourth nexus is restorative vision, the restorative justice continuum: from order, to rehabilitation, to shalom; and the Catholic social thought vision: the integrative Gospel, peace and liberation.

In restorative justice courses at Berkeley Law School, a question to which we repeatedly return concerns the extent to which restorative justice is a *reformist* movement, meant to tinker with the machinery of the prevailing criminal justice system, or a *transformative* movement that bespeaks broader intentions for a reordering of social perceptions, institutions, and modes of living.[71] A review of restorative justice literature reveals that there are adherents on all sides of this question, though most suggest, if not outright argue for, a restorative justice vision as a broader vision for social transformation. It is in that sense that I believe the fourth nexus, pertaining to restorative vision, asks of both restorative justice and Catholic social thought: What vision do you propose for a society marred by crime and violence?

In the Catholic social thought context the fourth nexus, concerning restorative vision, bespeaks the broadly integrative Gospel vision of peace and liberation. The U.S. bishops' document includes a section on Scriptural foundations of the Catholic-Christian approach to crime, violence, and restoration. Following specific Old Testament references to God's giving of the law, and the extension of justice and mercy, and references to Jesus' own ministry of healing and reconciliation, the bishops conclude with a quotation from John Paul II's July 2000 *Message for the Jubilee in Prisons*:

> What Christ is looking for is trusting acceptance, an attitude which opens the mind to generous decisions aimed at rectifying the evil done and fostering what is good. Sometimes this involves a long journey, but always a stimulating one, for it is a journey not made alone, but in the company of Christ himself and with his support... He never tires of encouraging each person along the path to salvation.[72]

Catholic social thought's themes of solidarity, the preferential option for the poor and vulnerable, and the promotion of peace and liberation from structural sin, speak of a broad restorative vision. And that is unsurprising, for when we stand back and take in the broad sweep of the Gospel's integrative vision of peace and liberation, we find therein not just Jesus and Cynthia, but Jesus and many men and women like her, and like ourselves, who require forgiveness and mercy and restoration, and find it in Him who is Prince of Peace. We find in the Gospel's own transformative, that is, redemptive, vision, the Jesus whose utmost act, going to the cross, testifies to his solidarity with those offended by violence, as well as his solidarity with those who offend. Jesus, at the point of his own death, forgave those who offended him (Luke 23:34; 43).

Challenges as Opportunities for Society, Church, and Academy

As I noted at the beginning, both restorative justice and Catholic social thought are best thought of as orientations and movements. I have presented broad themes from which my listeners can discern how insights from restorative justice and Catholic social thought can best be instantiated, or, to speak theologically, incarnated, in society, church, and academy. To conclude I will list some challenges that I see for society, church, and academy relative to the topic of restorative justice, examined from the lens of Catholic social thought. I present these challenges in the positive sense of opportunities, opportunities in light of Jesus' paschal mystery, which necessarily orients Catholic Christian social thought, opportunities to encounter Jesus and to be transformed by his restorative, redemptive action in our own lives.

In a society such as our own, with vast resources but a troubling tendency to incarcerate away the living signs of our broader cultural addiction to violence, the challenge is to go to the root of our social ills. But that is also an opportunity, an opportunity to harness the best of the American ethos, the diversity of our public square, to engage one another in a justice that is more relational, more restorative. That is not an easy task by any stretch of the imagination, and yet, Americans haven't given up on engaging in the public square as the current presidential election process demonstrates. What can each of us do? Well, we might begin by considering signing your name to a new ballot initiative amending California's Three Strikes Law. Beyond that, we can spread the word about restorative justice and Catholic social thought; write to our elected officials and advocate for restorative alternatives to strict punishment-only regimes.

The U.S. bishops' *Responsibility, Rehabilitation, and Restoration* outlines, I believe, a clear, well-reasoned Catholic approach to crime and violence, identifying 11 "policy foundations and directions," followed by seven further tasks particularly consonant with the Church's own mission:[73]

Policy foundations and directions:
- Protecting Society
- Rejecting Simplistic Solutions
- Promoting Serious Efforts Toward Crime Prevention and Poverty Reduction

- Challenging the Culture of Violence
- Offering Victims the Opportunity to Participate
- Encouraging Innovative Programs
- Insisting That Punishment Has a Constructive Purpose
- Encouraging Spiritual Healing and Renewal
- Making a Serious Commitment to Confront Addiction
- Treating Immigrants Justly
- Placing Crime in a Community Context

Seven tasks particularly consonant with the Church's mission:[74]

- Teach Right from Wrong, Respect for Life, Forgiveness and Mercy
- Stand With Victims and Their Families
- Reach Out to Offenders and Their Families
- Build Community
- Advocate Policies That Offer Real Alternatives to Crime
- Organize Diocesan Consultations
- Work for New Approaches

Any of these policy directions or mission tasks, however, ultimately require a spiritual orientation towards the conversion that stems from God's grace in Christ, through the Spirit of members of the Church, members of Christ's Body. Here I would simply restate the two lessons I drew out from Luke's account of Jesus and Cynthia: first, a Christian vision of justice requires that we *see* others first as persons (who have committed offenses) with whom we have a mutual relational claim. Second, Jesus' adjudication of Cynthia, "'so I tell you, her many sins have been forgiven; hence, she has shown great love' … [and Jesus] said to her, 'your sins are forgiven … your faith has saved you; go in peace.'" Jesus' adjudication reminds us that our duty, our very ability, to fulfill the Greatest Commandment, the love commandment, stems from our being restored, and our restoration of others to social and ecclesial communion. Particularly now, during Lent, we do well to reflect on how well we have responded to this challenge as opportunity. Restorative justice is a call to ongoing conversion in our own lives and in the lives of our family, work, friends, and community.

Academic research into restorative justice is important. While restorative justice ultimately is a praxis intended to effect restorative healing in the real contexts of crime and violence, as praxis it also requires continued reflection upon its premises and practices. The volume of restorative justice literature is growing, but more work needs to be done. In our own context here, a Jesuit, Catholic university, we do well to ask what further academic inquiry, from our own tradition, can contribute to the field. Unfortunately, the dominant approach to criminal justice, *lock them up and throw away the key*, seems to be believed by a majority of our citizens, including a good many Catholics. Part of the academy's task is to continue engaging in the kind of research that will publicize restorative justice's actual outcomes. The mission statement of the University of San Francisco (USF), *Educating Minds and Hearts to Change the World*, certainly supports engaging in the type of research, teaching, advocacy, and student formation that truly sees the Cynthias of our own community and proposes concrete means for restoring them and those whom they have harmed, is indeed an opportunity to incarnate our own values in the public square.

I thank you for the opportunity to speak with you, and invite questions and further dialogue both today, and beyond the time of our formal gathering. Please help to advance the challenge of restorative justice as an opportunity for advancing Catholic social thought's transformative Gospel vision.

Notes:

1. Translation from Donald Senior, ed., *The Catholic Study Bible: New American Bible* (Oxford University Press, 1990).

2. Adam Liptak, "One in 100 U.S. Adults Behind Bars, New Study Says," *New York Times*, Feb. 29, 2008, A1.

3. United States Conference of Catholic Bishops, *Responsibility, Rehabilitation, and Restoration: A Catholic Perspective on Crime and Criminal Justice* (USCCB Publishing, 2000). Also available at www.usccb.org/sdwp/criminal.shtml (last accessed January 19, 2008).

4. Bureau of Justice Statistics, United States Department of Justice Office of Justice Programs, "Prison Statistics, Summary Findings," www.ojp.usdoj.gov/bjs/prisons.htm (last accessed February 9, 2008).

5. The Sentencing Project, "Facts About Prisons and Prisoners" (December 2007; sourced from the federal Bureau of Justice Statistics), www.sentencingproject.org.htm (last accessed February 9, 2008).

6. *Ibid.*

7. Prison Policy Initiative, "U.S. Population," citing Peter Wagner, *The Prison Index: Taking the Pulse of the Crime Control Industry* (Prison Policy Initiative, 2003), www.prisonpolicy.org/graphs/uspopulation.html (last accessed February 9, 2008).

8. Bureau of Justice Statistics, "Prison Statistics, Summary Findings."

9. An incisive portrait of this problem, supported by extensive empirical findings, is found in Dorothy Roberts, "The Social and Moral Cost of Mass Incarceration in African American Communities," in *Stanford Law Review* 56 (2004), 1271-1305.

See also *Responsibility, Rehabilitation, and Restoration*, 10, noting that "recent studies show that African, Hispanic, and Native Americans are often treated more harshly than other citizens in their encounters with the criminal justice system (including police activity, the handling of juvenile defendants, and prosecution and sentencing). These studies confirm that the racism and discrimination that continue to haunt our nation are reflected in similar ways in the criminal justice system." *Responsibility, Rehabilitation, and Restoration* cites Ronald H. Weich and Carlos T. Angulo, *Justice on Trial: Racial Disparities in the American Criminal Justice System*, Leadership Conference on Civil Rights and Leadership Conference Education Fund (April 2000) and The National Council on Crime and Delinquency, *And Justice for Some* (April 2000).

10. Roberts, "The Social and Moral Cost of Mass Incarceration in African American Communities."

11. The Sentencing Project, "Facts About Prisons and Prisoners."

12. Prison Policy Initiative, "An International Incarceration Comparison" (and citing Peter Wagner, *Americans Behind Bars: The International Use of Incarceration*, 2005), http://www.prisonpolicy.org/graphs/internationalinc.html (last accessed February 9, 2008).

13. ACLU Capital Punishment Project, "Race and the Death Penalty," www.aclu.org/death-penalty, last accessed February 9, 2008.

14. Death Penalty Information Center, "Facts About the Death Penalty" (February 8, 2008), www.deathpenaltyinfo.org/FactSheet.pdf, (last accessed February 9, 2008).

15. Prison Policy Initiative, "U.S. Population," citing Wagner, *The Prison Index*

16. Prison Policy Initiative, "The Facts About Crime." PPI's references with respect to this analysis include the Bureau of Justice Statistics, as well as Alfred Blumstein and Joel Wallman, eds., *The Crime Drop in America* (Cambridge University Press, 2000).

17. Prison Policy Initiative, "The Facts About Crime," www.prisonpolicy.org/articles/factsaboutcrime.pdf, (last accessed February 9, 2008).

18. The Sentencing Project, "Facts About Prisons and Prisoners."

19. Prison Policy Initiative, "The Facts About Crime."

20. Howard Zehr, *The Little Book of Restorative Justice* (Good Books, 2002), 37.

21. The very first sentence of Kay Pranis's chapter on the values of the restorative justice movement offers a similar conclusion: "restorative justice as a field flows back and forth between practice that informs philosophy and philosophy that informs practice." Pranis, "Restorative Values," in Gerry Johnstone and Daniel W. Van Ness, eds., *Handbook of Restorative Justice* (Willan Publishing, 2007), 59.

22. In the U.S. Bishops' *Responsibility, Rehabilitation, and Restoration*, the section on the "Scriptural, Theological, and Sacramental Heritage" of the Church's approach to crime and criminal justice specifically identified the importance of various tenets from Catholic social thought, namely: Human Life and Dignity; Human Rights and Responsibilities; Family, Community, and Participation; The Common Good; The Option for the Poor and Vulnerable; Subsidiarity and Solidarity. *Responsibility, Rehabilitation, and Restoration*, 21-25.

23. Tony F. Marshall, "Restorative Justice: An Overview," in Gerry Johnstone, ed., *A Restorative Justice Reader* (Willan Publishing, 2003), 28.

24. See, e.g., Johnstone and Van Ness, eds., *Handbook of Restorative Justice*; John Braithwaite, "Principles of Restorative Justice," in Andrew von Hirsch et al., eds., *Restorative Justice and Criminal Justice: Competing or Reconcilable Paradigms?* (Hart Publishing, 2003); Gerry Johnstone, "Introduction: Restorative Approaches to Criminal Justice," in Johnstone, ed., *A Restorative Justice Reader*; Marshall, "Restorative Justice: An Overview," in Johnstone, ed., *A Restorative Justice Reader*; Daniel W. Van Ness and Karen Heetderks Strong, "Restorative Justice: Justice That Promotes Healing," in *Restoring Justice*, 2nd ed. (Anderson Publishing, 2001).

25. Howard Zehr, *Changing Lenses: A New Focus for Crime and Justice* (Herald Press, 1990), 81; also see Zehr, *The Little Book of Restorative Justice*.

26. Ibid.

27. See Van Ness and Strong, "Restorative Justice: Justice That Promotes Healing," 39, quoting John Braithwaite, *Crime, Shame and Reintegration* (Cambridge University Press, 1989), 172-173.

28. Most any criminal law casebook or treatise would identify the four main purposes of criminal law punishment as being retribution, deterrence, isolation, and rehabilitation. A general survey of principles of criminal law punishment appears in ch. 2 of Joshua Dressler, *Understanding Criminal Law*, 4th ed. (LexisNexis 2006).

29. See, e.g., Matthew W. Meskel, "An American Resolution: The History of Prisons in the United States from 1777 to 1877" in *Stanford Law Review* 51, 4 (April 1999), 839-865 or Michael Ignatieff, *A Just Measure of Pain: The Penitentiary in the Industrial Revolution, 1750-1850* (Pantheon Books, 1978). Also see Lorna A. Rhodes, "Toward an Anthropology of Prisons," in *Annual Review of Anthropology* 30 (2001), 65-83.

30. See, e.g., Karen O'Neill, "Organizational Change, Politics, and the Official Statistics of Punishment" in *Sociological Forum* 18, 2 (2003), 245-267.

31. See, e.g., Zehr, *Changing Lenses*; Van Ness and Strong, "Restorative Justice: Justice That Promotes Healing," esp. 31-32.

32. See, e.g., Mark Umbreit, *Victim Meets Offender: The Impact of Restorative Justice and Mediation* (Criminal Justice Press, 1994).

33. See, e.g., Jennifer Llewellyn, "Truth Commissions and Restorative Justice," in Johnstone & Van Ness, *Handbook of Restorative Justice*, 351-371. (Spring 2006) 19-21 at 21.

34. Class discussion, Restorative Justice class (Law 2318), Boalt Hall School of Law, University of California, Berkeley, February 6, 2008.

35. An assessment of the policy change appears in Crime and Justice Research Centre and Sue Triggs, New Zealand Ministry of Justice, *New Zealand Court-Referred Restorative Justice Pilot: Evaluation* (New Zealand Ministry of Justice, May 2005).

35. See Van Ness and Strong, "Restorative Justice: Justice That Promotes Healing," 39, quoting John Braithwaite, *Crime, Shame and Reintegration* (Cambridge University Press, 1989), 172-173.

36. Most any criminal law casebook or treatise would identify the four main purposes of criminal law punishment as being retribution, deterrence, isolation, and rehabilitation. A general survey of principles of criminal law punishment appears in ch. 2 of Joshua Dressler, *Understanding Criminal Law*, 4th ed. (LexisNexis 2006).

37. See New Zealand's 1989 *Children, Young Persons, and Their Families Act*. Except for murder/manslaughter, offenses are directed to the family group conferencing (FGC) system immediately, even prior to charges being brought. For more serious crimes an arrest and court appearance may come first, but then with referral to the FGC model. Those accused who deny any involvement are processed through a more traditional juvenile court trial, though in cases of a guilty verdict an FGC proceeding may occur before punishment is imposed.

  Additionally, Australia has adopted restorative justice models from its own indigenous community. See, e.g., Jim Consedine, "Aboriginal Australia: Betwixt and Between," in *Restorative Justice: Healing the Effects of Crime*, 109, 120. Canada has also successfully implemented restorative justice models. See, e.g., Julian V. Roberts and Kent Roach, "Restorative Justice in Canada: From Sentencing Circles to Sentencing Principles," in von Hirsch et al., *Restorative Justice and Criminal Justice*, 240-250. Scholars have compared the features of these models, centered on collaborative processes of restoration rather than correction, with similar features such as healing circles among Native American traditions in our own nation. See, e.g., Robert Yazzie, "'Hosho Nahasdlii' – We Are in Good Relations: Navajo Restorative Justice," *St. Thomas Law Review* 9 (1996), 117-124.

38. See, e.g., Johnstone and Van Ness, *Handbook of Restorative Justice*.

39. See, e.g., Balanced and Restorative Justice Project, "Balanced and Restorative Justice for Juveniles: A Framework for Juvenile Justice in the 21st Century," University of Minnesota (August 1997); Caren L. Flaten, "Victim-Offender Mediation: Application with Serious Offenses Committed by Juveniles," in Burt Galaway and Joe Hudson, eds., *Restorative Justice: International Perspectives* (Kugler Publications, 1996), 387-401; Executive Summary, "Face-to-Face with Urban Crime: Community-Based Restorative Justice in Minneapolis" (www.npcr.org/reports/npcr1046.html, 1/27/05).

40. See Sunny Schwartz, Michael Hennessey, and Leslie Levitas, "Restorative Justice and the Transformation of Jails: An Urban Sheriff's Case Study in Reducing Violence," *Police Practice and Research* 4 (2003), 399-410.

41. Presentation by Sunny Schwartz, RSVP co-founder and program director, to Restorative Justice class (Law 2318) at Boalt Hall School of Law, University of California, Berkeley, February 20, 2008.

42. My own list here adapts and combines the fourteen Catholic social thought themes identified in Peter J. Henriot, Edward P. DeBerri, and Michael J. Schultheis, *Catholic Social Teaching: Our Best Kept Secret* (Orbis, 1992), 2225, with William J. Byron's "Ten Building Blocks of Catholic Social Teaching," originally published in *America*, 31 October 1998 and reprinted in Thomas J. Massaro and Thomas A. Shannon, eds., *American Catholic Social Teaching* (Liturgical Press, 2002), 176-183.

  Other basic texts of Catholic social thought include: Charles E. Curran, *Catholic Social Teaching, 1891-Present: A Historical, Theological, and Ethical Analysis* (Georgetown University Press, 2002); Kenneth R. Himes, ed., *Modern Catholic Social Teaching: Commentaries and Interpretations* (Georgetown University Press, 2005); and David J. O'Brien and Thomas A. Shannon, eds., *Catholic Social Thought: The Documentary Heritage* (Orbis Books, 1992).

43. Zehr, *Changing Lenses*, 197.

44. See, e.g., Pontifical Council for Justice and Peace, *Compendium of the Social Doctrine of*

the Church (USCCB Publishing, 2004), § 156 at 68-69, citing John XXIII, Encyclical Letter *Pacem in Terris* (*Acta Apostolica Sedis* (AAS) 55 (1963), 259-64) and the Second Vatican Council, Pastoral Constitution *Gaudium et Spes*, § 26 (AAS 58 (1966), 1046-47). The U.S. Bishops identify the rights and responsibilities theme as the second of six Catholic social thought principles orienting their analysis of crime and the restorative justice alternative. *See Responsibility, Rehabilitation, and Restoration*, 23.

45. A helpful fundamental overview of Christian theological and social anthropology as drawn from Scripture and tradition occurs in J. Neuner and J. Dupuis, eds., "Humankind and the World," in *The Christian Faith in the Doctrinal Documents of the Catholic Church*, 7th ed. (Alba House, 2001), 163-194.

A helpful fundamental overview of Christian theological and social anthropology as drawn from Scripture and tradition occurs in J. Neuner and J. Dupuis, eds., "Humankind and the World," in *The Christian Faith in the Doctrinal Documents of the Catholic Church*, 7th ed. (Alba House, 2001), 163-194.

For scholarly commentary see, e.g., Anne M. Clifford, "Creation," in Francis Schüssler Fiorenza and John P. Galvin, eds., *Systematic Theology*, vol. I (Fortress Press, 1991), 193-248; and Karl Rahner, "The Hearer of the Message" and "Man in the Presence of Absolute Mystery," in *Foundations of Christian Faith* (Crossroad, 2004), 24-89.

46. From the Old Testament compare, for example, the older, pre-exilic Yahwist (Gen 2.4b-3.24) versus the post-exilic Priestly (Gen 1.1-2.4a) creation traditions within the opening chapters of Genesis, as well as the covenant theology of the Prophehtic texts, and the traditions of discernment within the Wisdom literature. Paul offers the most developed anthropology in the New Testament: humans are historical beings who are creatures of God's creation (Rom 1, 3, 11, 15; 1 Cor 1, 4; 2 Cor 1:12). Given Paul's theology of sin, his Christocentric and cruciform anthropology accents what Jesus, the One Man/New Adam accomplishes: correcting the wrong of the first man/Adam and re-creating us as a new humanity in Christ free to live a life of service and love (1 Cor 7, 9). See Neuner and Dupuis, "Humankind and the World."

47. Again, Donahue's "The Bible and Catholic Social Teaching" is an invaluable resource.

48. St. Thomas Aquinas offers the classical Catholic formulation of the natural law in *Summa Theologiae* I-II, q. 91, a. 2. Also see *Compendium of the Social Doctrine of the Church*, §140, or Stephen J. Pope, "Natural Law in Catholic Social Teachings," in Himes, *Modern Catholic Social Teaching*, 41-71.

49. The U.S. Bishops' *Responsibility, Rehabilitation, and Restoration* suggests a similar reading of the natural law, in terms of guiding individual conscience both *within* and *for the sake of* community: "we begin with a belief in the existence of a natural moral law that resides within the hearts of individuals and within the life of the community. This moral code is common to all peoples and is never fully excused by external circumstances. All are born with free will that must be nurtured and informed by spiritual, intellectual, emotional, and physical disciplines and by the community." *Responsibility, Rehabilitation, and Restoration*, 20.

50. *Responsibility, Rehabilitation, and Restoration*, 16.

51. "Human life and dignity" is the first of the Catholic social thought principles that *Responsibility, Rehabilitation, and Restoration* lists as duly influencing a Catholic response to crime and criminal justice. *Responsibility, Rehabilitation, and Restoration*, 21-23.

52. The rendering of justice as "fidelity to the demands of a relationship" comes from John R. Donahue's study of biblical justice themes, especially the terms *sedaqah* and *mispat* in the Old Testament, and the tracing of OT themes of covenant law and justice in NT texts. *See* Donahue, "The Bible and Catholic Social Teaching," in Himes, ed., *Modern Catholic Social Teaching*, 9-40. The "fidelity to the demands of a relationship" definition was first proposed by Donahue in "Biblical Perspectives on Justice," in John Haughey, ed., *The Faith That Does Justice* (New York: Paulist, 1977), 69.

53. This definition is my own, but it echoes Catholic social thought's perhaps most normative statement of solidarity, Pope John Paul II's Sollicitudo Rei Socialis (1987). There he claims that the fact of human interdependence imputes certain moral implications: its "correlative response as a moral and social attitude, as a 'virtue,' is solidarity ... a firm and persevering determination to commit oneself to the common good; that is to say to the good of all and of each individual, because we are all really responsible for all" (SRS §38, emphasis in the original text). Charles E. Curran's definition also is worth noting: "solidarity helps us to see the 'other' – whether that other is a person, people, or nation – not just as an object to be exploited but as our neighbor and helper, called with us to share in the banquet of life to which all are invited equally by God." See Curran, Catholic Social Teaching, 1891-Present, 36.

    I have explored this topic in "Cultivating Responsive Solidarity," presented at the Justice in Jesuit Higher Education Conference, John Carroll University, Cleveland, OH (October 2005). Available online: www.loyola.edu/Justice/commitment/commitment2005/presenters.html); and (with Timothy Brown) in "Incarnating Solidarity and Justice: Perspectives from Service-Learning in Philosophy and Ignatian Spirituality," presented at Catholic Social Thought Across the Curriculum, University of St. Thomas, St. Paul, MN (October 2003) (available online: www.stthomas.edu/cathstudies/cst/educ/03conference/papers/DenkBrown.pdf).

54. In addition to *Sollicitudo Rei Socialis*, other encyclical letters of Pope John Paul II such as *Redemptor* Hominis (1979), *Laborem Exercens* (1981), and *Fides et Ratio* (1998) also evidence the influence of personalist philosophy.

55. An assessment of the policy change appears in Crime and Justice Research Centre and Sue Triggs, New Zealand Ministry of Justice, *New Zealand Court-Referred Restorative Justice Pilot: Evaluation* (New Zealand Ministry of Justice, May 2005).

56. See Zehr, *The Little Book of Restorative Justice*, 44-47.

57. *Responsibility, Rehabilitation, and Restoration*, 23.

58. Byron, "Ten Building Blocks of Catholic Social Teaching," 180.

59. Bazemore and Umbreit, "A Comparison of Four Restorative Conferencing Models," 225-243.

60. Ibid. Also see Gordon Bazemore and Lori Ellis, "Evaluation of Restorative Justice" (397-423) and Hennessey Hayes, "Reoffending and Restorative Justice" (426-444) in Johnstone & Van Ness, *Handbook of Restorative Justice*.

61. Prison Fellowship International, "Introduction" to Restorative Justice Online website: http://www.restorativejustice.org/intro, (last accessed February 26, 2008) (emphasis added).

62. See, e.g., James Gilligan, *Violence: Reflections on a National Epidemic* (Vintage, 1996).

63. This point is one of eleven "Policy Foundations and Directions" charted by the U.S. Bishops in Responsibility, Rehabilitation, and Restoration, 29-31.

64. Various chapters in Part 4, "Restorative Justice in Social Context," of Johnstone & Van Ness, Handbook of Restorative Justice, echo this framing, emphasizing both "how restorative justice has been applied – and adapted to apply – in … various settings, but also … how restorative justice can play a role in transforming the nature of controlling institutions and … how the idea of restorative justice has itself been developed as a result of efforts to address a wider range of problems than juvenile and adult offending." Johnstone & Van Ness, "Restorative Justice in Social Context," 265.

65. See, e.g., Pranis, "Restorative Values," esp. 67-68

66. David Hollenbach provides an excellent contemporary analysis of this strand of Catholic social thought in *The Common Good and Christian Ethics* (Cambridge University Press, 2002), esp. ch. 3, "Recovering the Commonweal" (65-86) and ch. 5, "Christianity in a Community of Freedom" (113-136).

67. Among the U.S. Bishops' "Policy Foundations and Directions" are "promoting serious efforts toward crime prevention and poverty reduction" and other social and economic justice observations and recommendations. *Responsibility, Rehabilitation, and Restoration*, 29.

68. *Responsibility, Rehabilitation, and Restoration*, passim.

69. John Paul II, encyclical letter *Sollicitudo Rei Socialis* (1987), § 38.

70. *Responsibility, Rehabilitation, and Restoration*, 25.

71. Johnstone & Van Ness address this issue in "The Meaning of Restorative Justice," ch. 1 (5-23) in *Handbook of Restorative Justice*, 15-16.

72. *Responsibility, Rehabilitation, and Restoration*, 19, citing "Message of His Holiness John Paul II for the Jubilee in Prisons" (Vatican City, June 24, 2000).

73. *Responsibility, Rehabilitation, and Restoration*, 27-45.

74. Ibid, 47-53.

From Mutilation to Donation: Revising Moral Doctrine, Catholic Theology, Organ Transplantation and Social Policy

Dr. Albert R. Jonsen
Professor Emeritus of Ethics in Medicine, University of Washington

CATHOLIC SOCIAL CONCERNS LECTURE SERIES I March 29, 2005

T he transplantation of limbs or organs between humans was, until recently, physically impossible. Thus, its successful occurrence appeared only in myth, legend and miracle. A medieval story relates the miracle of Saints Cosmos and Damien, two holy physicians, who, at an angel's behest, removed the gangrenous leg of a patient and replaced it with the leg of a cadaver awaiting burial. This miracle, depicted in many medieval frescos, demonstrated that God alone performed the transplant; the doctors were merely agents of divine healing.

The miracles of nature arouse human curiosity and ingenuity. And, during the 20th century, the miracle of transplantation became one of the greatest achievements of modern medicine. Starting in the 1950s and continuing into the present, individuals whose vital organs, such as kidneys, heart and liver, have failed can be saved from certain death by the timely transplantation of an organ taken from another human. From the very first reports of success, this achievement was acclaimed as a "medical miracle." Unlike a theological miracle, however, which takes place suddenly, in a flash of faith and divine power, transplantation was a slowly evolving miracle. Also, unlike a divine miracle, which is an undiluted good and benefit to the one who receives it, the miracle of transplantation has always had its negative effects, its partial failures. And, finally, unlike a miracle that must, given its divine agent, always be unambiguously morally right, doubt has surrounded the moral propriety of moving organs from one person to another.

The purpose of this Lane Lecture is to trace the evolution of a particular teaching in Catholic moral theology, namely, the moral permissibility of taking a vital organ for transplantation from one person to another. The history of this teaching reveals a movement from one moral stance, condemnation, to another, commendation. It reveals a move from an individualistic to a social view of the problem and, finally, it shows an internal Catholic moral teaching that had a significant impact on secular moral judgment about the issue.

Catholic moral theology has been, since most ancient times, as deeply engaged in the life of the body as that of the soul. In particular, the work of medicine was considered a moral task, capable of being done virtuously or sinfully, and various medical procedures fell under the scrutiny of moral theologians. Since organ transplantation was not physically possible, it was not included in the treatises of the moralists. However, another procedure, amputation, was a standard part of the medical agenda. The moral theologians considered it under the general rubric of the Fifth Commandment of the Decalogue, *Thou shalt not kill*. They collected under that rubric not only acts of violence that killed but those that maimed or harmed the physical body. Since amputation of a crushed or partially severed limb was often the only means to save life, moral theologians had to ask whether this mutilation of the body was morally legitimate. In general, they noted that the human body was under God's dominion: thus, suicide and mutilation were a violation of God's dominion. Humans, however, have a delegated dominion: they must act to preserve the body in life and health. Thus, they concluded, a mutilation that was necessary to preserve the body was permitted. This concept was formulated as the "principle of totality:" any bodily mutilation was justifiable morally if and only if it contributed to the good of the whole body. St. Thomas Aquinas discusses this principle briefly.[1]

Two particular questions about mutilation dealt with male castration. A strict doctrine of sexual purity was often taught in the ancient church. One prestigious Church figure, the theologian Origen, was said to have castrated himself in order to preserve his chastity. This practice was never officially sanctioned, but Origen set a bad example for some zealous men. In the 12th century, for example, a papal document answers the question: whether a castrated man could be ordained a priest. The answer is yes, if his condition arises from a hostile act or a medical necessity but, "if done by his own hand, to avoid carnal vices, he should be considered ineligible, just as if he was an attempted suicide." A second moral problem concerned castration of children to preserve their voices for choral singing. This vile custom was tolerated in light of the *greater good* of divine worship until the mid-18th century.

The question of castration took an even more sinister turn in the early 20th century. The widespread ideology of eugenics, the planned improvement of the quality of the human race, had fostered the practice of sterilization of the mentally and morally unfit or feebleminded. A number of American states, led by California in 1909, enacted laws requiring castration by vasectomy and ovariectomy (operations invented for that purpose) of persons released from mental institutions. The German Eugenic Sterilization Act of 1933 initiated widespread sterilization. Eugenic sterilization stimulated the first official papal notice of the principle of totality. In 1930, Pope Pius XI issued an Encyclical on marriage entitled *Casti Connubii*. In it, he specifically noted the practice of eugenic sterilization. He stated the general moral principle: "people are not free to destroy or mutilate their members ... except when no other provision can be made for the good of the whole body." He then extended that principle to the authority of the state, which, he said, had no right or authority to order sterilizing mutilations. In 1936, the Holy Office, under his authority, issued condemnations of sterilization for contraception and for eugenic purposes.[2]

Medical transplantation was still in the laboratory in those years. The great French surgeon had advanced the practice by perfecting the reconnection of small blood vessels.

He incessantly attempted to transplant organs between animals. He succeeded surgically but failed medically, due to the inevitable rejection of foreign tissue between distinct individuals. In England, Sir Peter Medewar and his colleagues, struggled to save horribly burned RAF pilots by transplanting skin. In doing so, Medawar began to unlock the genetic locks that kept the tissue of one person from integrating into the tissue of another. Finally, in 1954, Drs. Joseph Murray and John Merrill at Boston's Peter Bent Brigham Hospital transplanted a kidney from an identical twin to his brother. Since they were genetically identical, the kidney was not rejected and the patient survived for many years. The *age of transplantation* was under way. Within a few years, drugs to combat rejection had been devised and transplant moved from identical twins to closely related persons. In 1967, the next great leap was taken: Dr. Christian Barnard of Capetown, South Africa, transplanted a heart into Philip Blaiberg who lived a year and a half. Within a decade, hearts, kidneys, livers, lungs, pancreas and guts were being transplanted all throughout the world.

We return from medical to moral history. The moral theologians now had a new topic to include in the treatise on mutilation: organ transplantation. The first moral problem that they noted was, quite naturally, the aspect of transplantation closest to the traditional doctrine: the removal of a vital organ from a healthy human being. Since the first decade of transplantation was almost exclusively one of taking organs from living persons to give to another (a practice made possible by the physical fact that a kidney can be removed from the body without impairing renal function: persons can live perfectly well with only one kidney and by the genetic fact that organs were best matched between relatives), the first question was: is it morally legitimate to remove an organ, not for the benefit of the person from whom it is taken (as in a medically necessary amputation) but for the benefit of another person. This was an unprecedented moral situation.

The response from the moral theologians was almost unanimous. Their judgment was that such a procedure was immoral: it simply violated the principle of totality. The harshness of the judgment was somewhat mitigated by the sad fact that many transplants, in those early days, were not successful. It was still a highly experimental and highly risky procedure. There was, however, one exception to the almost uniform condemnation. A graduate student at Catholic University of America, Fr. Bert Cunningham, wrote a bold doctoral thesis, contesting the judgment of his elders. Interestingly enough, he also had the jump on them, since he wrote in 1944, before transplantation had become possible. His was a rather speculative thesis (perhaps that was why he got away with it!). He did note two forms of transplantation that were being tried, one on an experimental basis, and the other very rare: The first was transplantation of an ovary into an infertile woman; the second was transplantation of a cornea from one living person to another (this latter was rare because corneas had been successfully transplanted from cadavers to

living person and it is hard to see why a sighted person would give up an eye).
Still, Cunningham took these rather marginal examples in order to raise the
larger question about a transplantation that was still in the future.[3]

Cunningham's thesis was that transplantation was not a violation of the
principle of totality. He drew on a doctrine of Catholic theology that was, at
that time, very much discussed: the doctrine of the Mystical Body of Christ.
This doctrine proposed that some scriptural references, largely from the
writings of the Apostle Paul, suggested that the church could be conceived as
an organic body, with Christ as the head and all Christians as members. Cunningham drew moral implications from this theological doctrine. He wrote,
"there exists an ordination of men to one another and as a consequence, an
order of their members to one another ... Thus, we contend that men are ordinated to society as parts to a whole and, as such, are in some way ordinated
to one another." This spiritual ordering allows any person to mutilate himself
physically for the good of another part of the mystical body (unless the
mutilation caused sterilization or great bodily harm). Crucial to this theological doctrine is the concept that this body is *mystical* in the sense that it is not
coincident with the visible church: it contains all humans, even those who do
not know that they are part of it, because Christ has redeemed all humans.
Thus, transplantation is morally legitimate between all humans.

Cunningham wrote, as I have said, before transplantation became a clinical
possibility. However, his thesis got some notice a decade later, when transplantation was much closer to reality. Pope Pius spoke to a convention of
histopathologists in 1952. He devoted his remarks to a discussion of experimentation and noted that one justification often given for experimenting on
individuals is that it is for the good of society. He then comments that this is
a distortion of the moral notion of community. "Community," he said, "exists
to facilitate exchange of mutual need and to aid each man to develop his personality in accord with his individual and social abilities. Community is not a
physical unity subsisting in itself and its individual members are not integral
parts of it."[4] Cunningham is not mentioned by name but his thesis is clearly in
the Pope's eye.

Two years later, Pope Pius XII addressed a group of ophthalmologists on
the topic of corneal transplants. Again, he does not directly cite Cunningham
but the allusion is clear enough. "We must note a remark," he said,

> [T]hat leads to confusion and which we must rectify ... that
> individuals could be considered parts and members of the whole
> organism that constitutes "humanity" in the same manner—or
> almost—as they are parts of the individual organism of a man. This
> is inaccurate. Integrity means the bodily unity of a physical organ-
> ism in which parts have no independent function except in relation
> to a whole ... in "humanity" each individual is a value in himself,
> although related to others.

The Holy Father does emphasize that he is not speaking of taking an organ for the sake of others; rather he devotes his remarks on that occasion to removing the cornea from a cadaver.[5] Still both of these allocutions emphasize an individualist rather than a communitarian interpretation of the principle of totality.

These papal statements played a significant role in the interpretation that the moral theologians of the first era of transplantation give to mutilation. Most of the leading theologians cite these statements as authoritative when they censure mutilation for transplantation. However, they fail to set the papal remarks in full context. The 1930 Encyclical of Pius XI was discussing the mutilation for the purpose of eugenic sterilization. The two allocutions of Pius XII, while endorsing an individualist interpretation of the principle of totality and condemning its extension to society, were given at a time when the Pope (and the rest of the world) were deeply concerned about totalitarianism, the political ideology that subordinates individuals to the state. He explicitly has the Nazi medical experiments in mind when making his remarks about the principle of totality in relation to experimentation.

In those early years, the center of theological attention was, as I have said, the legitimacy of taking an organ from a healthy body. This was also the center of attention for medical ethics and for the law. Never had doctors imagined that they could operate on a healthy body with impunity, much less take from it a vital organ. Dr. Murray himself told a conference on organ transplantation, "as physicians motivated and educated to make sick people well, we make a qualitative shift in our aims when we risk the health of a well person, no matter how pure our motives." At that same conference, a prominent British jurist expressed the traditional view of Anglo-American law: "a person cannot consent under the law ... to be maimed." The Catholic theologians were addressing a moral problem faced not only by Catholics but by every ethical doctor who must make a decision to retrieve a kidney or every judge who must decide whether it is legal to do so.[6]

In 1954, the year Drs. Murray and Merrill performed the first kidney transplant, a hint of change in the universally negative theological opinion appeared. In the United States, the Jesuit theological journal, *Theological Studies*, published several times a year a compendium of opinions by leading American Jesuit moral theologians. One of those theologians, Fr. John Connery, commented on Cunningham's thesis. "Personally," he said, "I am in favor of it." He did not consider Cunningham's justification based on the theology of the Mystical Body at any length. Rather he simply referred to an analogous issue. Theologians allowed a pregnant woman to undergo risky surgery in order to save her fetus; why should they object to a person undergoing similar risks to "sacrifice an organ for the good of another."[7]

Two years later, the most eminent Jesuit moralist, Fr. Gerald Kelly, devoted an entire article to "Pope Pius XII and the Principle of Totality." He noted that the Pope's condemnations of mutilation are, in their context, intended as condemnations of eugenic sterilization and of human experimentation under totalitarian coercion. They were not directly relevant to organ transplantation. Kelly fashions an argument that combines Connery's claim that a person can assume risk for the sake of another and Cunningham's thesis about the unity of the human race (abstaining from the more theological Mystical Body argument). He added a point of his own: Transplantation is justified by the law of charity, calling on persons to make sacrifices for the good of others, just as Christ had sacrificed himself for the salvation of the world. St. Thomas had affirmed that a person may even give his life for the good of another person. "Aquinas showed that in giving one's life for his neighbor, one prefers his own good of a higher order ... namely, not a physical good but the good of virtue." Thus, even the one who sacrifices an organ is the recipient of a good. Kelly concluded:

> Organ transplantation is licit provided it confers a proportionate benefit on the recipient without exposing the donor to great risk of life or depriving him of an important function ... the principle argument is the law of charity which is based on the natural and supernatural unity of mankind and according to which the neighbor is "another self." Thus arises the principle that we may do for the neighbor what we in similar circumstances may do for ourselves."[8]

Kelly wrote a second article in the next year, giving it the suggestive title, "The Morality of Mutilation: Toward a Revision of the Treatise." It had become clear, in his view, that the classical theological treatise about mutilation needed to be revised in light of the scientific achievements in transplantation. Not only could a kidney be taken from a healthy person with relatively low risk, that same organ would very likely save the life of another. The classical arguments about mutilation, including the papal statements, were valid in their contexts but were inadequate to deal with this new phenomenon. A new formulation was required. He suggested the formulation: "The rule of morality should be stated: ordinarily, direct self mutilation is permitted only for one's own direct good but, in exceptional circumstances, the law of charity allows it for the benefit of the neighbor."[9]

He concluded his article with a comment that, although some called for an explicit papal statement to resolve the controversy, he felt that the controversy itself was valuable. "We are learning much from the controversy and we will still learn more, and surely no harm will come from it if moralists avoid the moral errors at which papal statements have been leveled." Fr. Kelly was a strong advocate of respect for papal teaching but, at the same time, as a skilled theologian, he recognized that any papal statement called for careful interpretation in the light of context and circumstances.

The *revision of the treatise* took hold. One of the Church's most respected moralists, Bernard Haring, wrote in his major textbook, "It is surely the mark of the most profound reverence toward our neighbor to be willing to sacrifice an organ of one's own body for him in his necessity. ... In transplantation, the organ is not destroyed but lovingly transferred to one's neighbor in order to overcome a hazard to his life."[10]

The law of charity, so central to Catholic morality, took its place as the most basic justification of the previously condemned mutilation. In the secular world of medical ethics and law, the non-theological counterpart of charity, became the key concept supporting the morality of transplantation: the giving of a gift, a donation, and the gift that was given was *the gift of life*. The mutilating act of the surgeon now became the means whereby this gift was transferred. Consent to be a donor did, contrary to the ancient maxim, justify what would otherwise be a legal battle. This became the language used to encourage persons to offer themselves as sources of organs. A *gift relationship* existed between giver and recipient. In 1968, legislation was proposed under the title Uniform Anatomical Gift Act. This legislation, quickly adopted by all American states, authorized persons to donate organs at death and made people familiar with the donor card and the mark on the driver's license. Certain proposals to increase the availability of organs, such as allowing organs to be sold, were repudiated by arguing that such practices would undermine the gift relationship so important to the moral basis of transplantation.

A recent historian of transplantation sums up the importance of this concept:

> Altruism in organ donation has been the lynchpin of transplantation since its inception. The gift of life is a concept that comforts many donor families faced with the sudden and tragic death of a relative and allows them solace by realizing that the organs and tissues of someone they loved may live on in another.[11]

I do not claim that the considerations of Catholic moral theologians directly influenced the secular morality and legality of organ donation. The theological and the secular language and concepts grew up in the same atmosphere and certainly affected each other. In this lecture my point is to show how traditional concepts of moral theology undergo evolution due to circumstances and to critical evaluation of the contexts in which they originate. Unquestionably, the problem of evolution or development of moral doctrine is a complex one and calls for many more examples and much more analysis than this lecture can provide. Yet the brief story of the shift from mutilation to donation is one instructive example.

Notes:

1. *Summa Theologiae*, II-II, 65, 1.

2. *Casti Connubii*, 1930, 22-23; Holy Office 1936.

3. Bert Cunningham, *The Morality of Organic Transplantation. Studies in Sacred Theology*, 1944, no. 86.

4. *Acta Apostolici Sedis* 1952; 44: 786.

5. *Acta Apostolici Sedis*, 1956; 48: 446).

6. *Law and Ethics of Transplantation*. London, 1966, p.59, 3.

7. "Notes on Moral Theology," *Theological Studies*, 1954; 15:

8. *Theological Studies*, 1955; 16: 392.

9. *Theological Studies*, 1956; 17: 342.

10. *The Law of Christ*, III, 242.

11. N. Tilney, *Transplant: from Myth to Reality*. New Haven: Yale University Press, 2003, p. 262.

Is it Ethical to be Catholic?
Queer Perspectives

Rev. James Alison
Priest, author, theologian.

COMMUNITY IN CONVERSATIONS PROJECT I February 12, 2006

The question "Is it ethical to be Catholic?" is, to my mind, a somewhat surprising one, even when asking for queer perspectives.[1] It has had me scratching my head. You see, it would never have crossed my mind to wonder whether it is ethical to be Catholic, and I am not at all sure that I understand from where the question arises. I guess that the reason for my bafflement is that I have never met anyone who became a Catholic for ethical reasons. Every Catholic I know is so either because they were baptised as an infant and brought up that way, or because they converted to Catholicism later in life, and few of the conversion stories I've heard, have had to do with ethics. Mine is no exception. I became a Catholic when I was eighteen, at a time when there was no Pope (Paul VI had just died), and so, at my reception into the Church, I recited a formula of obedience to "Our Pope N." He has been one of my favourite Popes ever since. Every now and then, over the last twenty-five years or so, I have been tempted to want him back, though at the moment I am very happy with his substitute.

What brought me into the Church was a mixture of two graces. The first was falling in love with a Catholic classmate at school some years before my conversion. He was, and is, straight, but I perceived a certain warmth of personality in him, which seemed atypical of the world of Protestant schoolboys in which I lived, and I associated that warmth with his being Catholic. The second grace came at a time, shortly before going to university, when I was at a very low ebb, having just started to come out as a gay man in a very hostile, conservative evangelical environment. This grace I associate absolutely with the intercession of Padre Pio, coming, as it did, after I glimpsed something of the link between his stigmata and the sacrifice of the Mass. I knew then and have known since that the Mass isn't merely a memorial supper. I have always felt that this grace, which was accompanied by an astounding joy, literally blew me into the Church. It gave me the gift of the Catholic faith. Once it had fallen upon me, I knew myself to be involved in, and with, something that has been a love affair ever since, something that seems to open out and get bigger and better all the time. I was aware even then that my often-tortuous journey of self-acceptance as a gay man and my felicitous experience of becoming a Catholic were part of the same movement of joy. And God has been faithful, keeping the texture of those loves intertwined and slowly bringing them into one love and one blessing. God continues to nurture the heart that he chose to give me and keeps it safe from (the Lord alone knows how much of) my own erratic behaviour, slowness to trust and cowardice, as well as from the defamation and the hatred espoused by so many whose job it is to speak in God's name.

It certainly never crossed my mind back then to think that it was ethical to be Catholic. It seemed self-evident to me, with my English middle-class prejudices, that Protestants were much more moral people than Catholics. In the 1950s-style evangelical Protestantism of my background, the suspicion that the Pope was the Antichrist never lurked far beneath the surface. I remember some weeks of spiritual pain as I worked through the scar on my soul that had been left by my exposure to that lie and the fear that, by becoming a Catholic, I might be handing over my life to the service of evil. A couple of years later, I read that John Henry Newman had worked through just such a pain in his process of being brought by God into the life of the Church. And since then, other converts from the same background as me, have mentioned a similar painful passage. Here we are talking not, I think, about a level-headed discussion concerning what is good, but about a deep, existential terror that I might be sucked into the service of evil, and I would not know. Since that time, such moments of fear assail me every now and then, and they are compounded by the very deep fears of being evil which seem to be common among gay youths from religious backgrounds. I have learned to sit back, look at these assaults, giggle, and be aware that God is much bigger, more powerful, more gentle and more trustworthy than my own heart, that I should not take myself so seriously as to think that I could really get in God's way very effectively or for very long.

Then again, one of the reliefs about coming into the Church was precisely how it was *not* ethics obsessed. I remember realising, a year or so after becoming a Catholic, that one of the first things I had to learn, bizarrely, was how to sin. In the world where I was formed, being good was obligatory. And sinning, being bad, was a terrible letting down of the side, a sort of failure of English gentlemanliness. This created a constant struggle to live up to being good. It would seem that a strong belief in justification by faith alone seems to have, as its psychological counterpart, an extreme need to justify oneself. As a Catholic, I had to learn that sin is boringly normal, and that what is exciting is being pulled into learning new things, called virtues, which are ways in which a goodness, which is not ours, becomes connatural with us, and that this is something of an adventure. I had to learn how not to be so concerned with whether I was getting things right or wrong, but to learn to relax into the given-ness of things. I can scarcely tell you how strange it sounds in retrospect, but I was discovering that it is part of the mercy of the Catholic faith that those of us who are infected by spiritual haughtiness find ourselves being lowered slowly and gently into the mud of being one of ordinary humanity, and learning how it is this ordinary humanity that is loved just as it is. If there are any diamonds, they will be found amidst the clay, as the outworkings of the pressures in the clay, not perched on high, trying to avoid being infected by so much common carbon.

Part of my induction into being Catholic has been the discovery of the secret presence of Our Lady permeating everything. For many of us who were brought up Protestant, it can take a long time to make sense of devotion to Our Lady, a devotion which can seem psychologically weird and does not strike chords in us. But I have come to rejoice in and to love Our Lady and the difference she makes in the Church. She makes it impossible for the Church to successfully turn itself into either an ideology or a moralistic enterprise. She can never quite be co-opted into standing for something other than what she is. I have come to see her as being the link, the non-opposition, between the old creation and the new, between nature and grace, between the Israel of the Prophets and Patriarchs and the new, universal Israel of God. She is far too delicate to be clearly delineated and far too present to be dismissed. For me, our Lady makes elements of the faith three-dimensional, elements which can only be lived-into over time.

The feast of the Assumption, in particular, is one where my heart soars, and I have, over my twenty-seven years of being a Catholic, enjoyed two special moments of grace from Our Lady on the Solemnity of the Assumption. One, when out for a walk in Cochabamba, Bolivia, where a sense of the openness of heaven gave me the inspiration for the second half of my book, *The Joy of Being Wrong*. And, more recently, and even more surprisingly, a grace came when I was desperate to think of a way to finish my book, *Faith Beyond Resentment*. I was in Rio de Janeiro, running out of time before I had to hand in the manuscript, and I was utterly stuck, at the end of my tether, having spent Sunday, 15 August, failing to do anything on the computer other than play FreeCell and Solitaire. As I fell asleep, I was given the parable of Nicodemus, the Inquisitor and the boys in the square, which became the end of the last chapter of the book. I remember giggling, so preposterous did it seem as an ending for the book. I also remember thinking, as I wrote it out the next day, that Our Lady's love for her queer children, one of the best-kept yet best-known, secrets of the Church, is something which no amount of ecclesiastical homophobia can vanquish.

I recently came across what was, for me, an entirely new and wonderful avocation of Our Lady: Our Lady Un-doer of Knots. In Brazil, I stumbled upon a locally-carved statue of her, which I bought without knowing anything about the devotion. It turned out to come from Augsburg in Germany, taken from a painting by an unknown artist dating from 1700. What on earth, you may ask, was a devotion from a baroque part of Germany doing being sculpted in Salvador, the most African part of Brazil? I can only answer that this is part of the uncanny wonder of the Catholic Church. The image is of Our Lady of the Immaculate Conception holding a cord with knots, which she is undoing. This avocation gives me great peace, since it is clear to me that the knots concerning the relationship between grace and desire, sin and concupiscence, which have been so tied up in knots for gay people in the life of our Church, are being gently and carefully undone by hands blessed with far more patience and delicacy than I could hope to muster.

Well, I hope you can see why I was surprised by the question "Is it ethical to be Catholic?" Being Catholic for me has meant discovering myself on the inside of something where God and many wonderful people are doing things for me long before I can manage to do anything minimally presentable for others. In other words, the relationship between being Catholic and ethics is not a straightforward one, and I would like to give you a brief reminder of its strangeness before turning to look at how this impacts the queer perspectives which you have invited me to discuss.

A few years back, I attended the funeral of a well-known London parish priest, Father Michael Hollings, in Westminster Cathedral. The Requiem Mass was presided over by Cardinal Basil Hume, and there was a huge turnout. Father Michael had been a decorated military officer, well-known spiritual author, university chaplain and innovative parish priest. A complex man, widely but discretely known to be gay, he had, late in life, been suspended for some time following an allegation of molesting a youth. Although charges were never brought, Father Michael had asked the police that two other accounts of inappropriate behaviour be taken into account. I do not think anyone who knew him thought of him as flawless, but he was one of those people whose flaws were often transparent to grace, and people loved him, as was shown by the huge number of people, of all backgrounds, who came to his funeral. Cardinal Hume was in particularly fine form, directing his homily to Father Michael in his coffin, talking fondly, chidingly, infuriatedly, lovingly. What I, and others, came away with from this funeral Mass, and this is not something that any liturgist can just produce, was a palpable sense of the proximity, solidity and openness of eternal life. The Catholic faith is, in the first place, and above all, to do with eternal life. And I suppose it is important just to remember that. Why do any of us become Catholic and remain Catholic? Well, ultimately, because it is God's way of giving us eternal life, God's own life.

There is something special about this, something characteristic and odd. We find our hearts, minds and imaginations being opened up to perceive how YHWH, the God of Israel and Creator of all things, was present in the life, teaching and signs of Jesus of Nazareth in such a way that the very special rock-solidity of presence associated with YHWH was recognised in Jesus' own person. A group of not particularly distinguished people whom Jesus had chosen to be the witnesses to what he was about, found, after his death, that he was present to them in the way that was proper to YHWH, the Rock, the one who knows not death and who causes all things to be. These same ordinary people began to understand that this Rock, the one who makes all things to be and keeps them in unfrustratable being, had been present in Jesus all along, such that the day-to-day acting out of his life was a new and definitive glimpse at the inner life of God. His lived experiences show how much God loves us and wants to empower us to share his life, so that we can be much, much more than we ever thought possible.

This undistinguished group of people even became aware that when Jesus had nicknamed one of them, the notoriously volatile and unstable character Simon, "Rock," this wasn't just an ironic joke, but was part of the way that the Rock of Israel was going to make itself present in the life of humans. In other words, the rock-solidity of salvation made present by Jesus was not going to float in the air as some sort of spiritual doctrine for cognoscenti, but salvation was going to be made available to anybody through the witness given by a whole collection of highly implausible and improbable characters. In the midst of these characters, a certain derivative rock-quality, associated with the ministry of Peter, would also, always, be made available to all, as part of the indestructible opening up of the gates of Heaven on Earth. This indestructible quality resists all our death-bound-ness, all our waves of desire, patterns of hatred, fear and refusal of life. This gift of a continuing rock-quality, an un-snuffable, already-opened-for-us quality is largely independent of the highly mutable moral qualities of all of us, and it is also independent of the often undependable and mutable character of Simon Peter's successors.

From my perspective, John Paul was high on bluster and sounding firm and certain about everything, which made the quality of divinely-given *rockitude* rather more difficult to glimpse beneath the showier elements of his personality. That is until his last weeks, when he gave a glorious witness to the palpable abundance of eternal life. One of the things I especially like about Papa Ratzi is that he is a much more modest, self-effacing, even timid man, and this enables the rock quality, the authentic Petrine benchmark quality, to shine through rather more perceptibly. He knows that it is not about *him*, and I think that ordinary Catholics in Italy sensed rather quickly that the Petrine charism, the surety, is alive and shining in him.

I'd like to suggest that this rock quality permeates the Catholic faith in a whole lot of different areas. I sometimes describe it as the *just-there* quality, and I suppose we meet it most regularly in the liturgy where we are in the actual presence of Jesus. To me there is something quite wonderful about the quiet, serene, relaxedness, the lack of self-consciousness about Catholic worship, because we all know that Jesus is *just there*, giving himself for us and inviting us in. He's bigger than the flakiness of so many of our liturgies and the idiocy of so many of our homilies, and he's obviously bigger and better than the flawed-ness of our priests and, of course, of ourselves.

I know that this just-there quality, the *ex opere operato* nature of the sacraments, often leads us to the presumption of grace. For that reason, we typically spend too little time preparing our liturgies, give too little responsibility to proper musicians to organize real singing, spend too little time training preachers to know and love the Gospel text enough to preach from it, than we have any right to do. Yet this casual certainty of the self-giving of God to us, the knowledge that, however much we screw up, it is not our show but someone else's, seems to me to be an extraordinary gift, one that I associate with real faith. It is also one I associate with our Church order.

You see, I think that this very *given-ness*, this very just-there quality enables all of us to be more relaxed about popes, bishops, theologians, doctrines and so on than would be the case if we had to take such people desperately seriously, as though the matter ultimately depended on them getting it right.

We can be relaxed about Jesus in the Eucharist because we know that he is there, and that he will show himself to us as he will, in the way that is suitable for us and that we will be guided with love. We don't have to work ourselves up into knots of appropriate feeling, or self-consciousness, or liturgical perfection in order to *get it right*, because the real *getting it right* is being done by someone else; the most we can do is to be more or less appropriately respectful and grateful in our response.

I think the same is true about theological squabbles in the Church. We can relax about having to get it right because we know that the one who is making things right, who is bringing us into a new creation, does so hugely, safely, spaciously, gently. We can relax because, in the face of this unstoppable *just having happened*, this *just being there*, we are only tiny parts of the more or less chaotic response to whatever upheaval we are facing. We—popes, bishops, priests, theologians and every conceivable other sort of faithful—are all on the receiving side; all of us undergo it; we are not its protagonist.

I think this is huge and wonderful and specifically Catholic. The upheaval is bigger than any of us, all of us undergo it, and this means that over time we can learn to stand back from any and all of the things that we hold sacred, and see how the One who is happening in our midst, is beginning to reshape things. A sacredness resides in the signs of a new creation emerging in the midst of our own particular collapsing world. We can detect these signs; after all, we are not servants; we are on the inside of this project, not people to whom the project happens. Our Catholic faith is not a building project by a foreign corporation, which arrives and plants a huge factory on our street without any consultation or any legal guarantees, and then, in the face of our consternation, says: "You say you mind? Do we look to you as though we're concerned? We aren't doing this for your benefit!" Signs are genuinely difficult to interpret; what looks like good news for some people looks like the end of the world for others.

This *being shaken up as part of being saved* means that we can stop worrying about being wrong. Part of the joy in believing in the infallibility of the salvation that God gifts to the Church, is not having to hold too tightly to any notion of getting it right, and instead, being aware that we are on the rollercoaster where someone other than ourselves is getting it right, albeit with occasional contributions from us even, if we aren't entirely sure that the whole mess isn't against what sometimes seems to be our better judgement. This is because the *One who is getting it right* loves us and is getting through to us in ways that we do not at first understand, ways that take time for us to grasp are for our benefit. But we have been found and can trust that we will understand

and that it will make sense. We will be taken into all-truth even in the midst of our rows and disagreements.

Right now, for me, this knowing seems to be particularly important for those of us who are gay and lesbian Catholics. We are in the midst of a huge and emotionally charged row in our Church, a row that both seethes in silence and breaks out in strange and awful ways. What I find splendid is that, in the Catholic Church, faith prevents this row from being about ideology. Ideology is what you have when you don't have faith, when you don't recognize that there is *Another*, bigger than us, who holds all of us in his hand, and that ultimately we are safe; there is room; we can be wrong, and we can learn to get it right. If we don't know this, we are frightened of disagreement and need unanimity of opinion, of ideology: We need to enforce agreement; we need to establish who is in and who is out.

If we react like this, it means that our anchor is not in the rock beyond the veil. If it were, we would be happy to know that we can all be wrong together, and that our squabbling about what is right is a necessary part of the learning process for all of us. Through faith in the goodness and trustworthiness of the Creator, using human reason, we come to know what is objectively true. The great difficulty is learning how to be reasonable, learning to reason together, learning not to lynch each other, learning to detect when we are closing ourselves to the possibility of growth. We cannot reach resolution by lying and murdering in the name of what we take to be our identities, whether as individuals or as groups. How we conduct our rows and arguments is inseparable from what we discover to be true.

Something like this is going on at the moment for us, for gay and lesbian people in the Church. In the midst of frightening and violent struggles, shouting and name-calling, a certain sense of truth about who we are is beginning to become available to us. It becomes available to the degree we stop defining a particular group of people as evil just to hold on to a spuriously narrow sense of what is good. This is the only way anything about being human has ever been learned. It is only as we learn to see and love our neighbours as ourselves that we find out who we are, that we find out that we are much more than we thought we were.

Recently, the learning produced through just such a dynamic of seeing and loving our neighbours as ourselves has allowed a questioning, even at the highest levels of the Church, of the traditional way of looking at what was assumed to be a weird and evil behaviour. It is beginning to be possible to make a huge and new anthropological distinction between forms of behaviour that are a distortion of what people are, on the one hand, and forms of behaviour that can be a responsible part of what some people are, on the other[2].

We all understand that there are some distorted forms of behaviour into which males, particularly, and sometimes females, are initiated by force of circumstance, such as same-sex confinement, war, long journeys, imprisonment or strange religious cults. These distortions of behaviour may have a sexual component, but the sexual elements are symptoms; the real causes of these distortions are the misuse of power, the desire for dominance and/or financial advantage and the demarcation of property. The Church has always and everywhere considered these distortions of behaviour to be grave forms of depravity, never approved of under any circumstances.

What is beginning to become apparent is that there is a, more or less, regular minority of people of both sexes who, independent of circumstances, are principally attracted to people of their own sex at an emotional and erotic level. It is furthermore becoming clear that this is, in most cases, a stable and lifelong feature, that it is not, in any sense, a dysfunction and does not in any way diminish the viability of the persons who are this way. It is even beginning to become clear that such people are able to give and receive full-hearted love for each other, a love that is not just lust, nor defective, but is, quite simply, the real thing, which, when present, is recognised as a gift from, and an access to, God.

It is also beginning to become apparent that the attempt to describe these people by using the same ethical and descriptive tools as were used to describe the wayward form of behaviour is simply a category mistake. If you want to know what I mean by a category mistake, take a look at the famous picture of poor Private Lynndie England and her dog on a leash and the pile of humiliated male prisoners in Abu Ghraib. Then look at a picture, taken almost the same week, in 2004, that the Abu Ghraib photos became available, of two women walking down the steps of Boston City Hall waving a marriage certificate. Ask yourself: to which of these two images does the biblical category of *Sodom* rightly apply? The category mistake is to say: "Well, in some deep sense, they are both the same thing." Holding onto a category mistake as it becomes clear that something just is, ultimately constitutes a failure of faith, a refusal to allow ourselves to trust being pulled into the bigger picture, which is the new creation. And part of our trust in the Petrine gift, that key element of the Church, is that we know that ultimately, however much kicking and screaming goes on, God won't let such a failure of faith close down our access to that new creation.

Peter's job is to keep us together as we squabble over the extraordinary possibilities of truth and freedom which keep on being opened up for us, as God reveals to us who we are and how much we are loved. And, of course, keeping us together often means giving succour to brethren of weak conscience, those most frightened of change, those who most miss the apparent protection of the good old termite hill. As you would expect, it is such people who are most attracted to what they take to be the stability of the rock, and often enough they do quite a good job of hiding the fact that the stability of the Petrine rock derives from a Living Rock, one from which flows living water.

What I want to say at this point is: Now is not the moment to be despairing of the Church! I was taught at school that there is a so-called *J-curve* theory of revolutions, according to which, while people are really oppressed and downtrodden, right down at the bottom of the J, they don't rise up against the regime. It is only when their circumstances start to improve and the regime starts to lighten up that they finally rise up and throw off their shackles, at the beginning of the upward curve. And this, I suppose is what I make of the question you posed to me. From a queer perspective, why should we be wondering whether it is ethical to be Catholic now? We have just survived twenty-five years of John Paul, who, with all his qualities and virtues, seemed to me, at the distance from which I saw such things, a poor judge of character, and a man who gave succour to his sycophants. The result was that on his watch the Catholic faith seemed to become associated with a sort of totalising moral ideology in which we were simply a source of evil to be denounced and criticised.

It seems to me to be the height of perversity to get worried about whether it is ethical for us to be Catholic, just as it is becoming clear that we are in a much bigger and better space. The harshness of tone has gone, the temperature is going down. The visitation of seminaries seems, from what I have heard, to have been, in many cases, a less unpleasant experience than was feared. The long-awaited *Instruction* on not admitting gay people to the seminary seems to have fallen flat on its nose, with no indication that anyone in Rome is anything other than rather embarrassed by it. Certainly, there seems to be no inclination to make public agreement with the Instruction into the litmus test for episcopal appointments, which *Humanae Vitae* became under John Paul. The psychological backing for the Instruction met with well-nigh universal incredulity, and it seems that we are well on the way to a space where the issue of whether or not being gay is, as has been claimed, a psychological disorder, will be taken from the sphere of doctrine and placed where it belongs, in the sphere of the human sciences, with all the consequences which will follow from that.

Around the world, various forms of same-sex partnership laws appear to be becoming normal, Catholic countries having shown a great deal of ease in getting their heads around this. The result has been bishops everywhere (with, of course, some loud-mouthed exceptions) having learned, rather fast, to move from the vitriolic language and artificially dramatic displays of being shocked that such things should even be talked about, to something closer to adult discussion of the issues at hand. I rather think that Benedict is steering the very heavy John Paul emphasis on the family in a more productive direction. He appears to be keen that governments support the family; but, rather more subtly than John Paul, he is keen that this be a search for positive initiatives favouring the family. In other words, he has showed that it is possible to shift from an emphasis on the family, conceived of as over and against gay people, to one which needn't be over and against gay and lesbian people; indeed, we can interpret this as including us. True, in his recent encyclical, he privileges monogamous, heterosexual marriage as an especially blessed form of love; but we should not, I think, read the encyclical as a blow against same-sex love. It leaves room for us, and I suggest that we read it as an invitation for us to work out what the rich elements and gifts of same-sex love can be, and how we are to set about creating a Catholic culture of same-sex love.

It is up to us! That is where I think the ethical bit comes in. Are we going to allow ourselves to be given new life? What will be the shape of our moving from *creation into new creation*? This means working out what the holiness of life and of heart is for us, as gay and lesbian Catholics. It means noting that we are closer than ever to imagine that a rejoicing gay heart and a rejoicing Catholic heart can be the same heart, as well as a normal, healthy and holy thing. We can imagine a seminar reading *Brokeback Mountain* in the light of *Deus Caritas Est*, or vice versa. This could easily make sense to all those, straight or gay, who took part in such a session. One of the things, which as the Pope rightly insists, we might find ourselves learning, is how the development of our love should feed into, and be fed by, our development of charitable practices, of practical Catholic outreach to the poor, the sick, the imprisoned and the marginalised. It seems presumptuous of me even to mention it, here in this city of San Francisco, where the response to the HIV/AIDS pandemic on the part of many Catholic groups and individuals has been a beacon, but, even so, it is worth hammering home this point: Catholic faith without a love of the poor is not the real thing, and the Catholicity of gay love will be seen by our empowerment to love the dispossessed. No one will be able to take this away from us.

I am concerned, from an ethical position, that we are magnanimous victors. There are people in our Church who are seriously upset by the way Catholicism, in all its disputatiousness and diversity, is breaking out again under Pope Benedict. They are going to be terribly sore, as it becomes clear that the Church, in its stumbling, bumbling, chaotic way, is learning how to deal with the reality of honest, straightforward lesbian and gay people, how it is learning how to treat differences of opinion in this sphere as discussions, which do not merit exclusion from the life of the Church.

There are also a good number of priests and bishops, maybe a majority, who genuinely do not know what to do. They are themselves implicated, and they have never been able to face the issues of conscience, which come with understanding the deep fear about simply being gay. Perhaps they have been hoping against hope that Church structure would save them from having to face squarely their own truth. They are genuinely at sea. For them, the gentle, temperature-lowering way in which, as far as I can see, Pope Benedict wants to deal with this issue is, maybe for the first time in their lives, a permission not to have to get it right. It will take some time for people like this to say, "I just don't know what's right here, but let's try and help each other out of the hole." So, let us be gentle! Ethics is very much to do with how we extend mercy to the fearful, just as we have found ourselves the recipients of mercy when we have been frightened, tortured, annihilated by voices telling us how evil we were.

At this moment, the real ethical challenge for me as a Catholic is: I don't have an excuse any more. It is no good pretending that the Pope or the Church is really against me in the long haul, and so I have to fight him or them. Instead, I will have to grow up and learn to love, starting where I am, and being aware that the gift of a gay Catholic heart is a heavy responsibility, pregnant with love and opportunity.

Notes:

1. The title "Is it ethical to be Catholic? Queer Perspectives" was given to the author by the Lane Center, and he was invited to represent a positive answer to the question in the face of other panelists who represented the view that it is not ethical for a gay or lesbian person to continue to be a member of the Catholic Church.

   This paper has been previously published as the first chapter in the book *Broken Hearts and New Creations: Intimations of a Great Reversal* (London: Darton, Longman & Todd and New York: Continuum, 2010).

2. I take it that the recent Roman distinction, between transitory and deep-seated homosexual tendencies, opens up the possibility of eventual development in this direction.

Whose Holy Grail? Justice and Health Care in the Age of Genetics

Dr. Maura Ryan
Associate Dean, Arts & Letters, and Associate Professor, Department of Theology, University of Notre Dame

CATHOLIC SOCIAL CONCERNS LECTURE SERIES I April 26, 2005

think that it is safe to say that we are in the midst of a genomic revolution. The success of the Human Genome Project, the 13-year effort funded by the Department of Energy and the National Institutes of Health to map and sequence the human genome, is rapidly changing everything from the way we diagnose and treat disease to the way we understand health and "normality" to how we conceptualize our relationships to other forms of life. For a religious tradition such as Christianity, which has spoken of the human person as the crown of creation, genetic advances raise deep theological questions as we discover how little we differ genetically from other species, how very unremarkable human beings are genetically. Of course, here as everywhere, the devil is in the details, but considered just numerically, we have about the same number of genes as a laboratory mouse and slightly more than a mustard seed. The Human Genome Project is a stunning scientific achievement. Using samples from many donors, scientists have been able to *identify* all the approximately 30,000 genes in human DNA, and to *determine* the sequences of the 3 billion chemical base pairs that make up human DNA. According to the Department of Energy's primer on the genome project, "the order of the base pairs spells out exact instructions needed to maintain and reproduce a living organism, whether it's a person, a tree or microbe."[1] The Human Genome has been called the "Code of Codes," the "Book of Life," "Science's Holy Grail."

Although progress from research to clinical application has been slow, the long-range expectations for medicine are enormously exciting. In 2000, Francis Collins, who headed the Human Genome Project for the National Institutes of Health, predicted that within ten years, we will have tests (some performed even before birth) for identifying genetic predisposition to many of the major causes of death and chronic illness in this country—lung, colon and prostate cancer, coronary artery disease, diabetes, and osteoporosis.[2] By 2020, doctors will rely on individual genetic variations in prescribing drugs and choosing doses—cancer doctors will use drugs that precisely target a tumor's molecular fingerprint; by 2030, we will understand the genetic basis for aging and clinical trials will be underway to extend human life spans (an average lifespan of 90 is not unrealistic); by 2040, gene therapy and gene-based drugs will be available for most diseases.

Much has already been written on the ethical issues raised by the Human Genome Project. Not surprisingly, most of the attention within medical ethics (particularly in the U.S.) has focused on the issues of access and control of information: Who has the right to genetic information, to what uses can it be put, what are the commercial boundaries on genetic material, what is the scope of our responsibility to future generations, what are the limits, if any, on a parent's freedom to alter or enhance an offspring's genetic make-up? These are serious questions and they deserve attention. Indeed, Lee Silver, cell biologist from Princeton, argues that the single most significant driving force in future applications of genetic technologies will be the desire of parents to provide their children with the best possible future prospects. However, tonight I want to focus on an area which has received less attention: the implications of the genetic revolution for the multiple and unequal worlds of health care in which these technologies emerge. I want to shift the moral lens from the physician-patient relationship to the social or public health arena, to look at the questions of social justice posed by genetic advances in light of the potential for an ever-growing genomic divide between what Silver calls the genrich in this country (those who will have access to genetic breakthroughs) and the gennaturals (those who will live with the natural lottery); between the genetically rich and the genetically poor countries of the world. I want to ask: "How will advances in genomics improve health in developing countries? What do personalized medicine and gene therapy mean to one-third of the world's population, who live on less than $2.00 a day? How are genetic investments likely to impact health care for the 45 million people in this country who are currently uninsured or underinsured?"[3] How will we decide who will reap the benefits of the genetic revolution and who will bear the burdens? Whose Holy Grail"?

In what follows, I place the question of "genomic justice" in the context of Roman Catholic Social Thought, the more than 100 year reflection on what it means to build a just world, to seek the common good – to do not only what benefits individuals but to create conditions for human flourishing within community. To situate our discussion within this (or any other) religious tradition does not dissolve the complexity or dissipate either the ambiguity or the uncertainty raised by this revolution in medicine. It can, however, "provide a place to stand, a perspective from which to view and assess genomic advances and their application; it can provide a set of principles, a horizon of values for discernment."[4] More important, as I hope to show, our fundamental convictions lend a distinctive and necessary voice to the debate that will shape our genetic future.

10/90 Gap

A few years ago, I was teaching an undergraduate course in medical ethics and among my students was a young woman from Uganda. One particular day, we were engaged in a heated debate about the right to terminate treatment—we were arguing about a case involving a teenager with end-stage cystic fibrosis

and the question was who had the right to make the decision, the parents
or the teenager. I looked over at one point, and my Ugandan student (who
had been fairly quiet in the class up until then) was shaking her head, as if
in amazement. When I asked her what she was thinking, she said: "In my
country, if you had the treatment, you'd use it! How amazing it is to be in a
country where the ethical questions are all about what to do with the technology you have available and not why there isn't any treatment to offer at all."

The *two worlds* of health care in my Notre Dame classroom hint at the different worlds (multiple worlds) of health care within which genetic technologies are being developed and distributed.

A report published by the World Health Organization in 2002, *Genomics
and World Health,* begins by acknowledging what is often called the "10/90
gap": the reality that "90% of health research dollars are spent on the health
problems of 10% of the world's population."

According to WHO, several features of genomics research reflect and po-
tentially exacerbate this gap. Most genomics research was initially undertaken
in the public sector of developed countries. But a recent survey reports that
private-company spending on genomics has overtaken and is now substantially higher than government and not-for-profit spending. The concentration
of research funding in developed countries as well as in the private sector has
implications for setting research priorities and for accessing the products of
research. The private sector does not invest in research aimed at diagnostics
or therapeutics for diseases that are predominant in developing countries
because the populations that are afflicted and most likely to need them do not
have purchasing power. In order to ensure high returns on their investments,
companies tend to focus their research and development efforts on products
aimed at diseases and health problems that are most prevalent among the
populations of the developed countries. In 1997, for example, it was estimated
that low and medium income countries accounted for only 20% of the global
pharmaceutical market, even though they made up over 80% of the world's
population.[5] And the scale is enormous: The biotechnology industry has
doubled in size in ten years, generating 191,000 new direct jobs and 535,000
indirect jobs in 2001. Revenues for that year totaled more than $20 billion
directly and 28 billion indirectly.

Even public research funding is driven in large part by market concerns
(through the increasingly common practice of industrial-public partnership).
WHO argues that the "public research programs ... tend to be focused on
diseases such as cancer and cardiovascular diseases that are priorities in
developed countries." Whose economic interests drive global research priorities.[6] For example, the report notes, "it has been estimated that pneumonia,
diarrhea, tuberculosis and malaria, which together account for more than
20% of the disease burden of the world, receive less than 1% of the total
public and private funds devoted to health research. In 1988, out of the $70

billion global spending on health research, only $300 million was directed to vaccines for HIV/AIDS and $80 million to malaria research."[7] (All amounts are in USD) Jeffrey Sachs, Director of the Earth Institute at Columbia University, cites a 1998 study by the Wellcome Trust in the United Kingdom, which estimated that total malaria research worldwide runs at about $80 million per year. Since malaria kills between 1 and 2 million people per year, this amounts to around $40 - $80 of research spending per malaria death per year. This level of spending (per death) is a tiny fraction of the research spending on rich-country diseases.[8]

According to the Department of Energy, in 2002, there were 600 clinical gene-therapy trials involving 3500 patients going on worldwide. The vast majority takes place in the United States (81%) followed by Europe (16%). Most trials focus on various types of cancers (www.ornl.gov/hgmis/publicat/primer/).

It is not only research priorities that are heavily driven by the economic interests of the industrial North, but also the products of research. According to Genomics and Public Health, "of the 1,233 new drugs marketed between 1975 and 1999, only 13 were approved specifically for tropical diseases. Furthermore, of these, six were developed by the WHO, the United Nations Development Program (UNDP) and the UNDP/World Bank/WHO-supported Special Program for Research and Training in Tropical Diseases (TDR).[9]

Some observers, particularly from the two-thirds (90%) world, argue that the bias toward developed nations extends to the way we define and respond to ethical dimensions of research and distribution. Commenting on the way the ethics of HIV/AIDS research has been discussed, Zulfiqar Bhutta observes: "While issues of study design, ethical review and standards of care have been highlighted, the underlying socioeconomic deprivation and inequalities are largely ignored. ... While the concerns about research in developing countries have brought a welcome focus on this long-neglected area, the focus has been on regulatory issues, rather than on the basic problems that underlie the inequities in health and human rights in developing countries."[10] Some worry that the risks of inattention to vast disparities in public health infrastructure globally go even further, masking recognition that "genomics [has the potential to divert] precious resources away from the core issues of global public health, such as provision of clean water, safe food, proper sewage disposal, decent housing and access to maternal and child care."[11]

We do not need to look only to the developing world to find fear that pursuit of genomic advances will exacerbate existing injustices in the current health care system. Audrey Chapman, a bioethicist with the American Association for the Advancement of Science, captured well the risks in our current situation in the United States in a recent article on the ethics of inheritable genetic modifications, technologies that allow for the modification of a set of genes, which are then available to transmit to one's offspring.[12] Four factors lay the groundwork for concerns about assuring equity in access to the benefits of genetic therapies: the lack of a system of universal health insurance, patterns of inequalities of access to health care in the US; a projected scarcity of the availability of genetic services relative to demand; and the likely high cost of such interventions.[13] Chapman notes:

> Problems in obtaining access to health care are unfairly distrib-
> uted throughout our society. Blacks, Hispanics, and other minori-
> ties tend to receive lower quality health care than whites do …
> as a result of lower incomes, inadequate insurance coverage, and
> the absence of doctors in their areas of residence. Minorities are
> far more likely to be uninsured as compared to whites: minorities
> comprised 46 percent of the uninsured in 2000 although these
> groups represented only 24 percent of the United States population.
> In 2001, 37.7% of the uninsured were Hispanic and 20.2% African
> American, compared to 14% who were white."[14]

She cites a report issued by the Institute of Medicine (IOM) in 2002 to argue that a systemic *therapeutic discrimination* affects the health care that minorities receive. A review of 100 studies conducted over the past decade concludes, "Racial and ethnic minorities in the United States receive notably lower-quality health care, even when they have the same incomes, insurance coverage, and medical conditions as whites." The differences were especially significant for high technology interventions (organ transplants and open heart surgery). The IOM report attributes the disparities to subtle racial biases, the nature of health care facilities available in specific geographic areas and lower rates of long-term relationships with providers.[15] An earlier IOM study, in 1999, entitled *The Unequal Burden of Cancer*, raised similar concerns about inequities in research priorities. It concluded that NIH funding for research targeting minority and medically underserved populations was both inadequate and unequal in comparison to research targeting non-minority populations.[16]

Chapman is correct, I think, in assuming that "current limitations on access to health care, particularly high technology interventions, will also likely oper-ate with respect to genetic services."[17] Enhancement technologies, e.g., the abil-ity to give one's offspring enhanced physical, emotional or intellectual capaci-ties, are likely to be costly and (like in vitro fertilization and other reproductive technologies) to remain available, in the almost wholly unregulated private sector, to those who are willing and able to pay. Since effects of providing your children the best possible natures are cumulative, gaps have the potential to grow generationally. Even if universal health coverage were to be undertaken, underwriting access to some forms of genetic services, (e.g., gene therapy for muscular dystrophy) as Chapman points out, "the IOM report suggests that … the very groups who currently lack access to medical care, the poor and ethnic and racial minorities, are likely to still be disadvantaged."[18]

If concerns about a growing genomics divide, locally as well as globally, are at all founded, they join more general concerns about growing gaps between rich and poor, between prosperous nations of the industrial north and sustenance-level nations of the south, visible in Roman Catholic social teaching, especially in contemporary social encyclicals such as *Solicitudo Rei Socialis* and *Centessimus Annus*. In their pastoral letter on the economy, The U.S. Catholic Bishops make inequity the hallmark of economic disorder: "The obligation to provide justice for all means that the poor have the single most urgent economic claim on the conscience of the nation." (#86). But, what might it mean to provide justice for all in the context of genetic research and technology?

Here I want to turn to the Catholic tradition and briefly lay out three broad principles of discernment as a starting point for thinking about the obligations of justice in genomic advances: respect for human dignity, relationality, and solidarity.[19] These principles are not incompatible with the familiar principles of medical ethics. That is, respect for human dignity, respect for the fundamental equality of all human persons as *imago dei* (as representing the image and likeness of God), presupposes that we respect every competent person's right to make health care choices in light of his or her own needs and values; it presupposes the right not to be harmed, exploited or manipulated at the hands of a trusted provider and not to be discriminated against on the basis of genetic or any other disease or disability; and it presupposes respect for privacy in the use of genetic information. However, the Catholic tradition views the self in its totality, as a unity of body, mind and spirit. What this means is that no one of us can ever be reduced to our physical existence, or to our genetic make-up, nor is the pursuit of biological existence the only value to be recognized in setting social or scientific priorities. As Ann Richards, former governor of the great state of Texas (who, at 71, is as she said. "Still hell on wheels"), observed recently, the point is not just to live but to live well.

We could add that for the Catholic tradition, the point is to live well in relation to God and to others. Having been made for God, human beings are inherently social. As Karen Lebacqz puts it, "justice requires that we see ourselves as bound in a covenant of life with life, in which human freedom and choice is always coupled with a sense of social responsibility."[20] The principle of relationality brings individual rights and duties into conversation with the common good, asking how choices create conditions for the flourishing of all members of society. In the context of genetic technologies, a concern for relationality brings questions such as our responsibilities to future generations, how we set priorities for genetic research, how we weigh the advantages to be gained through genetic technologies against other means for addressing disease, disability and death; and how we will distribute genetic services in light of the multiplicity of needs and the limitations in resources, from the margins of analysis to the center. Finally, as the U.S. bishops argue:

> As individuals and as a nation … we are called to make a fundamental "option for the poor." The obligation to evaluate social and economic activity from the viewpoint of the poor and the powerless

arises from the radical command to love one's neighbor as one's self. Those who are marginalized and whose rights are denied have privileged claims if society is to provide justice for all. This obligation is deeply rooted in Christian belief.[21]

This special concern for the poor or those who are marginalized within community, which calls for active solidarity, follows from the Catholic tradition's emphasis on the importance of ensuring the capacity for humane participation in society for all members. The option for the poor is not an adversarial slogan that pits one group or class against another. Rather it states that the deprivation and powerlessness of the poor wounds the whole community. The extent of their suffering is a measure of how far we are from being a true community of persons.[22] *Solidarity* captures the sense in which the claims of justice exerted by the poor enjoin not only our emotions but our choices about how we will produce and use goods, as well as how we will organize our society, and they are claims to justice, a rightful share of what is owed to all, not simply to charity, not simply to a giving of one's surplus, but a reorientation of one's use of goods as well as the way we organize society to meet needs in light of the claims of the poor. In the context of genomics,

> Our enduring commitment to the disadvantaged and our option for the poor requires a careful and delicate balancing – for example, balancing the pursuit of the goods of genomics with efforts to ensure that the basic human needs of all our citizens [and those most in need around the world] are adequately met; balancing the pursuit of genomics with meeting the health needs of the poor and effecting reform of an unjust health care system; and ensuring that the benefits of genomics are as available to the disadvantaged as they are to all other citizens.[23]

Much more could be said about what these principles mean and what they imply for heath and medicine today. I want to offer just four reflections on the implications of this vision for justice in the genomic age.

One: As one philosopher noted recently, "justice begins by taking injustice seriously." If we are going to achieve any modicum of justice with respect to genomic developments in the long run, we must address what is now broken in our health care system. As we have argued, genomic advances will surely result in widening gaps between haves and have nots in our health care delivery system if we fail to address existing inequalities in access and quality of care. We must insist that our national leaders (and our candidates for office) answer to the need for universal health care coverage and quality care regardless of race, ethnicity or geography as a national priority every bit as compelling as the war on terror.

Two: Religious communities must take part in educated, substantive debates over how we as a nation ought to prioritize among areas of genetic research, how we ought to regulate genetic technologies in such a way that abuses and excesses can be controlled while the interests of parents in maintaining rightful authority in reproductive decisions can be honored; how we ought to weigh the priority of public health interests in prevention of disease across populations, with the promise of particular advances to address conditions for which other social and medical alternatives do not exist. Whatever we may hope for by way of universal health care coverage in the future, it is obvious that a simple case for equal access to whatever technologies are developed is unsustainable. It is also increasingly clear that the line between genetic interventions that are therapeutic and genetic advances that enhance human characteristics, while important in principle, is very fuzzy in practice, and that the availability of genetic interventions can easily *geneticize* our experience. Religious communities, in which human finitude is acknowledged and the presumption that we can avoid all human suffering is questioned, are uniquely positioned to debate the balance between investments in meeting basic human needs and improving quality of life across marginalized communities and pursuing high cost, high tech solutions to genetic disease and disability affecting individuals. As one theologian put it: "What genetics offers is a way to know the limits of participation and to make provision for inclusion when the person of limited capacity cannot independently earn a place.[24] Understanding this, religious communities are in a position to call attention to what sociologist Marque-Luisa Miringoff calls the subtle shift from a social welfare view (which seeks to adapt society for greater inclusion of those marginalized by disability through social welfare measures, laws and policies) to a genetic welfare view (which seeks to excise or biologically refashion those with disabilities).[25] Miringoff warns that rapidly developing and scientifically alluring genetic technologies are encouraging the adoption of a genetic welfare view, with resulting misplaced priorities: "while vast amounts of money are invested in genetic screening and reproductive technologies, mostly for middle- and upper-middle-class women, we fail to invest in basic forms of health care. As a result, poor women give birth to underweight, under-treated and chemically exposed babies, with similarly injurious forms of disease and developmental delay."[26]

Three: On the global front an option for the poor globally means above all to question the overriding control of market values in decisions concerning research and development priorities. Speaking both of the promises and the perils of our 21st century reality of global interdependence, Lisa Sowle Cahill argues that "a civic understanding of health, not merely a consumerist one, can emerge [must emerge] at the global level if information and communication technologies are used not only to serve the market, but to envision and realize shared goods of health care in a newly integrated world."[27] A study conducted by a team of Canadian researchers and published in the journal *Nature Genetics* in the fall of 2002 provides a good example of shifting the lens in genome research from its dependence on profitability and its dominant attention to the health problems of prosperous nations. In response to the

WHO report, *Genomics and World Health*, the team asked 28 experts in health
research, either from developing countries or specialists in public health in
the context of the developing world, to name the top ten biotechnologies
for improving health in the developing countries. At the top of the list were
"modified molecular technologies for affordable, simple diagnosis of infectious
diseases, recombinant technologies to develop vaccines against infectious
diseases, technologies for more efficient drug and vaccine delivery systems,
and technologies for environmental improvement (sanitation, clean water,
and bioremediation)."[28] The study showed not only that biotechnology is not
irrelevant for developing nations but also that some advances in biotechnology (e.g., in the areas of bioremediation and bioinformatics) are surprisingly
affordable especially when measured against conventional methods.

Related to this is a critique of what WHO calls *the culture of ownership* that
dominates the research and regulation environment in biotechnology. The
Genomics and World Health Report echoes the voices of many around the
world who are sharply critical of current intellectual property laws, which
allow patenting of genetic material. In their view, such laws disregard the
nature of genes (as naturally recurring information) and create monopolies on
genetic information that are counter to the public interest.[29] (Two models of an
approach that recognizes the common stake in genetic progress: The University of Ottawa and the University of Havana have decided to forego the royal-
ties of a jointly developed pneumonia-meningitis vaccine in instances where
it is used for strictly humanitarian purposes;[30] Canada's Newfound Genomics
devotes 1% of net profits to a charitable trust for the general population.[31])

The most compelling arguments in this vein have significant overlap with
Catholic social teaching on the universal destination of goods. Critics of the
rush to patenting (and overall inequity of access to the benefits of genomic
research) argue that the character of the Human Genome Project, as a multinational cooperative effort aimed at identifying a common genetic code makes
its discoveries *global public goods*. Cahill and others call for the creation of an
"international or transnational forum for creating and implementing global
policy," a forum that would be inclusive and participatory.[32]

An option for the poor globally also takes the form of encouraging the
creation of research collaboration between the genetically advanced or more
advanced countries (some, like China, Brazil, Cuba and India are developing
nations) and the genetically less advanced. Tikki Pang of WHO argues that,
while it is a positive step to ask how biotechnologies might serve public health
in the developing world, "It must be accompanied by a genuine willingness
on the part of developed countries and the pharmaceutical and biotechnology
industries to share knowledge and help poorer countries apply such knowledge to solving their health problems." Pang argues further that the "developed world must be prepared to invest more money in research in developing
countries, but … in a spirit of helping developing countries ultimately to
help themselves." In a symbolic illustration of the hope of partnership, WHO

released its report on genomics at a conference hosted by the Africa Human Genome Initiative, which drew "world renowned super-scientists" such as Nobel-winner David Baltimore along with leading African and South African scholars.[33] Pang and others endorsed the development of a Global Health Research Fund, heavily supported by public contributions from the U.S., which would make resources for research available through peer-reviewed application to every country.[34]

Of equal importance is the development of local capacity. This concern encompasses not only how partnerships might be forged between genetically sophisticated regions and genetically less sophisticated ones, but also how developments in biotechnology will interface with local and regional problems in health care delivery and infrastructure. *Genomics and World Health* makes the obvious but still important point that "any benefits that result from genomics research will be irrelevant to countries that do not have a functioning health care system in place."[35] Like efforts to bring affordable drugs to the AIDS-ridden nations of the South, strategies for mobilizing international cooperation for equitable access to biotechnologies must assist developing nations to address basic issues in health care delivery such as training, education and community organization. Along with the importance of such cooperation is support for the development of local capacity in bioethics, so that decisions about the conduct of research and the clinical application of developments in biotechnology incorporate and respect the religious and cultural values of those involved or affected. We can see some recognition of the importance of this kind of empowerment here in the U.S. in the NIH funded *Communities of Color and Genetics Policy* program, which seeks to engage minorities in policy development to address issues of particular relevance for African American and Latino communities."[36]

Four: It perhaps goes without saying that the greatest challenge in the context of justice and equity of access to genetic advances is how to mobilize action on behalf of the poor and the marginalized in the face of powerful counter-values, such as profitability, self-interest and market share, and in the face of powerful actors, such as multinational corporations; in other words, how exactly to transform interdependence into solidarity. Much attention is being given today to the need for transnational or global governance structures but little consensus about what such structures would look like or how exactly they would gain their authority. Drawing on the interconnection of human rights, global public health and biotechnology, some are arguing for the formation of an international supervisory agency (perhaps out of UNESCO) to oversee research and development in genomics. Such an agency would give regulatory power to documents such as the 1997 *Universal Declaration on the Human Genome and Human Rights.* Given the central place given to human rights in the Catholic social tradition, one way to take up the option for the poor is to join efforts to develop a workable vehicle for transnational solidarity around public health initiatives and to work toward its implementation.

However, in a recent article in the *Journal of Religious Ethics*, Cahill argues that the most important role for religious action on behalf of the poor today may lie outside of the arenas of law and regulation and cooperation through global advocacy networks. Religion can and should be a powerful force for education, for joining parties in opposition to inequities and violations of human rights, and for consolidating an alternate vision in the face of the all encompassing power of the market.[37] As an example of the potential, Cahill points to international grassroots organizing in opposition to the imposition of genetically modified foods on developing countries with insufficient attention to the potential to displace local crops on the one hand, and the role of corporate motives in promoting the technology on the other (an effort that joined religious groups, non-Governmental Organizations, Episcopal conferences, which ultimately reached policy makers). Similar grassroots actions brought international attention to the failure of U.S. and European pharmaceutical corporations to make affordable drugs available for countries devastated by AIDS, especially in sub-Saharan Africa, which ultimately led to positive changes in pricing policies and U.S. economic commitments to address AIDS.

Conclusion

I began by talking about the sense in which we live, in health care anyway, during a revolutionary age, an age in which we are opening new frontiers in the pursuit of health and redrawing the lines that mark the present boundaries. We see this in a dramatic way in the success of the Human Genome Project. We also see the way in which new biotechnologies risk widening old and scandalous gaps as many developing nations see themselves falling on the lean side of the genetics divide and as new risks of genetic inequality join old realities of differential access to health care here in our own country.

The Holy Grail is an interesting image; it was, after all, a chalice, a blessing cup, which in our tradition is meant for all. But the best image I have come across to capture the moral challenge of this age, the age of gene mapping, was used by the philosopher Albert Jonsen: He likens this age to the beginning of the colonial period:

> The ships that sailed from Europe five centuries ago not only mapped the world—they inaugurated social, political and economic events that radically changed humankind's view of itself and nations' views of their destinies. The rapidly redrawn map of discovery and colonization depicted areas of glorious achievement and areas of deplorable tragedy.[38]

Whether the map we are making will chart spheres of achievement or tragedy, of health for all or only for some, depends on the kinds of commitments we bring to the journey; whether we bring a commitment to profit, utility and individual liberty, or a commitment to respect for human dignity, solidarity and concern for the common good. How we will look back on the changes we have ushered in will depend on what sort of regard we have for what we encounter, what interests come into play, who wants the technologies, who profits from them and who bears the burdens, how they are regulated and finally whether we are willing to take the part of the poor against the voices that would drown them out. To borrow from Rosemarie Tong:

> It will depend on whether we (of the 10% world) are willing to continually remind ourselves what is wrong about a world in which some of us live well into our 80s and 90s, while others of us die before we had a chance to live; in which some of us go on diets and pay cosmetic surgeries, while others of us starve or beg for food; and in which some of us have access to life-saving technologies, abundant pharmaceuticals, and every manner and fashion of care-giver conceivable, while others of us drink contaminated water, breathe foul air, and lack the simplest of immunizations."[39]

Notes:

1. DOEgenomes.org

2. Lawrence Altman, Genomic Chief Has High Hopes, and Great Fears, for Genetic Testing, *New York Times* June 27, 2000 D6.

3. Tikki Pang, Equal Partnership to Ensure that Developing Countries Benefit from Genomics. *Nature* Genetics 33/1, 18.2003. See Ted Peters, ed., *Genetics: Issues of Social Justice* (Cleveland: Pilgrim Press, 1998); also Cynthia Crysdale, Christian Responses to the Human Genome Project, *Religious Studies Review* 26: 236-42.

4. Catholic Health Association, *Harnessing the Promise of Genomics*, 2004.

5. *Genomics and World Health*, The Advisory Committee on Health Research, World Health Organization, Geneva, 2002, 17.

6. *Genomics and World Health,* 18.

7. *Genomics and World Health,* 18.

8. See Michael Kremer and Jeffrey Sachs, A Cure for Indifference, *The Financial Times*, May 5, 1999 at http://www.brookings.edu/views/op-ed/kremer/19990505.htm. Even with an international commitment to battle diseases, which disproportionately affect the developing world, malaria funding remains inadequate in the judgment of Sachs and others. See Tamar Kahn, Fight Against Malaria Being Compromised, *Business Day*, November 5, 2002. Here it was noted that the UN Fund to Fight AIDS, TB and Malaria had committed only US$ 22 million (out of $616 mill. of total commitment) for malaria programs during its first round of funding. http://www.massiveeffort.org/showstory.aspid=2357.

9. Ibid.

10. Bhutta, *Ethics in International Health Research: A Perspective from the Developing World*, 116.

11. Tikki Pang, Equal Partnership to Ensure that Developing Countries Benefit from Genomics, *Nature Genetics* 33/1 (Jan 2003) 18.

12. Audrey Chapman, Should We Design Our Descendants? *Journal of the Society of Christian Ethics*, 23/2 (Fall/Winter 2003): 199-223.

13. Chapman, 210.

14. Chapman, 210.

15. Chapman, 211.

16. M. Alfred Haynes and Brian D. Smedley, Editors, *The Unequal Burden of Cancer: An Assessment of NIH Research and Programs for Ethnic Minorities and the Medically Underserved*, National Academies Press, 1999.

17. Chapman, 211.

18. Chapman, 211.

19. Here I am indebted to the formulation of these principles provided in the CHA educational program, *Harnessing the Promise of Genomics: A Catholic Vision Toward Genomic Advances* (CHA, 2004) for which I served as a consultant.

20. As quoted by Chapman at 202.

21. United States Catholic Conference, *Economic Justice for All*, # 87.

22. Ibid.

23. Harnessing the Promise of Genomics, p. vii.

24. Ann Lewis Boyd, Genetics and Social Justice, *Eubios Journal of Asian and International Bioethics* 12 (2002), 167-171.

25. As cited in Chapman, 212.

26. As cite in Chapman, 212.

27. Lisa Sowle Cahill, Biotech and Justice: Catching up with the Real World Order, *Hastings Center Report* 33/4 (2003): 34-44 at 42.

28. Addallah S. Daar, et.al. Top Ten Biotechnologies for Improving Health in Developing Countries, *Nature Genetics* 32 (October 2002): 229-232.

29. Genomics and World Health, 19.

30. Daar, et.al., 229.

31. Boyd.

32. Cahill, *Biotech and Justice*, 36.

33. Top Scientists to Attend Groundbreaking Human Genome Conference, press release, African Human Genome Initiative, March 2003.

34. Genome Research Can Save Millions in Developing World, press Release, WHO, April 30, 2002.

35. *Genomics and World Health*, 3.

36. Toby Citrin and Stephen Modell, *Genomics and Public Health*, Ch. 8.

37. Lisa Sowle Cahill, Bioethics, Theology, and Social Change, *Journal of Religious Ethics* 31/3 (2003) 363-398.

38. Albert Jonsen, *The Impact of Mapping the Human Genome on the Physician-Patient Relationship, The Human Genome and the Future of Health Care*, edited by Murray, Rothstein and Murray (Indiana University Press, 1996) 19.

39. Rosemarie Tong, Teaching Bioethics in the New Millennium: Holding Theories Accountable to Actual Practices and Real People, *Journal of Medicine and Philosophy* 27/4 (2002): 417-432 at 427.

For God and Country: Patriotism and Religious Identity

Rev. Thomas Massaro, S.J.
Professor of Moral Theology, Boston College School of Theology and Ministry

URBI ET ORBI LECTURE I September 25, 2008

I am grateful for the invitation to join you here today and to address this important topic. Patriotism is something we all experience in our own particular way, and it is not my intention to win you over to my particular views on the subject. Nor do I seek to enthrall you with the soaring but usually empty rhetoric often employed when speakers address love of country. My modest hope is to raise a few of the most obvious issues that arise when Christians, and particularly Catholics in the United States today, consider the relationship between their religious and national identities. What, then, are the relevant aspects of patriotism—cultural, historical and theological—which need to be recognized and assessed before Christians today can evaluate its operations, merits and problematic aspects? I will proceed by examining a series of four theses that summarize some of the received wisdom about patriotism and Christian identity.

But first, let me come clean about my own biography. As I do so, you might consider your own unfolding patterns of reflection on patriotism as well. As an ordinary child of a middle-class Catholic family in New York City, I would say that my life started on a rather solidly patriotic foundation. I suspect that I share with most of you strong memories of Memorial Day parades and Fourth of July celebrations with lots of flag-waving and patriotic flourishes, regular recitation of the *Pledge of Allegiance* at school and an unquestioned devotion to all things American. The parish I belonged to as a boy sported twin flags flanking the sanctuary, and nobody ever doubted the appropriateness of maintaining the stars and stripes right across from the gold and white papal flag. My family, my parochial school classmates, just about everyone I knew as a kid were self-consciously and proudly Catholics *and* Americans, no tensions, no conflict, nothing but pride in each of our dual identities. Even the Jesuit secondary school I attended, Regis High School in Manhattan, featured the motto, common to many Catholic educational institutions across the land, *Deo et Patriae*, for God and country. (Incidentally, that Latin phrase provided an excellent lesson in the form and proper use of the dative case for first and second declension nouns, a fact not overlooked in my freshman Latin course.)

But if you are like me, the unreflective national pride and patriotism of childhood met some inevitable challenges. For some of my age cohort or slightly older, it may have been the conduct of the horrific war in Vietnam or the disheartening Watergate scandal, which ushered in some initial doubts about our nation's policies, institutions and leaders. Maybe the U.S.A. was not always above reproach in all its operations at home and abroad. While the sixties and seventies were decades that called into question many previously unexamined dogmas, it was not until the final months of the 1970s, specifically my first semester of college in the fall of 1979, that my knee-jerk patriotism came to be challenged. The luck of the draw found me assigned to the prominent political philosopher George Kateb as my first academic advisor at Amherst College. Although I had no way of knowing this as a freshman, Professor Kateb had garnered quite a reputation for firm opposition to anything that smacked of irrationality in politics. Nationalistic fervor has been one of his prime bête noirs throughout his long career. The title of his most recent book, published in April 2008, is *Patriotism and Other Mistakes*. This captures very well his aversion to whatever might cancel out the better angels of our nature, which for Kateb is synonymous with what is eminently reasonable and rational. The undue influence of group loyalties serves to muddy the waters and leads us to policy mistakes and worse: abridgments of civil liberties, gross injustices, systematic discrimination and even brutal atrocities. What I heard from George Kateb in class lectures and in advising sessions is that we are on much more solid ground when the easily manipulated devotion to nation is supplemented, surpassed and even eclipsed by virtues such as toleration and reasonableness, and by processes such as dialogue, compromise and a commitment to humble inquiry.

I will say no more about my personal story beyond this: Kateb's admonitions about the dangers of patriotism prompted within my adolescent psyche considerable soul-searching. They have stayed with me throughout my adult life, haunting me in a gentle way, tugging at my conscience. But it was probably not until the aftermath of September 11, 2001 and the run-up to the Iraq war, which then started with the U.S. invasion in March 2003, that I recognized the full force of my professor's cautionary words. The insight that patriotic sentiment may at times lead us seriously astray has shaped practically all of my professional activities ever since, including my writing, teaching and other academic work, as well as the organized activism and advocacy I have engaged in of late. You need not go as far as the broad-stroked (but still mostly accurate) analysis of social critic Noam Chomsky to recognize that an exaggerated version of nationalistic sentiment accounts, at least in part, for many of the misadventures the U.S. has embarked upon in her history. As a theologian, I am most disturbed by the repeated abuse of the *just-war* theory to rationalize wars of choice in the name of principle, but many are the manipulations of patriotic sentiment that have lead us astray.

Based upon my own personal experience, then, here emerges the first of my four theses: *There are good and bad things about patriotism.* Rather obvious observation, I'll be the first to admit. While national pride and loyalty to one's country are certainly good things in themselves, and perhaps, ultimately, the indispensable glue that holds together so large an entity as a modern nation-state, my experience (and probably yours as well) suggests that there are limits that need to be observed. We hardly need the erudite arguments of George Kateb and others of like mind to persuade us that patriotism has a downside and that a patriotic stupor can cloud our collective judgments.

It would be impossible to make this point more succinctly than does the late Yale University chaplain William Sloane Coffin, Jr. Until his death in 2006, he was considered America's most prominent Protestant preacher. In an oft-quoted maxim, Coffin advises: "There are three kinds of patriots, two bad, one good. The bad are the uncritical lovers and the loveless critics. Good patriots carry on a lover's quarrel with their country." End-quote, and what a quote! The shortcomings of the extreme positions Rev. Coffin describes as *uncritical lovers* and *loveless critics* require no explanation. It is indefensible to close your eyes against any data that might contradict your dogmatically held views, whether you are positive or negative on patriotism or any other topic for that matter. But it may not be quite clear what it means to sustain a lover's quarrel with one's country. Allow me to mention two contemporary figures who appear to get this point quite right.

One is Donald Shriver, Jr., among the most esteemed social ethicists in American Protestant circles today. His most recent book is titled *Honest Patriots: Loving Our Country Enough to Remember its Misdeeds.* Shriver appeals to Americans to overcome their reluctance to be at all critical of their country, for any project of deliberate amnesia is a dangerous mistake, not a source of strength. Here Shriver builds upon his previous work on the topic of political reconciliation, especially his masterpiece *An Ethic for Enemies: Forgiveness in Politics.* Shriver encourages Americans to engage in a more accurate, deliberate and public process of remembering the major mistakes and injustices perpetuated by our government and other institutions throughout our national history. Acknowledging the mistreatment of Native Americans, of African Americans and other ethnic minorities, facing up to the use of force under false pretenses and war crimes, among other misdeeds, are necessary steps to true reconciliation with victims of injustice, and will in the long run make us stronger.

Somewhat similar is the call by theologian Geiko Müller-Fahrenholz for a reassessment of the role of key collective symbols in our national life. As a native of Germany with great affection for and considerable knowledge of U.S. public affairs, Müller-Fahrenholz offers a theological critique of U.S. civil religion from a European perspective in his intriguing and recent work *America's Battle for God.* His book culminates with a reminder that there are two sides to civil religion, a concept retrieved into public discourse by the great sociologist Robert Bellah four decades ago. These two complementary aspects are the priestly and the prophetic. While a *priestly* strand of civil religion serves the function of binding us together as a people and presides over our celebration of national unity and strength, it is incomplete and even dangerous without the *prophetic* dimension. This is the aspect of our shared civil religion that holds our nation up to the scrutiny of our highest principles and reminds us that we stand under the judgment of a Higher Power, however that is conceived. We expect to hear priestly style utterances in presidential inaugural addresses and annual state of the union addresses. The prophetic function is usually reserved to figures outside the corridors of power, with Martin Luther King, Jr. being perhaps the most vivid example of a prophet in our recent national experience. Our national life can only be healthy when it achieves legitimacy on both these scores. National power that is not fully answerable to ethical principles like democracy, peace making, self-restraint, equity and self-determination does not proceed with the appropriate authority that is worthy of our nation.

I suspect that I have so far told you precious little that you did not already know. Yes, there are bad kinds of patriotism lurking out there, and many of them are readily evident in our public life. The presidential campaign of 2008 has certainly supplied several glimpses of these that have been hard to ignore. For example, why did candidate Barack Obama have to prove his patriotism repeatedly in such absurd ways as insuring that a flag pin was fastened to his jacket lapel every morning? Obviously, it was because some opposing campaign operative figured that political advantage could be gained by accusing Obama of a deficit of patriotism based on how he accessorized or failed to accessorize his wardrobe. This seemingly trivial example illustrates a widespread and longstanding tendency in U.S. politics to level charges of un-patriotism at political opponents. We saw it in 1988 when the patriotism of candidate Michael Dukakis was called into question. The 2002 re-election bid of Senator Max Cleland of Georgia was thwarted when his opponent charged that he was not patriotic enough, despite the fact that Cleland was a Vietnam War veteran who lost three limbs in the course of his brave and exemplary military service. And the converse to attacking your opponents for a deficit of patriotism is the practice of wrapping yourself in the flag, sometimes almost literally, while campaigning for office. And so, the obligatory campaign stop at a flag factory has become a staple of U.S. presidential politics. The truth of Dr. Samuel Johnson's familiar quip, that patriotism is the "last refuge of a scoundrel," is nowhere more evident than on these shores.

You may be wondering why I have not yet supplied a rigorous definition of patriotism. Simply put, I have found patriotism to be one of those elusive things that is at once extremely familiar yet notoriously difficult to define. Beyond this, most people have an instinctive sense of what patriotism means even in the absence of a precise definition. One sound working definition would describe patriotism as love of one's country, the linguistic root of the word coming from the Latin *patria*, or fatherland, a word that ironically is feminine in gender in most Romance languages. Yet, mere love of coun-try does not capture the full semantic range of what we usually mean by patriotism. Is it perhaps more accurate to identify the heart of patriotism as being respect for country or perhaps concern for the honor of one's country? If we insist that patriotism is a matter of love, we need to explain how love of country compares and relates to other loves, such as love of one's family and love of God. Maybe patriotism, or love of anything as abstract as a modern nation-state, is only love in an analogous way.

Behind cotemporary nation-states, of course, lie concrete things like ancestral homelands, ties of blood and particular shared ways of life. But this is not uniformly so, and it is easy to argue that it is precisely the intangible things like governing ideals, ethical principles and national spirit that are the object of the nationalistic devotions of most people, at least in certain nations today. I would hasten to identify the United States, with its remarkable pluralism and rich immigrant history, as prime among these nations. In the end, I will leave to others the task of developing a rigorous definition and phenomenology of patriotism, as long as we remain cognizant that the term has meant many things to many people over many centuries and that patriotism continues to be ambiguous and even problematic today.

The mention of the phrase "love of God" just above brings us to my second thesis, which is nearly as obvious as the first. Patriotism presents something of a dilemma for Christians and requires careful discernment on the part of all religious people. Of course, anyone aspiring to the name Christian will insist that the God of Jesus Christ is alone worthy of our worship. While love of God by no means excludes other loves, for Christians other objects of devotion must ultimately be subordinated to our love of God, who alone is absolute and transcends all creatures of God. At least as far back as Saint Augustine's ruminations on the proper ordering of loves fifteen centuries ago, Christians have struggled with the tension between love of God and of country (or Empire or Kingdom or nation, as the case may be).

I want to put in a word here for alternative (perhaps even fringy) Christian positions that resist accommodation to state power. Those of us from particular Christian communities that have generally made their peace with this tension do well to recall that many sincere and genuine Christian voices continue to insist that there is something deeply incompatible between love of God and love of any political entity. Christian anarchists and traditions like the Mennonites that emanate from what is often called the "left wing of the Protestant Reformation" espouse the view that nationalism always amounts to a form of idolatry. As such arguments run, both nations themselves as well as excessive nationalism (that is, consciousness and celebration of national identity) easily become false gods and threaten to divert our allegiances from where they truly belong.

Even if we do not ultimately come down on the same side of the ledger as those who are thoroughly resistant to patriotism, Christians of the mainstream have to admit that weighty evidence can be marshaled to support the strong aversion of certain Christians to patriotism and celebrations of loyalty to nation. Modern history certainly documents that nationalism can be death dealing on a massive scale. How many millions have been slaughtered in the name of national aggrandizement, patriotic loyalties and humanly constructed boundaries, which arguably count for little in the eyes of God? In our honest moments, we must also recognize that a good measure, if not a preponderance, of scriptural evidence supports the presumption against patriotism. Consider the vicissitudes of the people of Israel in the Old Testament, for example. Insofar as it even makes sense to apply the modern notion of national identity to the collective entity that comprised the Jewish people after the Exodus, whatever praiseworthy developments unfolded in that history hardly hinged on the political institutions such as the monarchies the Israelites established. If we read attentively the prophets and historical books of the Old Testament, it soon becomes clear that ancient Israel, precisely as a nation, was nothing to be particularly proud of. The many manifestations of the anti-royal ideology evident in most parts of the Hebrew Scriptures cast considerable doubt on the proposition that patriotism is redeemable at all. Just recall the commentary on the costs of establishing the institution of kingship in I Samuel, chapter 8. Or thumb through the writings of the prophets who denounced the grave social injustices perpetuated by the royal establishment of the time. With national identity comes the inevitability of corruption and a fall from grace, as people struggle to keep their eye on what the First Commandment enjoins: to avoid all forms of idolatry and to dedicate oneself to the pure version of monotheism that alone is pleasing to the jealous God of Israel.

In the New Testament, Jesus, when pressed to identify the first and greatest commandment of Israel, summarizes the entire Decalogue as an enjoinder to love God with all one's heart, soul and mind. A review of this clarion call for single-hearted devotion to God as it appears in Matthew 22:37 might lead one to wonder just what is left over for other loves. Of course, no one seriously doubts that there are other legitimate objects of devotion. Jesus himself hastens to identify loving one's neighbor as oneself as a corollary. Nevertheless, the unquestioned priority of religious duty over all types of civic loyalties is affirmed time and again throughout Scripture. Readers of the New Testament see Jesus reaching beyond the boundaries of Israel, granting requests to a Roman centurion (Matthew 8: 5-13), reaching out to a Syrophoenician woman (Mark 7: 24-30 and Matthew 15: 21-8) and praising a Samaritan for his acts of compassion (Luke 10: 30-37). Saint Paul employs a variety of tropes and arguments to make the recurring point that our deepest allegiance can be to nothing other than Christ. He even employs a political metaphor in his claim that "Our citizenship is in heaven" (Philippians 3:20). In short, an attentive reader of the New Testament cannot miss the message that the loyalties we associate with patriotism are undergoing serious challenge in these texts, as all loves not centered in God are clearly and thoroughly relativized.

Now, contrary evidence could be cited to suggest that the tension between religious devotion and political allegiance is not quite as sharp as some imagine. Chapter 13 of Romans, where Paul urges subordination and even eager obedience to legitimate civil rulers, seems intent on smoothing over any conflict on this score. Scholars seeking to establish a middle path between utter accommodation of Christians to the political order, on one hand, and utter incompatibility and grounds for sharp resistance, on the other, usually point to the way Jesus handled the question about Caesar's coin. Remember the punch line of this controversial story that appears in all three synoptic gospels: "Render unto Caesar that which is Caesar's, and unto God the things that are God's" (Matthew 22:21; Mark 12:17; Luke 20:25). At the very least, following the promptings of Jesus here entails a critical distancing from the powers of the state. Those who heed this advice will tend to sit lightly in whatever civic entity they find themselves.

But some take it further. There is a prominent strand within Christian thought that insists that we remain no more than resident aliens on this earth, existing in constant tension with culture, including the secular life of modern nation-states. To recognize the ultimate Lordship of Christ means to reject all civic loyalties and memberships. Although today this Christian tradition of radical rejection of earthly authority, even to the point of anarchy, is a small minority voice, it comprised the dominant viewpoint of the earliest generations of Christians. If the mainstream of contemporary Christianity is characterized by a both/and approach to God and nation, the fledgling Christian community before the time of Emperor Constantine in the early fourth century was very much in the either/or camp. The reality of periodic persecutions reinforced what they saw as a stark choice: you belonged to Christ *or* you belonged to the Empire; any attempt at straddling the fence was impossible. Taking their cues from Revelation 13 and other New Testament texts that portrayed government as demonic in nature, our forebears in faith walked the path of non-cooperation and even active resistance to imperial power in all its forms. For reasons of principle or simply because the option to engage the dominant culture was less than readily available in that era, the early church of the catacombs staked out a rather sectarian stance.

All this changed with a series of stunning fourth-century events: the conversion of the Emperor Constantine, his Edict of Toleration and the eventual establishment of Christianity as the official religion of the Roman Empire. Not everyone rejoiced that the sharp tension between Christianity and Empire was resolved in this way, for it led to uneasiness with how facilely Christianity developed an imperial theology that too readily justified Roman power and fit all-too-neatly, hand-in-glove with the agenda of a ruling elite. Many authentic Christian voices remained uncomfortable with leaning so heavily on the Empire that had executed its Lord and Savior as a common criminal.

Saint Augustine, himself a citizen of the Roman Empire, made the great contribution of introducing terminology that captured the tensions felt by fifth-century Christians. He talked about this duality of consciousness in terms of the two cities to which Christians belong simultaneously. As we long for the full establishment of the City of God, we slog through life in the Earthly City. This distinction between *civitas Dei* and *civitas terrena* helps us make sense of many aspects of human experience, including the relationship between our temporal and ultimate ends. At the very least, Augustine's categories allow us to abide the unresolved schizophrenia that accompanies holding multiple loyalties. At best, they guide our ordering of loves, permit us to obey civil authorities within the limits of Christian conscience and still allow us to dissent from unjust laws or resist tyranny when we discern a duty to do so. In setting up a schema that preserves the full range of relevant values and remains firm in setting priorities, Saint Augustine insures that the earthly political order is neither idolized nor demonized. Christian citizens are in a position to follow the call of both Acts 5:29 (where Peter and the apostles proclaim: "Better for us to obey God than men") as well as Jeremiah 29:7 (which enjoins the conflicted Israelites to "promote the welfare of the city to which I have exiled you"). Still, our ultimate loyalty is reserved for God alone. Duties to political entities, while important, are subordinated to even more solemn higher purposes.

I have probably tipped my hand that I approve wholeheartedly of Augustine's stance and the tradition of reflection he inspired regarding faith and politics. Here love of God and regard for one's earthly homeland are portrayed as compatible, though perhaps in a perennially uneasy relationship. The both/and is affirmed without losing the force of the either/or. The simultaneous membership we hold in earthly and eternal communities may not precisely determine the various courses of action we pursue, but it does set the basic framework for life in human society. While this Augustinian paradigm has served the Christian mainstream well for centuries, I would hasten to make one request. All things being equal, I would prefer a dash more cosmopolitanism than is customarily present while flavoring my personal portion of the soup of Christian patriotism. Allow me to explain this point, leaving behind the broth metaphor I employed to introduce it.

It seems particularly regrettable to me that Christians in recent centuries so easily slip into a version of tribalism that seeks pro forma religious sanction for what usually amounts to ethnic or national self-interest. If our particular political community identities a goal worth attaining, or even one worth fighting for, then God *must* be on our side in the struggle, as this flawed argument runs. Following this logic, the horizons of our social concern shrink all too readily into the confines of national borders, ceding the moral high ground of universal love and good will that should be the overriding focus of engaged Christians. Maybe this is due to the ways Medieval Christianity absorbed feudal ideals, such as fealty, in such a way that the practice of loyal service of vassals to the lords who protected them evolved eventually into an unquestioned allegiance to country. The version of patriotism we subsequently inherited thus includes, among other elements, the tradition of *pro patria mori*. This Latin phrase describes a willingness—even an eagerness presumed to be noble in nature—to die for one's country with few questions asked regarding precisely what principles make the offer of one's life necessary and laudable.

These developments beg to be reexamined in light of two things. First, this pattern of behavior fails to honor our supreme allegiance to the God who stands above all nations and judges their ways. Second, it devalues principles and causes that transcend the projects of particular nations and that rightly stake a weightier claim upon us than mere national interest. If there are things worthy of solemn sacrifices in today's world, they more likely go by names like "human rights" and "solidarity with the poor" than the "sovereign nation of X" or the "Republic of Y." If there is a distinctive Christian supplement to patriotism as it is practiced today, I would then hasten to identify a more thoroughgoing cosmopolitan agenda as the missing dimension. If Christians truly believe that our individual destinies are linked to the fate of all of humanity, then the key questions become the following: How should we enlarge the scope of our concerns for people and causes of justice around the world? How may we practice the most universal form of love in a renewed stance of solidarity, one that is compatible with our particular loyalties in this complex world? It is about time that we took seriously the claim that has echoed through Roman Catholic as well as World Council of Churches social teaching documents in recent decades: in this age of globalization, the common good is now universal in scope, and the only adequate practice of social responsibility is one that accounts for all our neighbors, without exception, whether they belong to our nation or not.

My third thesis brings the question of patriotism home to the Roman Catholic community in the United States. It is this: Patriotism presents a particular dilemma for U.S. Catholics, especially in light of our distinctive history. The ever-thorny challenges of staking out the terms of dual membership in church and civil society have been especially difficult for American Catholics to navigate. Although Catholics seem eminently secure and well adjusted to American culture today, indeed enjoying the status of the single largest religious denomination in the U.S. for many decades now, it was not always thus. At the time of U.S. independence, Roman Catholicism claimed only a fraction of one percent of the population. In most of the original colonies, public Catholic worship was forbidden. Progress towards initial toleration and eventual full-throated acceptance was fitful and slow in coming. As relative latecomers to these shores, the Catholic community had to deal with the forces of suspicion, nativism, and blatant discrimination in educational and employment opportunities and even violence in the form of personal attacks and church burnings.

There is no doubt that the Catholic minority in America, challenged to forge a convincing loyalty to their new homeland, deeply desired to make the project of Americanization work. In seeking to prove their loyalty to their adopted land, generations of Catholics became super-patriots. Exaggerated displays of love of country grew comical at times, as generations of Polish, Italian, Irish and other Catholic immigrants and their descendants appeared especially eager to wear on their sleeves the proof of their successful assimilation. But the ardent desire to achieve a dual identity at once as loyal Catholics and patriotic Americans came at a price and contained an implicit irony.

Participation in the horrific sequence of bloody wars of the twentieth century became the paradigmatic act to demonstrate loyalty to the United States and its ideals. That ethnic Catholics felt particular pressure to exceed ordinary standards in answering the call to national duty is a dynamic confirmed by depictions of Catholic GIs in films, literature and other vehicles of popular culture. Stereotypes though they be, the gung ho Italian-American private from Brooklyn, the Boston-Irish doughboy volunteering for hazardous duty and the German-Catholic farm boy from the Midwest vowing with all his might to defeat Hitler's forces—all are enduring icons of a faith community eager to prove its patriotism. But the tragic irony is that, in seeking to demonstrate that their loyalty to America was beyond reproach, they found themselves putting on the shelf many of the teachings of the man they acknowledged as their Lord and Savior. The mental calisthenics of the just-war theory notwithstanding, exceptional service in bloody conflicts is not the ideal way for a religious community to earn its stripes of ethical approval. Sure, Catholics in the U.S. had answered all doubts about their primary allegiance being to a foreign potentate in Rome, but their unquestioned loyalty to Uncle Sam may just have eclipsed their practice of discipleship to the Prince of Peace.

For those familiar with Catholic theology and social philosophy, it comes as no surprise that Catholics make good company men and women. Our heritage of communitarian commitment and our high regard for the common good, something we seem to have retained even amidst the highly individualistic culture of America today, makes us good candidates for the kinds of public service that come with a request for no questions asked. Anecdotal evidence suggests that CIA and FBI recruiters are particularly eager to receive job applications from Catholics because of their perceived disposition toward obedience and staunch patriotism.

But just when it may have seemed that Catholics had definitively given in to the temptation to conflate the purposes of God and of country, the critical edge seemed to reappear. The grace note I am referring to involves the leadership of the U.S. Catholic bishops during the decade of the 1980s. This decade of stunningly public church activism witnessed our hierarchy's advocacy for reform of U.S. policies in economic and defense-related matters, and culminated in the publication of two major pastoral letters: *The Challenge of Peace* in 1983 and *Economic Justice for All* in 1986. These bold initiatives of challenging morally objectionable structures and policies marked the definitive coming of age of the U.S. Catholic Church as a community no longer content merely to prove its patriotism, but now confident enough to wage an informed and constructive lover's quarrel with American institutions. Although more recent chapters in the story of the U.S. Catholic Bishops Conference are far less encouraging, the bold leadership the bishops provided in challenging public policies from the distinctive moral perspective of Catholicism was extremely encouraging evidence that our church could still muster up a good dose of the prophetic from time to time.

We would be remiss to overlook the contributions of previous generations of U.S. Bishops on issues of church and state, for their leadership is most relevant to issues regarding patriotism. In a Catholic church that struck a virulently anti-modern stance from the time of the French Revolution until the Second Vatican Council, it was certainly not easy to serve as a bishop in a liberal society with secular institutions that were repeatedly condemned by popes and councils. The 1864 *Syllabus of Errors* of Pius IX, the anathemas of the First Vatican Council, the repeated condemnations of modernism by Pius X, all were constant reminders that to be an American Catholic with aspirations for cultural assimilation was to be walking a fine and uneasy line. But this is exactly what our great church leaders did, starting with the first U.S. Bishop, John Carroll (1735-1815). He dared to hope that the whole Church would one day adopt the U.S. style of religious freedom as not only compatible with Catholic life but positively the most beneficial style for Catholicism itself. Of course, it would only be at the Second Vatican Council in 1965, and then only under the strong influence of the American Jesuit, John Courtney Murray, that the principle of religious liberty would win out over the long insistence of the Restorationists that an established Catholic church remain the norm to which all the faithful aspired. With the Vatican II *Declaration on Religious Freedom* (or *Dignitatis Humanae*), religious pluralism was no longer condemned or merely tolerated but openly embraced. We must not forget that it was in the rich soil of a thriving American Catholicism that the seeds of this stunning development of church doctrine were planted generations earlier.

While some church leaders of the pivotal nineteenth century weighed in primarily on institutional matters such as the separation of church and state, among them Cardinal James Gibbons (1834-1921) of Baltimore and Isaac Hecker (1819-1888), the founder of the Paulists, others offered guidance on matters of religion and society more broadly conceived. Although U.S. Catholics for several generations tended to cluster in ethnic enclaves and urban ghettos shared with kindred souls, the Catholic community was blessed with such leaders as Bishop John Ireland (1838-1918), who opposed all versions of sectarianism and preached a mutually beneficial relationship between Catholicism and American society. Despite the presence of doubters, Ireland and his supporters demonstrated how the national and spiritual allegiances of U.S. Catholics do go hand in hand, without undue friction. This is sometimes called the gospel of *compatibilism*, for it contends that being Catholic and being American are indeed compatible, and, more than that, mutually reaffirming. Because of the courageous pioneers who articulated such novel ideas, American Catholicism was able to wrestle in constructive ways not only with questions about patriotism but also with the key matter of religious liberty, a distinctive contribution that Justice John Noonan, citing a term used by James Madison, recognizes as "the lustre of our country."

Of course, this positive portrayal of the achievement of the U.S. Catholic community has its dissenters. Our distinctive style of civic engagement strikes some of the faithful as unduly accommodationist or even relativistic, as if we are overly eager to sweep under the rug any evidence of incompatibility between Catholic and American identity. Actually, even for those of us who are eager to celebrate these achievements, it is not at all hard to find objectionable elements of American culture, national ethos and public policy. A short list would include: consumerism, vulgar materialism, disregard for the environment, callousness to human suffering abroad, hasty resort to the use of force and economic imperialism, just to name a few indictments of the dominant American way of proceeding. The American way of life features an underside, one that must not be overlooked. It seems to me that the proper response is not to fall into a crass anti-Americanism, but rather to adopt a stance of *more-than-Americanism* that holds up higher ideals than we now espouse or achieve, and that challenges the country we love to do better on these scores. The ultimate gift and legacy of the vicissitudes of our history as Catholics in America is that we are free to be something other than completely alienated from or thoroughly uncritical of America. Indeed, U.S. Catholics are uniquely well positioned to continue this project of critical engagement with the culture of a nation that is quite imperfect, but still one we can proudly call our home.

I have by now no doubt stolen all of the thunder from my fourth and final thesis, which requires little explication at this point. It is this: A chastened patriotism, tempered by reason and deliberation and a variety of other virtues and loyalties, is the best option. Now the most direct way to develop this point might be to recount just how badly things go when unchecked patriotic fervor gets the better of us. We know from the recent experience of the Obama campaign cited earlier that certain appeals to patriotism easily degenerate into sheer triviality or even silliness, usually in service of other agendas related to the symbolic wrangling of the culture wars. Perhaps the notion of patriotism has been so tarnished and abused as a wedge issue in recent public life that it is no longer salvageable as a constructive force in our society. After all, a perceived deficit of patriotism has landed many people of conscience in jail or worse, from the days of the Alien and Sedition Acts in Federalist America through the protests of Henry David Thoreau and other opponents of unjust wars over the course of the past two centuries, and right up to today. The flames of patriotism have scorched many dissenters who sought to render service to America by pointing out its faults. How quickly loyalty to one's nation devolves into extremism and simplistic slogans such as *America, love it or leave it* and *My country, right or wrong.*

But it is consoling to recall that this need not be the case. A well-tempered patriotism need not crowd out loyal dissent. An open-eyed version of patriotism is fully capable of recognizing a loyal opposition when it sees one. Indeed, to disregard or dismiss opposing voices that challenge one's country to achieve higher ideals may just be to display the worst kind of anti-patriotism. Deliberately turning a blind eye to the shortcomings of one's nation can only harm the land one pretends to love. Further, the prejudices and irrationalities that are commonly associated with patriotic fervor are by no means necessary components of loyalty to country; they are mere accretions that can be purified out with an adequate application of attention and effort. So we can dare to hope for better, and it is not impossible to find reasons to support such a hope.

What do true patriots look like today? They are people with long enough memories to recall the value of conscience and civil liberties even in times of national trial. They love peace enough to recognize that restraint and self-control are a greater credit to a nation than muscular self-assertion. They balance their love of country with enough cosmopolitan regard that they reject a narrow agenda of self-aggrandizement in favor of the universal common good of all humankind. Above all, they resist the temptation to use patriotism itself to change the subject from uncomfortable topics regarding their nation's faults and misdeeds.

Above all, if it is to be a constructive force in our national life, patriotism must not exist in a vacuum, for it requires numerous correctives to accompany it. The same people who appeal to love of nation as a motive for action should be mindful of the full range of values and virtues that deserve to be cultivated and enacted: items like respect for other cultures and peoples, attention to the demands of social justice and openness to changing social mores. In lonely isolation, patriotism cannot play the constructive role we need to meet the contemporary challenges of a complex and increasingly globalized society. But with proper augmentation by the myriad sets of loyalties felt by people today, including Christians who center their lives on the living God of Jesus Christ, patriotism can be a constructive force that will *bind* our nation together, not *blind* it with arrogance and self-centeredness. At its best, patriotism is fully compatible with the blessed life of the Christian proclamation. Whether the abstract noun of patriotism delivers on this promise is fully in the hands of concrete people like us.

Admittedly, I have hardly gone out on a limb in selecting and developing the theses I have presented. Just to recap, these were the four: First, there are good and bad things about patriotism. Second, patriotism presents something of a dilemma for Christians and requires careful discernment on the part of all religious people. Third, patriotism presents a particular dilemma for U.S. Catholics, especially in light of our distinctive history. Fourth, a chastened patriotism, tempered by reason and deliberation and a variety of other virtues and loyalties, is the best option. I trust that I have kept my promise to refrain from soaring but empty rhetoric, and I continue to suspect that I have told you little that you did not already know. But I will declare success if I encouraged you to think about these matters just a bit harder, or to consider anew the value and operation of patriotism in the landscape of your own sets of values. Clarifying the place of patriotism in the lives of any of us, but especially of Catholics in the U.S. today, is a crucial item on any agenda for developing a stance of responsible and faithful citizenship.

Flannery O'Connor's Vision of Faith, Church, and Modern Consciousness

Most Rev. George H. Niederauer
Archbishop of San Francisco

LANE CENTER LECTURE SERIES I September 28, 2007

My days as a teacher of college English are long past, and now I am a Roman Catholic archbishop, who agreed to speak, from that viewpoint, about a woman and a writer whom I admire greatly, Flannery O'Connor. I remember, though, what Flannery O'Connor wrote after meeting Paul Hallinan, the new Archbishop of Atlanta, whom she admired. She said: "Usually I think the Church's motto is *The Wrong Man for the Job*; but not this time."1 That pungent little verdict suggests much of what I believe is wonderful and valuable in Flannery O'Connor: the savvy, sly wit; the dead-on-honest observation; the faith, strong in spite of all; and the Christian realist's hope that this time it might be better, but not easily, and not likely for long.

Flannery O'Connor died during the Church's Second Vatican Council, while the bishops were writing anew what she had always known: the Church is the Body of Christ, the People of God, that laypeople are its flesh and blood and that the clergy and religious orders are its servant-leaders. While Flannery O'Connor was a supreme artist in fiction, this afternoon I want to suggest how she was, and is, a particularly valuable witness to the Catholic Church and its leaders in this country. Hers is the testimony of a watchful, honest, faith-filled, eloquent lay person, and she had much to say about the experience of living her faith within the Roman Catholic Church, especially in a society and a culture that had marginalized genuine Christian faith and practice. I invite you now to listen with me to what she said in her letters about several closely connected aspects of Roman Catholic experience: 1) the experience of being a believer, a disciple of Jesus Christ; 2) the cost of discipleship; 3) the power of grace in the experience of the believer; and, 4) the experience of the Church as the setting of that life of faith and discipleship, a setting that she saw as all too human as well as divine in origin.

Besides O'Connor's letters, collected and edited by Sally Fitzgerald, in *The Habit of Being*, I will make references to a recent work by Paul Elie, *The Life You Save May Be Your Own*, a study of four mid-twentieth century American Catholic writers: Flannery O'Connor, Thomas Merton, Walker Percy, and Dorothy Day. Elie drew the title for his study from the title of a Flannery O'Connor short story. I am also indebted to George A. Kilcourse, Jr., for his work, *Flannery O'Connor's Religious Imagination: A World with Everything Off Balance*.

Flannery O'Connor said of herself as a writer: "I feel that if I were not a

Catholic I would have no reason to write, no reason to see, no reason ever to feel horrified or even to enjoy anything." (p.114) The Church, she claimed, was "the only thing that is going to make the terrible world we are coming to endurable." (p. 90) Why? Quite simply because the Church taught as its central doctrine the Incarnation, the belief that God became human and creaturely, with us, in Jesus Christ. Flannery O'Connor believed that teaching, and for her, its truth transformed everything in life: She said: "the ultimate reality is the Incarnation, the present reality is the Incarnation, and nobody believes in the Incarnation; that is nobody in your audience. My audience are the people who think God is dead. At least these are the people I am conscious of writing for." (P.92)

Thus there follows the clash of consciousness between O'Connor and her audience, the clash between the believers and the non-believers, between contradictory sets of assumptions about human experience.

She claimed the Incarnation as the principle of her spirituality: "if you believe in the divinity of Christ, you have to cherish the world at the same time that you struggle to endure it." (p. 90) But beyond shaping her personal spirituality, Incarnation directed her strategy as a writer. She asserted that, "the writer has to succeed in making the divinity of Christ seem consistent with the structure of all reality. This has to be got across implicitly in spite of a world that doesn't feel it, in spite of characters who don't live it." (p. 290) Incarnation even helps explain an aspect of O'Connor's writing that is particularly challenging for many readers: The grotesque. She said: "The Incarnation makes us see the grotesque as grotesque." (p. 227) Paul Elie gives us this analysis of freakish and grotesque characters in O'Connor's fiction:

> The grotesque character or freak plays various roles in her work, serving a broad range of dramatic purposes. The freak is an image of human nature deformed by sin, as is the Misfit in *A Good Man is Hard to Find*, or an instance of human nature transformed by God's grace, as Hazel Motes is at the end of *Wise Blood*. The freak is a figure for modern man, like the psychologist Rayber in *The Violent Bear It Away*, reduced by the scientific worldview to an aggregate of tendencies and statistics; or a character deliberately distorted by the author, like the tattooed O.E. Parker in *Parker's Back*, so as to startle the unwitting reader to attention.

Christ as the light of the world, as light on the world, makes the believer see things differently, even contrarily. This observation brings to mind the words of Christ to the Pharisees regarding material wealth: "You justify yourselves in the eyes of others, but God knows your hearts: For what is of human esteem is an abomination in the sight of God." (Luke 16:15)

Flannery O'Connor claimed that faith was essential to her, but she never claimed it was easy. She described the mid-twentieth century as particularly uncongenial to genuine Christian faith:

> [T]he religious sense seems to be bred out of [people] in the kind
> of society we've lived in since the 18th century. There is no sense
> of the power of God that could produce the Incarnation and the
> Resurrection. They are all so busy explaining away the Virgin birth
> and such things, reducing everything to human proportions, that
> in time they lose even the sense of the human itself, what they were
> aiming to reduce everything to. (p.299)

The New Yorker magazine reviewed, rather dismissively, Flannery
O'Connor's short story collection, *A Good Man is Hard to Find*, after which she
wrote a friend regarding the review: "It was a case in which it was easy to see
that the moral sense has been bred out of certain sections of the population,
like the wings have been bred off certain chickens to produce more white
meat on them. This is a generation of wingless chickens, which I suppose is
what Nietzsche meant when he said God was dead."

Years later, when her novel, *Wise Blood* was re-issued, she wrote in an introductory author's note: "*Wise Blood* was written by an author congenitally innocent of theory, but one with certain preoccupations. That belief in Christ is
to some a matter of life and death has been a stumbling block for readers who
would prefer to think it a matter of no great consequence." O'Connor said that
some writers had even enshrined this lack of faith as a prerequisite for the
artist's vision: "It is popular to believe that in order to see clearly one must
believe nothing." (p. 147) As a young student, Flannery O'Connor's antidote
to that false assumption was what she called "Christian skepticism," and she
recommended it to others: "Learn what you can but cultivate Christian skepticism. It will keep you free - not free to do anything you please, but free to be
formed by something larger than your own intellect or the intellects of those
around you." (p. 478) Also, "What kept me a skeptic in college was precisely
my Christian faith. It always said: wait, don't bite on this, get a wider picture,
continue to read." (p. 476)

On another occasion, Flannery O'Connor dealt with this conflict between
faith and unbelief and its effect on the writer who is a believer:

> I don't think you should write something as long as a novel
> around anything that is not of the gravest concern to you and every-
> body else, and for me this is always the conflict between an attrac-
> tion for the Holy and the disbelief in it that we breathe in with the
> air of our times. It's hard to believe always but more so in the world
> we live in now. There are some of us who have to pay for our faith
> every step of the way and who have to work out dramatically what it
> would be like without it and if being without it would be ultimately
> possible or not.

So the believer needs patience and passion. According to Flannery
O'Connor, faith naturally waxes and wanes, and we must not panic or jump
to conclusions because of that. She wrote: "[L]et me tell you this: faith comes

and goes. It rises and falls like the tides of an invisible ocean. If it is presumptuous to think that faith will stay with you forever, it is just as presumptuous to think that unbelief will." (p. 451) She was especially fond of the prayer addressed to Christ in the gospel: "Lord, I believe; help my unbelief." (p.92) She wrote: "It is the most natural and most human and most agonizing prayer in the gospel, and I think it is the foundation prayer of faith." (p. 476) The Christian must yearn for and seek out faith, not just grudgingly take delivery of it if God sends it along: "Faith is a gift, but the will has a great deal to do with it. The loss of it is basically a failure of appetite, assisted by sterile intellect." (p. 451) But Christian faith cannot remain in the intellect; it must be lived for, with, and in Christ. Flannery O'Connor declared: "What people don't realize is how much religion costs. They think faith is a big electric blanket, when of course it is the cross. It is much harder to believe than not to believe." (p. 354) This cost of believing, of discipleship is crucial to an understanding of genuine Christian faith, as opposed to the casual, superficial, cultural Christianity that she so deplored. Genuine Christian faith transforms the meaning and value of everything; cosmetic Christianity merely brightens Sunday morning and highlights the tiny compartment of life labeled "religion." Flannery O'Connor would have appreciated the distinction made by the Protestant theologian, John MacMurray:

> The maxim of illusory religion runs: "Fear not; trust in God and He will see that none of the things you fear will happen to you"; that of real religion, on the contrary, is "Fear not; the things that you are afraid of are quite likely to happen to you, but they are nothing to be afraid of.[2]

Flannery O'Connor pointed out that, in her fiction, there are no halfway positions for the characters: "Everything works toward its true end or away from it. Everything is ultimately saved or lost." (p. 350) At this point let me pause a moment to cite a crucial passage from the Gospel of Mark, a passage that sets forth the cost of discipleship and the paradox of values at the heart of this Christian faith, in the sense of all being saved or all being lost:

> He began to teach them that the Son of Man must suffer greatly and be rejected by the elders, the chief priests, and the scribes, and be killed, and rise after three days. He spoke of this openly. Then Peter took him aside and began to rebuke him. At this he turned and, looking at his disciples, rebuked Peter and said, "Get behind me, Satan. You are thinking not as God does but as human beings do." He summoned the crowd with his disciples and said to them, "Whoever wishes to come after me must deny himself, take up his cross, and follow me. For whoever wishes to save his life will lose it, but whoever loses his life for my sake and the sake of the gospel will save it. What profit is there for one to gain the whole world and forfeit his life? What could one give in exchange for his life?" (Mark 8:31-37)

Let me make three brief observations on this teaching of Jesus, then consider Flannery O'Connor's reflections of it. First, when Peter tries to argue against Jesus' first prediction of his death on the cross, I believe there is a good reason why Jesus addresses him as "Satan." Peter in that moment reminds Jesus of what Satan had tried to do in his three earlier temptations, that is, argue for a short cut, easy version of salvation, which would eliminate any need for living, dying, and rising for others. (Flannery O'Connor made numerous trenchant observations about easy, short-cut religion.) Second, the cost of discipleship is described as triple in form: 1) self-denial; 2) carrying (sharing in) the cross; 3) following in the steps (the example and teaching) of Jesus.

The third point is the paradox at the heart of Christian faith and life: the "saved" life vs. the "lost" life. Here is one way of understanding that paradox (so prominent in Flannery O'Connor's fiction): each of us can save his or her life in a worldly sense, i.e., we can go off and make the best self we can of ourselves, for ourselves, by ourselves, with no real reference to Christ, but if we do that we lose the life we could have had in following him. Or, we can let go to grace, choose the lost life, become the person we were created, redeemed, and called to be in Christ, i.e., get lost in Christ, which, for a Christian, is to be saved - but, of course, we lose the self we could have become through self-absorption and self-fulfillment.

Now back to O'Connor on these points. In regard to the value of self-denial in following Christ, Flannery O'Connor made the following observation on members of the Beat Generation as opponents of materialism: "They call themselves holy but holiness costs and so far as I can see they pay nothing. It's true that grace is the free gift of God, but in order to put yourself in the way of being receptive to it you have to practice self-denial." (p. 336) She defended asceticism, a value less and less popular in our time: "Accepting oneself does not preclude an attempt to become better. Self-torture is abnormal; asceticism is not." (p. 458)

In regard to suffering, to meeting and bearing the cross in following Christ, she said of her stories: "It is necessary to throw the weight of circumstances against the character I favor. The friends of God suffer, etc." (p. 120) She claimed that her stories were "about original sin" (p. 74), and that they were misunderstood by readers who missed the faith context.

> The stories are hard because there is nothing harder or less sentimental than Christian realism. I believe that there are many rough beasts now slouching toward Bethlehem to be born and I have reported on the progress of a few of them ... and when I see these stories described as horror stories I am always amused because the reviewer always has hold of the wrong horror. (p. 90)

The wrong horror leaves the reader aghast at how destructive divine grace seems to be of worldly values. The right horror is grace rejected from a nice worldly life. In one letter Flannery O'Connor observes, "Human nature is so faulty that it can resist any amount of grace and most of the time it does. The

Church does well to hold its own; you are asking that she show a profit. When she shows a profit, you have a saint, and not necessarily a canonized one."

Paul Elie points out that Flannery O'Connor, a Catholic writer living in and writing about the overwhelmingly Protestant South, often indicated what she thought the Catholic Church and the Protestant South had in common: "the Bible, a religious heritage, an awareness of human limitation, a respect for the concrete and the actual, and a recognition that 'good and evil in every culture tend to be joined at the spine. '"

But how does one know that one has chosen the lost life of Christ over the saved or worldly life? Flannery O'Connor gave the standard, the only, answer—charity or love, but she gave anything but a standard spin to that answer. She was fond of Gerard Manley Hopkins' simple, two word response to Robert Bridges' request for advice on how to open himself to faith: "Give alms." (pp. 164 and 476)

The following of Christ is the living of Christian love, and she declared: "You will have found Christ when you are concerned with other people's sufferings and not your own." (p. 453) But she knew how hard-won and elusive this love is, and how easily it is confused with its cheap imitations: "To expect too much is to have a sentimental view of life and this is a softness that ends in bitterness. Charity is hard and endures." (p. 308) Again: "It is what is invisible that God sees and what the Christian must look for. Because he knows the consequences of sin, he knows how deep in you have to go to find love." (p. 308) Nevertheless, she was confident, saying: "I believe love to be efficacious in the long run. (p.97)

To what did Flannery O'Connor credit this ultimate victory of love? She looked to the operation of God's grace, redeeming power, in the world, in his creatures, often in spite of them. Believers have to choose the lost life over and over again, not once and for all. She wrote in this regard:

> I don't think of conversion as being once and for all and that's that. I think once the process is begun and continues that you are continually turning inward toward God and away from your own egocentricity, and that you have to see this selfish side of yourself in order to turn away from it. I measure God by everything I am not. I begin with that. (p. 430)

How did Flannery O'Connor's "Christian realism" respond to the experience of the suffering of innocent human beings in the world around us? A group of Dominican nuns who ran a Free Cancer Home in Atlanta, Georgia, prevailed upon a very reluctant O'Connor to introduce and edit a memoir they intended to publish about Mary Ann, a terribly disfigured but very cheerful little girl, who had lived and died among them. What follows is Paul Elie's analysis of Flannery O'Connor's response to this challenge:

> A child like Mary Ann, she observed, is obviously grotesque, and in the modern world such a child is thought to discredit the

goodness of God. How can a good God allow such a child to die? the Ivan Karamazovs of the world ask. How, moreover, can a good God allow such a child to be born? The modern unbeliever prides himself on his realism, his willingness to recognize suffering and to ponder the problem of evil directly. But in O'Connor's estimation such an outlook is not realistic; it is naive, sentimental, and even dangerous. It is the believer, not the unbeliever, who is the realist. In a child like Mary Ann the believer sees the likeness of every human person—deformed, limited, imperfect. In human deforming the believer sees the raw material of good. In human suffering the believer sees the grounds of our common humanity, recognizing that it is through suffering, above all, that human beings are stirred to the love of one another, and to the love of God, who showed his love for humanity through his willingness to suffer as one of us.

Flannery O'Connor's characters wrestle with grace because she believed we all do. She said: "All human nature vigorously resists grace because grace changes us and the change is painful. Priests resist it as well as others." (p. 307) God's grace reaches down past our self-satisfaction and self-absorption to where we yearn for him. She wrote: "God rescues us from ourselves if we want him to." (p.118)

Flannery O'Connor knew how difficult it was to portray these operations of grace to contemporary readers: "Part of the difficulty of all this is you write for an audience who doesn't know what grace is or doesn't recognize it when they see it. All my stories are about the action of grace on a character who is not very willing to support, but most people think of these stories as hard, hopeless, brutal, etc." (p. 275) Again she said: "For me this is always the conflict between an attraction for the Holy and disbelief in it that we breathe in with the air of the times." (p. 349) In a lecture entitled "The Catholic Novelist and the Protestant South," Flannery O'Connor described the situation of the Christian disciple who is poet or storyteller in what is, for me, a lovely and powerfully suggestive image:

> The poet is traditionally a blind man. But the Christian Poet, and the storyteller as well, is like the blind man Christ touched, who looked then and saw men as if they were trees - but walking. Christ touched him again and he saw clearly. We will not see clearly until Christ touches us in death, but this first touch is the beginning of vision, and it is an invitation to deeper and stranger visions that we shall have to accept if we want to realize a Catholic literature.

O'Connor was not sanguine about the tastes and capacities of general audiences for fiction in her day. She wrote to a friend, describing her talk at a ladies' book club: "The heart of my message to them was that they would all fry in hell if they didn't quit reading trash." About the fiction of the time she said, "There's many a best seller that could have been prevented by a good teacher."

But what about the believer's experience of Church? Our present age has been described as one in which people place a high value on spirituality and a low value on religion, especially organized religion. Of particular interest, then, is Flannery O'Connor's thinking about the experience of Church, the assembly of believers. She valued the Roman Catholic Church highly, but she observed it acutely, warts and all. If the Church made life endurable, it also provided much that had to be endured. She wrote: "You have to suffer as much from the church as for it. The only thing that makes the church endurable is that somehow it is the body of Christ, and on this we are fed." (p. 90) She went on to explain why we suffer from the Church: "The operation of the church is entirely set up for the sake of the sinner, which creates much misunderstanding among the smug." (p. 92) God, then, is as patient with the entire church as he is with each lost sheep, and many of us Catholics have very little patience with either.

The Catholic Church is made up of imperfect pilgrims on a long, difficult journey, and Flannery O'Connor described them well: "The Catholic Church is composed of those who accept what she teaches, whether they are good or bad, and there is constant struggle through the help of the sacraments to be good." (p. 346) T.S. Eliot says, in *Choruses From The Rock*, that modern people don't like the church because "She is tender where they would be hard, and hard where they would be soft."[3] (Think of issues like abortion, euthanasia, welfare reform, capital punishment, etc.) I believe Miss O'Connor might have appreciated Eliot's remark.

Within the visible church, the Holy Spirit is constantly acting in the lives of its members, individually and collectively. Thus, the Church cannot be accurately judged or evaluated by what her critics observe externally. Flannery O'Connor pointed that out to one of her friends in these words:

> You judge [the Church] strictly by its human element, by unimaginative and half-dead Catholics who would be startled to know the nature of what they defend by formula. The miracle is that the Church's dogma is kept pure *both by and from* such people. Nature is not prodigal of genius and the Church makes do with what nature gives her. At the age of 11, you encounter some old priest who calls you a heretic for inquiring about evolution; at about the same time Pere Pierre Teilhard de Chardin, S.J., is in China discovering Peking man. (p. 366)

The human element in the Church was a frequent target of Flannery O'Connor's wit, as when she proposed this motto for the Catholic press of her day: "We guarantee to corrupt nothing but your taste." (p.138) More seriously, she quoted Saint Augustine's advice to the "wheat" in the Church not to leave the threshing floor of life before the harvest is complete, just because there is so much of that disgusting chaff around! (p. 330) In this connection, she slyly suggested what the difficulty may be for more sensitive Catholics (referring to one young woman in particular): "She probably sees more stupidity and vulgarity than she does sin and these are harder to put up with than sin, harder on the nerves." (p. 330)

Meanwhile, the world goes on judging the Church in utilitarian fashion, using the same standard it would apply to the Rotary or the Kiwanis. Miss O'Connor challenged this approach: "Any Catholic or Protestant is defenseless before those who judge his religion by how well its members live up to it or are able to explain it." (p. 345) The surface is easy to judge, she was saying, but not the interior operations of the Holy Spirit. She illustrated this principle with a touching reference to the vocation of Catholic priests, whom she often found to be overworked and unimaginative. She wrote:

> It is easy for any child to find out the faults in the sermon on his way home from Church every Sunday. It is impossible to find out the hidden love that makes a man, in spite of his intellectual limitations, his neuroticism, his lack of strength, give up his life to the service of God's people, however bumblingly he may go about it. (pp. 307-308)

While Flannery O'Connor defended her Church against superficial and unfair judgments, she was neither a whitewasher nor a fatalist, and she was an implacable foe of complacency. She believed that the Church must struggle toward greater virtue as surely as each of its members. She wrote quite forcefully in this regard: "It's our business to change the external faults of the Church—the vulgarity, the lack of scholarship, the lack of intellectual honesty—wherever we find them and however we can." (p. 308) Let me give three examples of Church faults she criticized and wished to see corrected. They are in order of increasing severity, I believe.

First, she condemned smugness as *The Great Catholic Sin*. Perhaps 45 years later, something else would head her list, but smugness would probably still be listed. She wrote of this smugness in these words: "I find it in myself and I don't dislike it any less. One reason Guardini is a relief to read is that he has nothing of it. With a few exceptions the American clergy, when it takes to the pen, brings this particular sin with it in full force." (p. 131) [Aside: About twenty years ago a bumper sticker appeared on cars, saying: "If you feel God is far away, guess who moved." If Flannery O'Connor had lived to see one of those signs on a Georgia road, I like to think that she would have skewered the sentiment as very smug, even as she chuckled at the rampant vulgarity of bumper sticker theology.] Related to smugness is glibness, which she described as "the great danger in answering people's questions about religion." (p. 307) Again, a sense of mystery will give the Christian apologist a sense of humility: if I am convinced that I have the truth about God I am much more likely to be obnoxious about it, than if I am convinced that God's truth has me.

Flannery O'Connor expressed impatience with the kind of Catholicism, and Catholic fiction, which kept everything nice, shallow, cute, and safe. She described what she called "A nice vapid-Catholic distrust of finding God in action of any range and depth. This is not the kind of Catholicism that has saved me so many years in learning to write, but then this is not Catholicism at all." (p. 139) Genuine Catholicism, she felt, must be as radical and demanding as its Founder's teaching.

Another Catholic fault O'Connor described is, I believe, an evergreen reality in the Church: A Jansenistic disdain for human weakness and struggle, and a distrust of questions, speculations, and discussions of any depth. Of the pseudo-faith of such persons she said:

> I know what you mean about being repulsed by the Church when you have only the Mechanical-Jansenist Catholic to judge it by. I think that the reason such Catholics are so repulsive is that they don't really have faith but a kind of false certainty. They operate by the slide rule and the Church for them is not the body of Christ but the poor man's insurance system. It's never hard for them to believe because actually they never think about it. Faith has to take in all the other possibilities it can. (pp. 239-231)

In considering such people's self-righteous judgments of others, she made an acute observation: "Conviction without experience makes for harshness." (p. 97) By contrast, Christians who have struggled with their demons are better equipped to show compassion toward others.

Finally, some reflections on Flannery O'Connor's deep distaste and contempt for modern, sanitized, "empty" religion. Because she embraced an imaginative vision of religion as the mystery of God's saving action intersecting with all that is earthly, Flannery O'Connor remarked to one correspondent as follows: "All around you today you will find people accepting 'religion' that has been rid of its religious elements." (p. 365) Elsewhere she described this development in more detail. She wrote:

> One of the effects of modern liberal Protestantism has been gradually to turn religion into poetry and therapy, to make truth vaguer and vaguer and more and more relative, to banish intellectual distinctions, to depend on feeling instead of thought, and gradually to come to believe that God has no power, that he cannot communicate with us, cannot reveal himself to us, indeed has not done so, and that religion is our own sweet invention. (p. 479)

The issue of religion bled dry of its content is the feature of what is probably the most famous story about Flannery O'Connor. As a very young and unknown writer, she visited New York and was taken to a party at the home of Mary McCarthy, ex-Catholic and ex-believer, a sophisticated and accomplished novelist, essayist, and critic. What follows is O'Connor's description of the encounter:

> We went at eight and at one, I hadn't opened my mouth once,

> there being nothing in such company for me to say … Having me
> there was like having a dog present who had been trained to say
> a few words but overcome with inadequacy had forgotten them.
> Well, toward the morning the conversation turned on the Eucharist,
> which I, being the Catholic, was obviously supposed to defend.
> Mrs. Broadwater [Mary McCarthy] said when she was a child and
> received the Host, she thought of it as the Holy Ghost, He being
> the most 'portable' person of the Trinity; now she thought of it as a
> symbol and implied that it was a pretty good one. I then said, in a
> very shaky voice, 'Well, if it's a symbol, to hell with it.' That was all
> the defense I was capable of.

Paul Elie remarks of this exchange: "The closing remark is the most famous
of all O'Connor's remarks, an economical swipe at the reductive, liberalizing
view of religion."

She locates one important moment in the development of this religious trend
in this country. With some amusement she recalls a talk she gave at a college:

> I told them that when Emerson decided in 1832 that he could no
> longer celebrate the Lord's Supper unless the bread and wine were
> removed, that an important step in the vaporization of religion in
> American had taken place. (p. 511)

For some readers, one of the most surprising, even jarring, features of
O'Connor's fiction, is its consistently comic character, even as the stories and
novels pursue such serious themes of faith and grace. Paul Elie describes an
experience the author had when in New York, on a visit to the Cloisters (the
museum of medieval art in Fort Tryon Park): "She was *greatly taken* with a
wooden statue on display in one of the chapels. It was the Virgin holding the
Christ child and both were laughing; not smiling, laughing." Elie concludes:
"It was a piece to emulate as well as admire; like her own work, it was religious and comic at the same time."

The betrayal of religion is downright diabolical in Flannery O'Connor's
view, and so it is portrayed in her fiction. For her, the crucial choice facing each of us is between the lost life with Christ and the worldly saved life
without him. Thus, the most fiendish of temptation is to offer a saved, worldly
life, but to offer it under the guise of being generically Christian (though
with no Christ content whatsoever). In this connection Paul Elie describes a
type of character that appears over and over again in O'Connor's stories: "the
middle-aged busybody who knows exactly what she thinks, who sees all and
understands nothing." One example is the character of Mrs. May, in the story
Greenleaf. At one point in the story, Mrs. May comes upon Mrs. Greenleaf in
the woods, murmuring over and over again, "Jesus, Jesus, Jesus." O'Connor
wrote: "Mrs. May winced. She thought the word, Jesus, should be kept inside
the church building, like other words inside the bedroom. She was a good
Christian woman with a large respect for religion, though she did not, of

course, believe any of it was true."[4]

As I close these remarks on what Flannery O'Connor has to say to the Church about faith, modern consciousness, and living together as Church, I think of her simple statement: "I write because I write well." We are here this afternoon because we all agree with her, and her works live because multitudes, who are not here, agree with us. She writes well. But there is so much more than that to be said of her. One thing will suffice for me now: How wonderfully different Flannery O'Connor was from Mrs. May. She thought that the name of Jesus, the reality of Jesus, belonged everywhere, indeed, was everywhere. And about the Christian faith Flannery O'Connor was the polar opposite of Mrs. May, because she, of course, believed all of it was true.

Notes:

1. Flannery O'Connor, *Habit of Being, Letters Edited And With An Introduction by Sally Fitzgerald* (New York: Favor, Straus, Giroux, 1979), p. 474.

2. Cited by William Barry, S.J., in "The Kingdom of God and Discernment" (*America*, Vol. 57, No.7, September 26, 1987), p. 159.

3. Eliot, Thomas Stearns, *Complete Poems and Plays* (New York: Harcourt, Brace, 1952), p. 106.

4. Flannery O'Connor, *The Complete Stories* (New York: Ferror, Straus and Giroux, 1971), p. 316.

Jesuit Hybrids, Catholic Modernities, Future Pasts

Rev. Stephen Schloesser, S.J.

Associate Professor, Department of History, Boston College. Fr. Schloesser served as Lo Schiavo Chair in Catholic Studies and Social Thought at USF from 2005-2007.

INAUGURAL LECTURE OF THE JOSEPH AND ANNA LO SCHIAVO CHAIR IN CATHOLIC THOUGHT I September 1, 2005

n the year 1924, the Jesuit paleontologist Pierre Teilhard de Chardin
(1881-1955) was forty-three years old, having spent years excavating
fossils and teaching in Spain and Egypt after the First World War. During the war, Teilhard declined the safer route, which would have been
to serve as a military chaplain. Instead, he volunteered for the infantry
and served as a medic on the front lines where he saw some of the worst
that humanity is capable of. Returning to civilian life as a research scientist,
Teilhard talked about his travels in the Middle East and his theories regarding
evolution. His Catholic listeners were both fascinated and troubled: fascinated by the exotic stories of travel and discovery; troubled because one could
not be both a believer in the Catholic faith and in evolutionary theory. Or so it
seemed in the postwar period.[1]

In response to repeated questions about how to reconcile scientific inquiry
with the doctrine of Original Sin, Teilhard prepared written notes. These
notes mysteriously made their way to Rome's Holy Office of the Inquisition,
today's Congregation for the Doctrine of the Faith, and an investigation was
launched.[2] After a lengthy inquiry, Teilhard's license to teach at the Institut
Catholique was permanently revoked. This was only the beginning: for three
more decades he would be forbidden to publish or teach; he would not be
allowed to live in Paris; and he spent the remainder of his life exiled from
France, first in China and then, after the Communist revolution, in New York,
where he eventually died and his body remains buried.

During the great crisis of conscience provoked by these events, Teilhard
wrote to a close Jesuit friend:

> They want me to promise in writing that I will never *say* or write
> anything against the traditional position of the Church on original
> sin ... I feel I should, in conscience, reserve for myself (1) the right
> to carry on research with professional men; (2) the right to bring
> help to the disturbed and troubled.[3]

To my mind, these lines, written in 1924, sum up succinctly what it means
to be a Jesuit scholar, and, by extension, what it means for an intellectual
institution to be in the Catholic and Jesuit traditions. Teilhard's first *right*, to
carry on research with professional peers, followed logically from the longstanding Catholic tradition that the object of Truth is ultimately Being itself, a
vision extending back at least as far as St. Thomas Aquinas (1225-1274) who

imported the metaphysics of Aristotle (384 BCE-322 BCE), via Jewish and Muslim commentators, for medieval Christian use.[4] For this tradition, if one is a religious believer, the object of Truth is ultimately God. Unlike nominalist traditions, skeptical about whether the mind ever grasps extra-mental reality, Thomas held to the conviction -- some have said an overly naive one -- that we can know things as they are.[5]

Faith and reason, ultimately, cannot contradict one another. This exceedingly optimistic stance was defined dogmatically at the First Vatican Council (1869-1870): "Even though faith is above reason, there can never be any real disagreement between faith and reason, since it is the same God who reveals the mysteries and infuses faith, and who has endowed the human mind with the light of reason."[6] In soaring poetry, Pope John Paul II (1920-2005), so recently deceased, made this claim even stronger: "Faith and reason are like two wings on which the human spirit rises to the contemplation of truth; and God has placed in the human heart a desire to know the truth—in a word, to know himself—so that, by knowing and loving God, men and women may also come to the fullness of truth about themselves."[7] This basic Catholic conviction leads logically to Teilhard's first claimed right: the right to carry on research with intellectual peers --- what today we call "academic freedom."

If this first right is quintessentially Catholic, the second right is particularly Jesuit: "to bring help to the disturbed and troubled." In Teilhard's time, the disturbed and troubled were those who could not find the intellectual means with which to reconcile their positions as believing Catholics and as scientifically informed moderns. It seemed that one could not, for example, be both Catholic and a believer in evolutionary science. Similarly, one could not be both Catholic and a proponent of liberal democracy, an opposition that would baffle almost any Catholic today.[8] When Teilhard said that he had a *right* to bring help to the disturbed and troubled, he might have added that he had, as a Jesuit, a *duty*, an *obligation*, a *vocation* to do so. Throughout the writings of St. Ignatius Loyola (1491-1556) and the early Jesuits we find these two words used over and over to specify the Jesuit's proper mission: "to help" (or "to aid") and "to console."[9]

Thus, to be Catholic and to be Jesuit is not the same thing. The Jesuit tradition is a specific species of the genus Catholicism, a species with a particular relationship to the hierarchical institution. That relationship emerges out of the Society of Jesus's unique and unrepeatable historical origins in sixteenth-century Renaissance Humanism. A Jesuit has one foot in the Church and one foot in "the world" or, using now-classic terminology, a Jesuit bridges "Christ and culture."[10] There are, of course, many other Catholic traditions with their own unique historical origins and trajectories, and a number of these set Christ and culture in opposition to one another: St. Benedict's monastic tradition, St. Dominic's medieval tradition, the early-modern Jansenist tradition, and today's Legionnaires of Christ. These are all Catholic traditions, but they differ strongly, some even radically, from the Jesuit tradition, which is a

Renaissance Humanistic tradition of reconciling Christ and culture.

We do not live in Teilhard's day; but then again, there is a way in which those days have made an uncanny return. Ten years ago, who would have imagined that the theory of evolution would once again become a national site of contest between science and religion?[11] And who could have predicted that Teilhard would today be regarded as a conservative in that debate? (He did, after all, argue for divine intelligence in the evolutionary process, albeit a divinity that often seemed to work itself out in violent ways.) Forty years after the death of John F. Kennedy,[12] who could have imagined that it would be controversial once again to reflect on the simultaneous practice of Catholicism and democracy --- that is, a world in which the values of some must be compromised with those of others?[13]

But conflicts between Catholicism and evolution or Catholicism and democracy are not the fundamental conflicts between the Church and culture today --- those were largely settled at the Second Vatican Council. Rather, today's hot-button conflicts reside in the arenas of gender, sexuality, and reproduction, principal avenues of twentieth-century technological and cultural innovations which are advancing even more rapidly in our own new century. Those who are disturbed and troubled today largely want to know how the Church and culture can correspond on these issues. This seems to me a key question --- if, indeed, a volatile one --- for any intellectual institution that today thinks of itself as Catholic and Jesuit.

Being a historian by trade and training, I want to offer some images from the past for our consideration. I hope they can let us creatively re-imagine ourselves as those who possess rights *and* duties, first, to pursue truth with our intellectual peers; second, to help the disturbed and troubled.

Jesuit Hybrids

A hybrid is the grafting of one species onto another to produce a third. It used to be difficult to talk to my students about the concept of hybridity; unless they were biology majors, they just couldn't grasp it. But in today's world of escalating gasoline prices, hybrids are a household name. Just last week, Californians lined up to get the new permits allowing solo drivers in certain hybrid makes to use the diamond lanes.[14] The USF Jesuit Community now owns two Prius hybrids. But Jesuit hybrids go way back before Toyota...

By "Jesuit hybrids" I mean the early-modern Jesuit practice of grafting Catholicism onto found cultures.[15] For example, here is an image of Fr. Giulio Mancinelli (1537-1618) in Constantinople (today's Istanbul): back then it was the capital of the Ottoman Empire; today it is the contested border of the New Europe.[16] In 1583, Fr. Mancinelli was sent by Pope Gregory XIII (1502-1585) and the Jesuit General Claudio Acquaviva (1543-1615) to the Islamic capital where he seems to have accommodated himself to the local culture with ease: when in New Rome, do as the New Romans do.[17] My undergrads love this image of the Jesuit priest smoking hookah as hookah lounges have become newly chic.

Or we could look at the Jesuits at the Imperial Court of the Mughal Emperor Akbar the Great (1542-1605) in India.[18] Perhaps our most popular visual association with this court is the Taj Mahal, a tomb built for a Mughal emperor's wife. The Islamic influence is explicit, with its horseshoe-shaped Moorish arches as well as Arabic script. The Jesuits opened an art school at the court (as they did throughout their missions[19]), and one of the art works produced at the school is of St. Jerome (347-420) seemingly asleep beneath a Bodhi tree with a copy of the Bible in his hand. Jerome, iconic in the Renaissance for having translated the original Biblical languages into an authoritative Latin Vulgate, became a symbolic figure for Renaissance Humanists (e.g., Desiderius Erasmus [1466-1536]) seeking authentic ancient sources and producing definitively accurate translations.[20] We find numerous pictorial depictions of him from the 1400s through the 1600s, including those of Antonello da Messina (1430-1479) in Sicily, Albrecht Dürer (1471-1528) in Nuremberg, El Greco (1541-1614) in Spain, and Georges de La Tour (1593-1652) in France.[21] However, this Jerome under the Bodhi Tree is different: it is St. Jerome hybridized with Siddh rtha Gautama Buddha (d. ca. 411-400 BCE), seated beneath the Bodhi tree at the Sri Mahabodhi Temple, achieving enlightenment.

Another production from the same Jesuit court school depicts a Madonna and Child. Done by the artist Basawan (1550-1610), it uses Arabic calligraphy and architecture to situate the Madonna within a Mughal court setting. But there is a foreign element in this work: the Madonna bares her breast to suckle the baby. No other portrait of women that I have encountered, by Basawan or by one of his imitators from the same period, displays a woman this way. The bare breasts of the Madonna *are* a foreign element --- an element from Italian Renaissance paintings emphasizing the humanity of a God become incarnate.[22] The Italian-Mughal hybridization served both parties: the Jesuits used the portrait to preach a Renaissance Humanistic Christ, and the Mughals used the image to assert their divine right kingship.

Farther East, the Jesuit mission to the Chinese was an enormous undertaking that has been the subject of numerous studies.[23] The Jesuits initially tried imitating the Chinese to whom they were sent by donning the robes of Buddhist monks. When locals came in and tossed them out an upper story window, the Jesuits discovered that Buddhist monks were not always held in high regard, having earned reputations among some for luxurious living and sexual improprieties. So the missionaries changed their strategy and adopted the garb of Confucian imperial court scholars: pictured here are Fathers Matteo Ricci (1552-1610), Johann Adam Schall von Bell (1591-1666), and Ferdinand Verbiest (1623-1688).[24] Fr. Ricci, in particular, is well known to the USF community, thanks to the presence of the Ricci Institute for Chinese-Western Cultural History in the University's Center for the Pacific Rim.[25]

The more I read about Fr. Jean-Joseph-Marie Amiot (1718-1793), the more I want to study him.[26] He lived in the imperial court at Beijing until his death, producing the first dictionary of the language spoken by the Manchurian Tartar Monguls, as well as volumes on Chinese music, court dance, and the life of Confucius (traditionally 551-479 BCE). He was also a prolific composer, and Fr. Amiot and his fellow court Jesuits wrote music in indigenous genres (for example, funerary rites) which they studied and mastered. When I used to play my students excerpts from the Mass written by the court Jesuits in Beijing, I always began by showing them a bit of Beijing Opera from the movie *Farewell My Concubine* (1993) --- without it, the students had no clue about making sense of these sounds.[27] Now, thanks to YouTube, I can show them a number of video clips (by entering "Confucius ceremony") that prepare them for listening to the seventeenth-century Jesuits' music.

Ricci and his companions applied Jesuit strategies of cultural accommodation that extended those formulated by Fr. Alessandro Valignano (1539-1606) for Japan.[28] The Jesuits accommodated themselves to the cultures they found because they genuinely *reverenced* what they found. A really wonderful small volume of excerpts from the *Jesuit Relations* --- that is, the letters sent back to Europe from the North American missionaries "relating" what they had discovered --- has recently been published.[29] Clearly presented, it introduces undergraduates to the complexity of seventeenth-century attitudes toward indigenous peoples. My own students have been shocked at just how much the Jesuits were fascinated by, and how much time they spent meticulously noting (for some students much too meticulously), what they found: new plants and animals, native religious beliefs, spoken languages, marriage customs, and healing rituals, including the game of lacrosse. Certainly, they did not approve of everything they found; but I doubt that any reader can come away unimpressed by the passionate reverence the Jesuits had for what they encountered and the care they took to relate it faithfully.

This specifically Jesuit vision, a vision that strove to seek God in all things, grew out of various influences. Let me underscore three of them:

First, the early Jesuits inherited the medieval metaphysics that came through "Aristotle's children."[30] The world is one Great Chain of Being, and, insofar as anything exists, it participates in Being, which is both Good and True.[31] In this vision, creation is (in the formulation of the Jesuit theologian Karl Rahner) "always already graced" simply by the fact of its existence.[32]

Second, the early Jesuits were trained in Renaissance Humanism, the turn to the *humanum* recovered from Greco-Roman antiquity, a primarily urban celebration of the human body, civic participation, and classical literature reborn.[33] As the historian John O'Malley reminds us in a recent essay published in *America* magazine, Jesuit education's fundamental curriculum was based, shockingly enough, on reading the literature of such pagans as Plato, Cicero, and the like.[34] Jesuit Renaissance humanism, focusing on the Incarnation in

Jesus Christ, celebrated humanity here-and-now, using pagan antiquity to overcome a Christian dualism that dominated medieval thought.[35] If you are lucky enough to gain access to USF's archives, survey the course bulletins for St. Ignatius College (today's USF) from 1907-08; you will see that the Renaissance program of studies was still alive and well here just after the great earthquake of 1906, thanks to the bedrock foundation of the *Ratio Studiorum*.[36]

Third, the early Jesuits lived in the Age of Discovery. The illustrations from *A Voyage to Brazil* (1578) by Jean de Léry (1536-1613), a Reformed pastor turned explorer, display the shared passion for conveying the wonders of the New World back to Europe. The same passion can be said for the *Briefe and True Report of the New Found Land of Virginia* (1588) published a decade later by the English astronomer and mathematician Thomas Harriot (c. 1560-1621).[37] Everything was new and marvelous for these early adventurers, and the prospect of unfathomable riches lured the colonizing investments that made such voyages possible.[38]

The Jesuits shared their contemporaries' wonder with what they found in these new worlds. But Jesuit fascination also had a unique source as it flowed directly out of the *Jesuit Constitutions*. Note, for example, the directive found in paragraph #449:

> When a plan is being worked out in a college or university to prepare persons to go among the Moors or Turks [i.e., into Muslim cultures], Arabic or Chaldaic would be expedient; and Indian would be proper for those about to go among the Indians; and the same holds true for similar reasons in regard to other languages.[39]

The notion of respecting another's difference so much that you would undertake in advance the mastery of foreign alphabets and logograms is inscribed within the *Constitutions*.

To conclude: although certainly there were other influences, these three produced a specifically Jesuit species of Catholicism, a hybridizing one: the Catholic conviction that all being is always already graced; the Renaissance Humanistic turn to this material world; and the fascination with "the Other" in the Age of Discovery.

If I had to summarize this Jesuit vision in just one word, it would be St. Ignatius's own --- *reverence* --- found repeatedly in his *Autobiography*, in the *Spiritual Exercises*, and in the *Constitutions*.[40] The early Jesuits approached the stranger with reverence. They did not view the cultures that they encountered through the eyes of alienation or dualism. Rather, both in their formal education and in their contemplative meditations, early Jesuits embraced a theology of reconciliation, a conviction that Christ and culture, faith and reason, grace and nature, God and the world were ultimately at one. They fostered a reverence for what they found, and they creatively hybridized what they found with what they brought, producing distinctively new Catholic cultures.

Catholic Modernities

The preceding examples come from early-modern times. How did Jesuit hybridization manifest itself in later modernity? In ways all too human, it played out both triumphantly and tragically. We are aware of the Jesuit successes — we are gathered here this evening to celebrate the sesquicentennial of one of them.

However, there were also conflicts and betrayals when others saw Jesuit hybridizations of Catholicism and modernity as an illegitimate and unacceptable blurring of boundaries. Here again, the example of Matteo Ricci and the Chinese mission provides an excellent illustration. The so-called "Chinese Rites" were Jesuit adaptations of certain Confucian rites—for example, the veneration of both ancestors and Confucius—for use in Christian services.[41] Critics of the Jesuits saw this accommodation of pagan cultural elements as fitting into a much larger Jesuit problem, that is, "laxism" in religion and morals.[42]

The status of the Jesuits' strategies began to fluctuate with whoever happened to be in power in Rome. In 1645, Pope Innocent X (1574-1655) decreed that Chinese rites were no longer to be used in the liturgy. In 1656, Pope Alexander VII (1599-1677) reversed that decision and permitted the rites. In 1704, Clement XI (1649-1721) voided Alexander VII's reversal and reinstated Innocent X's restrictions. Eleven years later, the papal bull *Ex illa die* (19 March 1715) closed down the Jesuit Chinese mission. Clement XII (1652-1740) renewed the ban in 1735. In 1742, Benedict XIV (1675-1758) renewed the ban and required all missionaries to take an oath to observe it. (He also called Jesuits "disobedient, contumacious, crafty, and reprobate men.") Clement XIII (1693-1769) reversed this trend and defended the Jesuits "in perpetuity" with the "plenitude of [his] Apostolic power." Alas, "perpetuity" and "plenitude" are relative terms. In 1773, Clement XIV (1705-1774) suppressed the Jesuits — also "perpetually" --- and ruthlessly imprisoned the Jesuit General, Father Lorenzo Ricci (1703-1775), in Castel Sant'Angelo's papal prison.[43] Mercifully, death ended Ricci's misery two years later.

However, since Catherine the Great (1729-1796), Empress and Autocrat of all the Russias, refused to publish the papal decree in her territories, the Suppression did not take legal effect there. A remnant of Jesuits survived and ministered to the Polish Roman Catholics who, in 1795, suddenly found themselves subjects of Catherine's Orthodox empire after Russia, Prussia and Austria divided up and absorbed their nation. Twenty years later, having survived Napoleon Bonaparte (1769-1821) and his near-destruction of both the papacy and the Church in Europe, Pius VII (1742-1823) desperately needed aid in negotiating the new post-Napoleonic world. With the help of the Russian remnant, he restored the Society of Jesus in 1814 to assist him and his successors in what would become an intransigent campaign against "modernity" until at least the death of Pius IX (1792-1878) and the ascent of Leo XIII (1810-1903) to the papacy[44]

It would take until 1939, however --- a full 235 years after Clement XI's 1704 ban of the Chinese Rites --- for the Roman authorities to reverse the course. Why 1939? The policy shift was interwoven with the ominous last years of the 1930s: the growth of Japanese militarism, the unstable situation in China, and the imminent end of the European colonial empires in Asia and elsewhere. The Japanese Empire invaded China in 1937; in March 1939, Pius XII (1876-1958) succeeded to the papacy; on September 1st, Hitler's Germany, Japan's ally, invaded Poland; and on December 8th, the Pope had the Congregation for the Propagation of the Faith issue its instruction *Plane compertum*.[45] In response to this overture, China established diplomatic relations with the Vatican in 1943. Just as the Chinese Rites controversy was initially entangled in seventeenth- and eighteenth-century political and colonialist intrigue, so too was its conclusion enmeshed in twentieth-century imperialist global warfare.

Stepping back from the numerous political and economic issues, if we look at the key theological issues at stake in the Rites Controversy, we can see the problem is inherent in Jesuit accommodation through hybridization. Where Jesuits, in general, discern a graced world to be reverenced, their opponents have historically charged that Jesuits over-accommodate culture and over-assimilate Christ.[46]

At the turn of the twentieth century, during the so-called Roman Catholic Modernist Crisis, Jesuits again paid a heavy price for hybridization.[47] The Irish Jesuit, George Tyrrell (1861-1909), was expelled from the Society in 1906 and suspended from the sacraments in 1907.[48] The next year, Cardinal Désiré-Joseph Mercier, the primate of Belgium, attacked Tyrrell in his 1908 Lenten pastoral letter as the archetypal Modernist; in reply, Tyrrell wrote a trenchant work entitled *Medievalism*, assaulting intransigence and arguing for a Church open to historicity and change.[49] Tyrrell's book was recently re-printed by Christian Classics; its back cover matter describes it as "a brilliant expose of the Church's tradition."[50] This tells us something about the fluid fortunes of "tradition" and "heresy."[51]

The following year, Tyrrell died tragically young at the age of 48. Although his close friend, the former Jesuit Henri Bremond (1865-1933), said he had heard Tyrrell's confession and administered Extreme Unction, Tyrrell was not permitted a Catholic burial. Bremond accompanied Tyrrell's casket to the graveside and blessed it --- a modest act for which an English bishop suspended him from sacramental ministry.

Abbé Bremond had made his Jesuit novitiate in England, been ordained in 1892, and worked as a writer at the Jesuit journal *Études*.[52] However, as the Modernist Crisis began to boil with the 1903 ascendancy to the papacy of Pius X (1835-1914), Bremond left the Society (while remaining a priest) in 1904. He would become an astonishingly prolific writer, his most important work being a magisterial multi-volume history of French mysticism that remains a standard scholarly reference today.[53] After the First World War, he was also inducted as an "immortal" into the Académie Française.

A second wave of Vatican repression began in the postwar era of the late 1940s and continued throughout the 1950s. During this period of the "Nouvelle théologie" movement and of Pius XII's *Humani Generis* (12 August 1950) which singled out Teilhard de Chardin's thought for censure, the Jesuit theologians Henri de Lubac (1896-1991) of France, Karl Rahner (1904-1984) of Germany, and John Courtney Murray (1904-1967) of the United States were silenced.[54] Each attempted, within the sphere of his particular research specialty, to bridge the yawning gulf between Catholicism and modernity --- one that could no longer be ignored in the wake of the Second World War's unprecedented horrors and now the Cold War threat of nuclear annihilation.[55] In a highly ironic historical twist, the Second Vatican Council would transform the ideas of these silenced Jesuits (and of course others, most especially Fr. Yves Congar, O.P.) into Church teaching.[56]

In the beautifully illustrated volume, *Spirit of Fire*, Ursula King recounts Teilhard de Chardin's long and tragic conflict with Jesuit superiors and the Church.[57] As I noted at the start of this lecture, Teilhard was denied permission to publish what he wrote or to accept any French teaching position (including one offered at the prestigious, and thoroughly secular, Collège de France) until his dying day. As I understand it, when he died in New York City in 1955 and was buried at the Jesuit novitiate in upstate New York, the novices were not allowed to accompany the casket to the gravesite. Whether fact or Jesuit urban legend, the point is clear: religious superiors in both the Church and the Society considered Teilhard to be virulently contagious. And indeed, as his writings began to pour off the presses almost immediately after his death (without any need now of ecclesiastical approval), you could say they "went viral."[58]

The British intellectual historian, Nicholas Boyle, has recently noted Teilhard's posthumous yet powerful "subterranean influence" in the Council's final document, *Gaudium et spes* (*The Church in the Modern World* [7 December 1965]), about to celebrate its fortieth birthday.[59]

> At the same time, the human race is giving steadily-increasing thought to forecasting and regulating its own population growth. History itself speeds along on so rapid a course that an individual person can scarcely keep abreast of it. The destiny of the human community has become all of a piece, where once the various groups of men had a kind of private history of their own.
>
> Thus, the human race has passed from a rather static concept of reality to a more dynamic, evolutionary one. In consequence there has arisen a new series of problems, a series as numerous as can be, calling for efforts of analysis and synthesis.[60]

In their attempts to hybridize Catholic modernities by mediating Christ and culture, these Jesuits were thoroughly traditional. Through it all, it seems to me, Jesuits have been singularly ardent defenders of a distinctive, and I would say, absolutely central, Catholic belief: namely, that *faith is not incompatible with reason*. The First Vatican Council may have defined this dogma; but Jesuits are among those who have most concretely defended it, even in, and perhaps most especially in, those moments when the Church silenced them for it. In the late-modern period they remained faithful to their early-modern foundation as ministers formed to hybridize Christ and culture.

Futural Pasts

So far, I have tried to argue two points: first, the Jesuit species of Catholicism is marked by a strong, perhaps even extreme, belief in the compatibility of Christ and culture. Second, Jesuit accommodations resist other Catholic voices that draw strong distinctions or oppositions between the Church and "the world." If Catholicism is a big tent, Jesuits stand somewhere close to the door with at least one foot jutting outside. I have used this brief historical survey to argue that this location in the margins, border zone, or boundary waters is not an accident or an aberration. Rather, it is an essential trait resulting from the Society's historical origins as a Renaissance Humanistic movement. In short: reconciliation has been the Society's particular "charism" from the laying of its cornerstone.

I now want to make a third and final point about the present and the future. As I see it, the primary lasting cultural legacy of twentieth-century modernity has been an irreversible revolution in the areas of sexuality and gender.[61] What does it say, after all, that until the ratification of the Nineteenth Amendment in the summer of 1920, women in this country could not vote; and yet this evening, as we are gathered here in California, the two U.S. senators from this state are Diane Feinstein and Barbara Boxer; and Congresswoman Nancy Pelosi represents this city's 8th District in the U.S. House of Representatives (serving also as the minority leader)? We might also note the Supreme Court justices Sandra Day O'Connor (appointed 1981) and Ruth Bader Ginsburg (appointed 1993); and the current and past U.S. Secretaries of State, Condoleezza Rice (appointed this past January 2005) and Madeleine Albright (appointed 1997). As we are in the city of San Francisco, we could also note the pioneering political career of the first openly gay elected official in California, city Supervisor Harvey Milk (elected in 1978 and assassinated later that same year); and that of Representative Barney Frank who publicly disclosed his same-sex orientation in 1987. Frank won the 4th District congressional seat previously occupied by Jesuit Fr. Robert Drinan in 1981, and he has served Massachusetts in that capacity for the past quarter century.

The sexual and gender revolutions of twentieth-century modernity will only become more complicated in the twenty-first century. Issues categorized before under the simple rubric of sexual reproduction are now interwoven with stem cell research and the potential for genetic manipulation. Combining this observation with the previous points I have made leads me to this conclusion: a Jesuit institution not only can but *ought to be* the place that approaches these tectonic shifts in culture with reverence. Although such accommodation might mean uneasy and even tumultuous relationships with other Catholic traditions, a Jesuit institution should act out of the long historical view instead of short-term resistance, fear, and sometimes panic.[62]

I would like to offer two examples of "futural pasts," that is, moments in the past that can illuminate the present and suggest a future path forward.[63] The first of these is actually the immediate past, having ended (if in fact it has actually ended) just two months ago. The second example occurred seventy-five years ago.

Futural past 1: 2002-2005—
The Bostonians

My reflections here emerge out of some very powerful experiences from the recent past. I have spent the last six years [1999-2005] living in Boston and teaching at Boston College --- astonishing times to live in that city and work at that institution. I doubt that any of us there have fully processed the experience which, in many aspects, has been traumatic.[64] For me, this historical moment was something akin to living through other traumatizing periods, like the post-1918 decade (which is the primary subject of my research) or 1968.[65]

The entire chain of events seems to have been set in motion by the terrorist attacks on 11 September 2001. Almost immediately afterward, the sexual abuse scandal began to break in the *Boston Globe* and roiled the archdiocese throughout the year 2002: the first newspaper report was published on 6 January; Cardinal Law's resignation was accepted by the Vatican on 13 December.[66] A year later came the gay marriage decision by the Massachusetts Superior Court in late 2003; it was followed by a long year during which attempts to pass an amendment in the state legislature intersected with the bitterly acrimonious campaigns for the 2004 national presidential election.[67] Finally, again intersecting with the fall 2004 elections (because President George W. Bush was running for re-election and his brother Jeb was the Governor of Florida), the Terri Schiavo case galvanized opponents on both sides until her death on 31 March 2005.[68] In a remarkable coincidence suggesting yet again that truth is stranger than fiction, Pope John Paul II, whose own long-term illness had become the focus of parallel debates over "ordinary" and "extraordinary" means of life support, died two days later (2 April 2005).

These events were lived with a frightening immediacy at Boston College due to the Theology Department's specialization in moral theology. First, the Massachusetts Superior Court decision on gay marriage was followed by a constitutional convention called to amend the Commonwealth's constitution to outlaw gay marriage altogether. The convention provided an amazing, sustained civics lesson for my History students, and not just because of the pumped-up crowds and out-of-state buses gathered around the front steps of Beacon Hill's State House, a short subway ride away. It began with the fact that the constitution had been the brainchild of John Adams, the American founding father. Adams had made it almost impossible for future citizens to amend the document, due to his renowned mistrust of human intentions and motives --- a mistrust fundamentally at odds with the visions of other revolutionaries.[69] The ironic lesson for my students was that Adams's conservative skepticism of human motives ended up preserving an extremely liberal court ruling two centuries later. But that's another story...

During this convention, my Jesuit colleague at Boston College, moral theologian Fr. James Keenan, was asked to testify on behalf of those who opposed amending the constitution. In his testimony, Fr. Keenan distinguished between what he termed the Church's "theology of chastity" and its "theology of justice." While acknowledging that the Church's theology of chastity forbids same-sex activity (let alone marital unions), he argued that the Church's theology of justice insists that human beings have certain non-negotiable rights. These include access to health care, insurance, retirement, and so on. Thus, he concluded, the Church's theology of justice (Catholic social teaching) could not be used to argue against the extension of civil marriage protections to same-sex couples in an immediate, predetermined, or unmediated way.

A month later, the legal counsel for the Massachusetts Catholic Conference provided a "Memorandum on Erroneous Testimony on Catholic Teaching" regarding the testimony of Fr. Keenan and two other priests (including Jesuit Fr. Thomas Carroll).[70] The Conference's response used the Church's theology of chastity to deny that opposing legalized same-sex marriage is "unjust discrimination" by quoting the U.S. bishops: "No same-sex union can realize the unique and full potential which the marital relationship expresses. For this reason, our opposition to 'same-sex marriage' is not an instance of unjust discrimination or animosity toward homosexual persons."[71] I would note that these same arguments were replayed in Spain during this past year, culminating in the legalization of gay marriage there just eight weeks ago.[72]

Meanwhile, again a remarkable and ironic coincidence: here at the University of San Francisco, on 3 June 2003, exactly one day after the Massachusetts Catholic Conference statement just mentioned,[73] the University's trustees voted "to extend healthcare benefits to all adults legally domiciled with USF employees ... [establishing] USF as the first Jesuit university in the nation to make a healthcare commitment to same-sex partners, non-married other-sex partners, and financially dependent family members such as parents or siblings." Although "some argued that extending healthcare benefits to same-sex partners violated Catholic doctrine," for University President Fr. Stephen A.

Privett, S.J., "the extension of health care benefits to this population was an ethical imperative, supported by Catholic doctrine."[74] An amazing divergence of approaches on the east and west coasts within a single 48-hour period!

As I noted above, these events of 2003 and 2004 began to intersect with the Terri Schiavo case, one that only ended two months ago with the autopsy results released in mid-June.[75] One of the main Catholic voices arguing on behalf of Michael Schiavo was another Jesuit colleague of mine at Boston College, moral theologian and bioethicist Fr. John Paris. Fr. Paris held that Terri Schiavo's life was being supported by extraordinary means and he argued, employing distinctions made in traditional Catholic teaching, that Michael Schiavo had no moral obligation to keep these means in place. He voiced his position in various venues, most conspicuously by appearing on MSNBC and CNN.

In response, given these bitterly divided times in our nation, both Fr. Paris and the Boston College Theology Department received a great deal of email and faxed messages. Much of it was hate mail, and much of it was shocking in its violent language and vulgar imagery. Its viciousness was overwhelming, as was the depth of rage directed by some at the Society of Jesus. I don't know whether Fr. Paris has saved those documents, but they would make an invaluable archive for future historians as they try to understand the chaos we have been living through.[76]

My observation of these events has persuaded me that "Catholic social thought" as it has been formulated since at least 1931, straddling somewhat arbitrary distinctions between theologies of "chastity" and "justice," is no longer adequate to our historical epoch. This epoch, as I suggested at the beginning of my remarks, is fundamentally marked by an irreversible revolution over the past century in areas of sexuality, gender, and reproduction.[77]

As a recent article entitled "The Coming Death Shortage" has underscored (with some rather dark humor), advancing technology will continue to erode any meaning left in distinctions like "artificial" and "natural"[78] (Indeed, just a year before he ascended to the papacy, Cardinal Ratzinger noted the difficulty of grounding arguments in "natural law": "Unfortunately, this instrument has become blunt. Accordingly I do not intend to appeal to it for support in this conversation."[79]) Moreover, the distinction between "ordinary" and "extraordinary" means will be measured, not in terms of technological complexity, but rather in numbers of dollars. In a world where limited available resources are acquired by those with financial means, whose access to increasingly expensive procedures for prolonging life will be enabled and whose will be denied? These are questions provoked by "the coming death shortage."

Futural past 2: 1930-1931—
A Tale of Two Encyclicals

I have pointed to the year 1931 as having special historical significance for our present confusion, and I would like to conclude now by returning to that year. Let's recall the events: on "Black Tuesday," 29 October 1929, the New York Stock Exchange collapsed. Almost immediately afterward and continuing throughout 1930, unemployment began to rise sharply in Germany which was still saddled with financial problems stemming from the Great War settlements a decade earlier. In 1931, as the Great Depression settled in and banks and governments collapsed throughout Europe, the Nazis experienced a spike in popularity. In 1932, German unemployment had reached 25%; Nazis won 37% of the popular vote for parliament; Franklin D. Roosevelt was elected president of the United States; and the Japanese invaded China. The following year, Hitler was appointed chancellor of Germany. The Nuremburg Laws soon followed. These were epochal times.

On New Year's Eve in 1930, Pope Pius XI published *Casti Connubii* ("Chaste Wedlock," 31 December 1930), a wide-ranging encyclical now usually remembered for being the first explicit papal condemnation of contraception. (Just two days before, the Pope had been featured on the cover of *Time* magazine. The highly laudatory feature article, "Souls, States, and Helicopters," called him "a spiritual diplomat, in many respects the earth's most potent individual."[80]) *Casti Connubii* was in large measure a Catholic response to the approval of contraception by the Anglican Communion's Lambeth Conference earlier that year. Five months later, Pius XI issued another encyclical entitled *Quadragesimo Anno* ("Forty Years," 15 May 1931). This encyclical celebrated the fortieth anniversary of Leo XIII's *Rerum Novarum* ("Of New Things," 15 May 1891), the founding document on human labor that finally came to grips with what had already been more than a century of industrialized capitalism and its attendant problems.[81]

Consider how *Quadragesimo Anno* is traditionally classified as a "social encyclical" while *Casti Connubii* is not. Issues in both encyclicals intertwine; for example, *Quadragesimo Anno* argues that a male (husband and father) should receive a just wage because it allows him to support a family so that the female (wife and mother) need not work outside the home. (In fact, the reality of the Great Depression job market, at least in the United States, turned many women into families' primary wage-earners precisely because they were more economical for employers; that is, they were paid less for the same amount of labor.[82]) Even in this single example, a theoretical distinction between "economic" and "gender" realities was somewhat arbitrary. Or as one of my colleagues once quipped, "Anyone who thinks marriage is not about property has never negotiated a divorce."

It is illuminating to sit down and read these two 1931 works side-by-side, as I did a couple years ago with a number of bright students. The students interpreted *Casti Connubii* as a "theology of chastity" condemning contraception, civil divorce, and women working outside the home. They identified it with the political right. But I encouraged them to notice that it also condemned the forced sterilization of those considered inferior, which brought it into opposition with a popular plank of Progressivist American eugenicists (and later the Nazis).[83] Eugenicist ideology had been legally upheld four years earlier by the U.S. Supreme Court in *Buck v. Bell* (1927), infamous for Justice Oliver Wendell Holmes's notorious judgment: "Three generations of imbeciles are enough."[84] *Casti Connubii* also condemned laws that restricted marriages between persons considered to be of different racial descent. (In a sign of the times, 1931 was also the year in which California would pass a sweeping state code prohibiting marriage between Caucasian and Asian races. A statute in 1933 broadened the scope to prohibit marriages between whites and Malays.[85] Soon afterward, the Nazis passed the Nuremburg Laws [1935] also regulating racial "mixture" in marriage.[86]) By insisting instead that marriage is about the rights of human beings (instead of racialized bodies) to marry in freedom, the encyclical today appears far more progressive than Progressivist California. It resists easy pigeonholing.

Quadragesimo Anno, on the other hand, was written in response to the collapse of laissez-faire capitalism and the onset of widespread economic depression. It embodies a "theology of justice" which students identify with the political left, along with its descendants, from John XXIII's *Peace on Earth* (11 April 1963) to John Paul II's *On Human Labor* (14 September 1981). I point out to them, however, that one of the most notable features of *Quadragesimo Anno* is found in paragraphs 94 and 95 which approvingly reference the Fascists' Labor and Anti-strike Law (1926) enacted five years earlier, prohibiting both lockouts and strikes. Insofar as it considers right-wing solutions as legitimate responses, this allegedly left-wing encyclical also resists easy pigeonholing.

In those fateful first five months of 1931, we can already see the problems inherent in distinguishing too sharply between matters of gender and economics, between a "theology of chastity" and a "theology of justice." By 1965, this fissure manifested itself clearly in *Gaudium et* spes in which concerns about the effects of population growth ("social teaching") and solutions deemed contrary to the moral law ("moral teaching") are inextricably linked.[87] Seventy-five years is long enough for such a fragile and factually inadequate theoretical paradigm to have unraveled; but perhaps it is not yet long enough for us to have sorted out a solution.[88]

Regardless, my sense is that this widening incoherence has had three serious outcomes.

First, Catholic discourse about sexuality and gender has become associated with magisterial "teaching" while that on economics or war or the death penalty has become associated with "social thought." "Teaching" implicitly connotes a sense of necessity and obligation whereas "thought" suggests merely "optional advice." Second, this theoretical distinction in categories has become embodied in an ideological divide between parties --- an often bitterly contentious one --- constituting a Catholic right and left.[89] Third, because the paradigm does not cohere in practice, Catholics, tending to reject one or the other strand of these discourses, increasingly do not think of the Church as a "teacher" at all. The now infamous line in a 1961 *National Review* gossip column --- punning on the title of John XXIII's encyclical *Mater et Magistra* (15 May 1961) --- has become more than a quip: "Going the rounds in conservative circles: 'Mater sì, Magistra no.'" [Mother yes, teacher no].[90]

Remembering Teilhard's two rights seems to me an urgent need today. Preserving the right to research with scholarly peers and the right to help the disturbed and troubled may have the side effect of conserving something else. It may help restore a sense of Catholic intellectual traditions as a teaching authority – that is, as a "teacher," one to whom a "disciple" would turn in times of need for guidance, direction, and wisdom.

Conclusion

There is something wonderful about the presence of the Matteo Ricci Institute here in USF's Center for the Pacific Rim. (For the Institute's existence we owe a great debt of gratitude to the late Fr. Ed Malatesta, S.J. [1932-1998]). Today in 2005, the near future is racing towards China and India. And that future has already arrived at USF, now ranked as the fourteenth most diverse college in the nation, with 22% of its student body self-identifying as being of Asian descent.

The Ricci Institute also reminds us of what is absolutely central in the Jesuit species of Catholicism. (And so, it seems to me, it is intimately linked with the Lane Center for Catholic Studies and Social Thought.) The story of the Chinese Rites reminds us that Jesuit eyes are trained to *reverence* any culture that they encounter as creation always already graced. In addition, the Chinese Rites also serve as a historical reminder of the hard price that has been paid for this hybridizing vision. In the long run, the example of the Chinese Rites seems hopeful to me. They signify the impassioned Jesuit historical witness to Catholic tradition: a sturdy belief that both faith and reason aim at a single Truth.

Exactly forty years ago, the Second Vatican Council addressed itself to humanity's existential concerns which cross all boundaries of space and time:

> Meanwhile every man remains to himself an unsolved puzzle, however obscurely he may perceive it. For on certain occasions no one can entirely escape the kind of self-questioning mentioned earlier, especially when life's major events take place. To this questioning only God fully and most certainly provides an answer as He summons man to higher knowledge and humbler probing.[91]

This is the truth that the University of San Francisco, situated on the shores of the Pacific Rim, has served for 150 years.

May it serve 150 more.

This paper was written in August 2005; it was revised and annotated in August 2010. For purposes of verification, all internet references supplied in the endnotes were accessed on 11 August 2010.

Notes:

1. The conservative Jesuit journal, *La Civiltà Cattolica*, published a series of articles in 1919 and 1920 responding to the question of "Evolution or the Stability of Species?" and came out against evolution. See Mariano Artigas, Thomas F. Glick, and Rafael A. Martínez, *Negotiating Darwin: The Vatican Confronts Evolution, 1877-1902* (Baltimore, MD: Johns Hopkins University Press, 2006). See also Don O'Oleary, *Roman Catholicism and Modern Science: A History* (New York: Continuum, 2006).

2. Most recently presided over by then Cardinal Josef Ratzinger, the CDF is now headed by the former archbishop of San Francisco, now Cardinal William Levada, who had resigned as archbishop effective 17 August 2005, i.e., just two weeks before this lecture was given.

3. Teilhard quoted in Ursula King, *Spirit of Fire: The Life and Vision of* Teilhard *de Chardin* (Maryknoll, N.Y.: Orbis Books, 1996).

4. Richard E. Rubenstein, *Aristotle's Children: How Christians, Muslims, and* Jews Rediscovered Ancient Wisdom *and Illuminated* the Dark Ages (Orlando, FL: Harcourt, 2003).

5. "Indeed the chief objection that can be brought against scholastic theology is not its lack of humanism, but its persistent tendency to make man appear more rational, human nature more noble, the divine order of the universe more open to human inspection, and the whole complex of man, nature and God more fully intelligible, than we can now believe to be plausible... Thomas Aquinas died in 1274, and it is probably true that man has never appeared so important a being in so well-ordered and intelligible a universe as in his works." R. S. Southern, *Medieval Humanism and Other Studies* (New York: Harper & Row, 1970) 49; 50.

6. First Vatican Council (1869-1870), Session 3 (24 April 1870), Dogmatic Constitution *De fide catholica*, c. 4, "De fide et ratione" [On faith and reason]; in *Decrees of the Ecumenical Councils*, ed. Norman P. Tanner, 2 vols. (London: Sheed & Ward; Washington, DC: Georgetown University Press, 1990), vol. II: 808. Compare John Henry Newman lecturing on "The Idea of a University" in the 1850s: "if anything seems to be proved by astronomer, or geologist, or chronologist, or antiquarian, or ethnologist, in contradiction to the dogmas of faith, that point will eventually turn out, first, not to be proved, or, secondly, not contradictory, or thirdly, not contradictory to any thing really revealed, but to something which has been confused with revelation." Newman, *The Idea of a University Defined and Illustrated in Nine Discourses Delivered to the Catholics of Dublin in Occasional Lectures and Essays Addressed to the Members of the Catholic University*, ed. Martin J. Svaglic (Notre Dame, IN: University of Notre Dame Press, 1982), 351.

7. John Paul II, *Fides et Ratio* (14 September 1998), introductory "Blessing." www.vatican.va/holy_father/john_paul_ii/encyclicals/documents/hf_jp-ii_enc_15101998_fides-et-ratio_en.html

8. For the problem of liberal democracy, see Stephen Schloesser, "Against Forgetting: Memory, History, Vatican II," *Theological* Studies 67 (2006): 297-301; reprinted in John W. O'Malley et al., *Vatican II:* Did Anything Happen?, ed. David G. Schultenover (New York: Continuum, 2007). For the papal reaction to France's 1905 Act of Separation of church and state, see Schloesser, *Jazz Age Catholicism: Mystic Modernism in Postwar Paris, 1919-1933* (Toronto: University of Toronto Press, 2005) 53-54.

9. On the ministry of "consolation," especially with regard to Blessed Pierre Favre, S.J., see John O'Malley, S.J., *The First Jesuits* (Cambridge, MA: Harvard University Press, 1993).

10. In his classic study, H. Richard Niebuhr distinguished five paradigms exploring the relationship between "Christ and culture": Christ against Culture; Christ of Culture; Christ above Culture; Christ and Culture in Paradox; Christ transforming Culture. See Niebuhr, *Christ and Culture* (New York: Harper, 1951). For further reflections on these positions, see Stephen Schloesser, "The Unbearable Lightness of Being: Re-Sourcing Catholic Intellectual Traditions," *Cross Currents* 58/1 (Spring 2008): 65-94. Niebuhr's thought applied and developed distinctions first explored by Ernst Troeltsch in *The Social Teaching of the Christian Churches*, tr. Olive Wyon, 2 vols. (London: Allen & Unwin; New York: Macmillan, 1931), originally published as *Soziallehren der christlichen Kirchen und Gruppen* (Tübingen, 1912).

11. During the time this lecture was prepared the question of evolution was a prominent issue. *The New York Times* published an op-ed essay written by Cardinal Christoph Schönborn, O.P., archbishop of Vienna, entitled "Finding Design in Nature" (7 July 2005); a followup article appeared two days later: "Leading Cardinal Redefines Church's View on Evolution" (9 July 2005). Other news headlines in the *Times* give a flavor of that year: "Judge in Georgia Orders Anti-Evolution Stickers Removed From Textbooks" (14 Jan 2005); "2 School Boards Push On Against Evolution" (19 Jan 2005); "[President] Bush Remarks Roil Debate on Teaching of Evolution" (3 August 2005).

12. American Catholic church historian Mark S. Massa, S.J., considers Kennedy's famous 1960 "Houston Speech" in which the presidential candidate famously said that nothing (including religious principles) should take precedence over a president's oath to uphold the laws of the land. Massa writes that it was "a breathtaking reversal of the traditional understanding of Christian responsibilities in the public sphere. . . . Political pundits at the time (and since), as well as religious scholars, have noted the problematic theological implications of such a statement. Political and cultural considerations of the time certainly make Kennedy's statement understandable and perhaps even compelling. But given current Catholic concern over the 'naked public square' that relegates religious considerations to the non-public sectors of our culture, the ironic possibilities that it was the first Catholic president himself who 'secularized' the White House here are rich and sobering." Massa, *Catholics and American Culture: Fulton Sheen, Dorothy Day, and the Notre Dame Football Team* (New York: Crossroad, 1999), 18.

13. In the summer of 2005, the nomination of John Roberts, a Roman Catholic, as Chief Justice of the Supreme Court, sparked numerous reflections in the press. For

example, see: "Court Nominee's Life Is Rooted in Faith and Respect for Law," *The New York Times* (21 July 2005); "Why Roberts's religion matters," *Boston Globe* (1 August 2005); "Catholic Justice: Quit tiptoeing around John Roberts' faith," *Slate* (1 August 2005). Such considerations made a second round after the fall nomination of Samuel Alito: "Alito Could Be 5th Catholic on Current Supreme Court," *The New York Times* (1 November 2005); "Why Catholics? The political advantages of Catholic justices," *Slate* (1 November 2005); "Should senators ask Alito about the role of his faith? If confirmed, he would become the fifth Catholic among the nine justices on the Supreme Court," *Christian Science Monitor* (4 November 2005); "Court Could Tip to Catholic Majority. Some Say Slant Is Dangerous; Others See Historic Victory," *Washington Post* (7 November 2005). David Brooks caught the spirit of the times in an especially acute way: "Confirmation battles have come to seem of late like occasions for bitterly divided Catholics to turn political battles into holy war Armageddons. Most of the main Democrats on the Judiciary Committee are Catholics who are liberal or moderate (Kennedy, Biden, Durbin, Leahy), and many of the most controversial judges or nominees are Catholics who are conservative (Scalia, Thomas, Pryor). When they face off, you get this brutal and elemental conflict over the role morality should play in public life. Roberts is indeed a Catholic (if he's confirmed, there will be four on the court, three Protestants and two Jews), but he's not the sort to spark the sort of debate that leads to bitter Catholic vs. Catholic meshugas. He's not a holy warrior, and his wife is active in the culturally heterodox Feminists for Life." Brooks, "A Competent Conservative," *The New York Times* (21 July 2005).

14. Scott Horsley reported on the new law for National Public Radio on 17 August 2005: see "Reconsidering Hybrids in the Carpool Lane" www.npr.org/templates/story/story.php?storyId=4803134.

15. For a succinct overview of "cultural hybridity," see Peter Burke, *Cultural Hybridity* (Cambridge: Polity Press, 2009). For a sense of the concept's development from 1994-2005, see also: Homi K. Bhabha, *The Location of Culture* (London: Routledge, 1994); Robert Young, *Colonial Desire: Hybridity in Theory, Culture and Race* (London: Routledge, 1995); Tariq Modood and Pnina Werbner, eds., *Debating Cultural Hybridity* (London: Zed Books 1997); Deborah A. Kapchan and Pauline Turner Strong, eds., "Theorizing the Hybrid," special issue of *Journal of American Folklore* 112/445 (1999); Marwan M. Kraidy, *Hybridity: or the Cultural Logic of Globalization* (Philadelphia: Temple 2005).

16. For this image of Mancinelli and many others see the richly illustrated volume by Philippe Lécrivain, S.J., *Les missions jésuites: pour une plus grande gloire de Dieu* (Paris: Gallimard, [1991] 2005).

17. Charles A. Frazee, *Catholics and Sultans: The Church and the Ottoman Empire, 1453-1923* (New York: Cambridge University Press, 1983), 73-74.

18. For the following, see Gauvin Alexander Bailey, *The Jesuits and the Grand Mogul: Renaissance Art at the Imperial Court of India, 1580-1630* (Washington, DC: Freer Gallery of Art, Arthur M. Sackler Gallery, Smithsonian Institution, 1998); and Bailey, "The Indian Conquest of Catholic Art: The Mughals, the Jesuits, and Imperial Mural Painting," *Art Journal* 57/1 (Spring 1998), 24-30. For the mission, see *Letters from the Mughal Court: The First Jesuit mission to Akbar (1580-1583)*, edited with an introduction by John Correia-Afonso, 2nd ed. (St. Louis, Mo.: The Institute of Jesuit Sources; in cooperation with Gujarat Sahitya Prakash, Anand, India, 1981); and

Lécrivain, *Les missions jésuites.*

19. Gauvin Alexander Bailey, *Art on the Jesuit Missions in Asia and Latin America, 1542-1773* (Toronto: University of Toronto Press, 1999); *The Jesuits and the Arts, 1540-1773*, eds. John W. O'Malley and Gauvin Alexander Bailey; original Italian edited by Giovanni Sale; 1st English ed. (Philadelphia: Saint Joseph's University Press, 2005).

20. See for example the work of Desiderius Erasmus of Rotterdam: *Patristic Scholarship: The Edition of St. Jerome,* edited, translated and annotated by James F. Brady and John C. Olin (Toronto: University of Toronto Press, 1992).

21. Eugene F. Rice, *Saint Jerome in the Renaissance* (Baltimore: Johns Hopkins University Press, 1985).

22. Leo Steinberg, *The Sexuality of Christ in Renaissance Art and in Modern Oblivion*, with a postscript by John W. O'Malley, 2nd ed., rev. and expanded (Chicago: University of Chicago Press, 1996).

23. *Bibliography of the Jesuit Mission in China: ca. 1580-ca. 1680,* eds. Erik Zürcher, Nicolas Standaert, and Adrianus Dudink (Leiden,The Netherlands: Centre of Non-Western Studies, Leiden University, 1991); Lionel M. Jensen, *Manufacturing Confucianism: Chinese Traditions & Universal Civilization* (Durham: Duke University Press, 1997); Sangkeun Kim, *Strange Names of God: The Missionary Translation of the Divine Name and the Chinese Responses to Matteo Ricci's "Shangti" in late Ming China, 1583-1644* (New York: Peter Lang, 2004); Liam Matthew Brockey, *Journey to the East: The Jesuit mission to China, 1579-1724* (Cambridge, Mass.: Belknap Press of Harvard University Press, 2007); Florence C. Hsia, *Sojourners in a Strange Land: Jesuits and their Scientific Missions in Late Imperial China* (Chicago: University of Chicago Press, 2009). For Tibet, see Trent Pomplun, *Jesuit on the Roof of the World: Ippolito Desideri's Mission to Tibet* (New York: Oxford University Press, 2009).

24. For illustrations, again see Lécrivain, *Les missions jésuites.*

25. For a forthcoming biography, see R. Po-chia Hsia, *A Jesuit in the Forbidden City: Matteo Ricci 1552-1610* (New York: Oxford University Press, 2011).

26. Nicolas Standaert et al., *Les danses rituelles chinoises d'après Joseph-Marie Amiot: aux sources de l'ethnochorégraphie* (Namur: Presses universitaires de Namur; Bruxelles: Éditions Lessius, 2005);

27. *Amiot: Messe des Jésuites de Pékin,* performed by Musique des Lumières XVIII-21, Ensemble Meihua Fleur de Prunus, and Francois Picard. Audio CD ASIN: B000N-QDE7C (Naïve 2007); *Vêpres à la Vierge en Chine*, performed by Jean-Christophe Frisch, Musique des lumières Ensemble XVIII-21, and Choeur du Beitang. Audio CD ASIN B00019IC5K (K617 2004).

28. Josef Franz Schütte, SJ, *Valignano's Mission Principles for Japan. Vol. 1: From His Appointment as Visitor until His First Departure from Japan (1573-1582). Vol. 1, Part 1: The Problem (1573-1580); Vol. 1, Part 2: The Solution (1580-1582)*(St. Louis: The Institute of Jesuit Sources, 1980-85); J. F. Moran, *The Japanese and the Jesuits: Alessandro Valignano in Sixteenth-century Japan* (New York: Routledge, 1993);

Pedro Lage Reis Correia, "Alessandro Valignano [sic] Attitude Towards Jesuit and Franciscan Concepts of Evangelization in Japan (1587-1597)," *Bulletin of Portuguese/Japanese Studies* 2 (2001): 79-108; Augusto Luca, *Alessandro Valignano (1539-1606): la missione come dialogo con i popoli e le culture* (Bologna: EMI, 2005); Adolfo Tamburello, M. Antoni J. Uçerler, and Marisa Di Russo, *Alessandro Valignano S.I.: uomo del Rinascimento, ponte tra Oriente e Occidente* (Roma: Institutum Historicum Societatis Iesu, 2008). See also chapters in *The Jesuits: Cultures, Sciences, and the Arts, 1540-1773*, ed. John W O'Malley

(Toronto: University of Toronto Press, 1999); and *The Jesuits II: Cultures, Sciences, and the Arts, 1540-1773*, eds. John W. O'Malley et al. (Toronto: University of Toronto Press, 2006).

29. The *Jesuit Relations: Natives and Missionaries in Seventeenth-century North America*, edited with an introduction by Allan Greer (Boston: Bedford/St. Martin's, 2000). For the original comprising seventy-three volumes see: *The Jesuit Relations and Allied Documents; Travels and Explorations of the Jesuit Missionaries in New France, 1610-1791*; the original French, Latin, and Italian texts, with English translations and notes; ed. Reuben Gold Thwaites, 73 vol. (Cleveland: Burrows Bros. Co., 1896-1901).

30. Rubenstein, *Aristotle's Children*.

31. For a representative statement of the Jesuit analogical approach in the seventeenth century, see the work by Cardinal (Saint) Robert Bellarmine, S.J., *The Ascent of the Mind to God by a Ladder of Things Created*, tr. T. B. Gent.; first published at Doway, 1616; with an introduction by James Brodrick (New York: Benziger Brothers, 1928). For the now-classic study of the concept, see Arthur O. Lovejoy, *The Great Chain of Being* (Cambridge, MA: Harvard University Press, 1936).

32. Karl Rahner, *Foundations of Christian Faith: An Introduction to the Idea of Christianity*, tr. William V. Dych (New York: Crossroad, [1978] 1982), 122. For a succinct overview of this principle, see Roger Haight, S.J., "Expanding the Spiritual Exercises," *Studies in the Spirituality of Jesuits* 42/2 (Summer 2010), esp. 4-22.

33. Thomas M. Lucas, S.J., *Landmarking: City, Church, & Jesuit Urban Strategy* (Chicago: Jesuit Way, 1997).

34. John W. O'Malley, S.J., "Jesuit History: A New Hot Topic," *America* (9 May 2005). Available at www.americamagazine.org/content/article.cfm?article_id=4175.

35. An assessment of the policy change appears in Crime and Justice Research Centre and Sue Triggs, New Zealand Ministry of Justice, *New Zealand Court-Referred Restorative Justice Pilot: Evaluation* (New Zealand Ministry of Justice, May 2005).

35. For extended reflections on representations of the Incarnation in Renaissance Christian humanism, see also John O'Malley's postscript in Steinberg, *The Sexuality of Christ in Renaissance Art*.

36. *The Ratio Studiorum: The Official Plan for Jesuit Education*, translated and annotated by Claude Pavur, S.J. (St. Louis: The Institute of Jesuit Sources, 2005); *The Jesuit Ratio Studiorum: 400th Anniversary Perspectives*, ed. Vincent J. Duminuco (New York: Fordham University Press, 2000); *Ratio studiorum: plan raisonné et institution des études dans la Compagnie de Jésus*, presented by Adrien Demoustier and Dominique Julia; translated by Léone Albrieux and Dolorès Pralon-Julia; annotated and commented on by Marie-Madeleine Compère; Latin-French bilingual edition (Paris: Belin, 1997).

37. Jean de Léry, *History of a Voyage to the Land of Brazil, Otherwise called America*, tr. Janet Whatley (Berkeley: University of California Press, 1990); Thomas Harriot, *A Briefe and True Report of the New Found Land of Virginia* (Rosenwald Collection

Reprint Series) (New York: Dover Publications, 1972).

38. Lorraine Daston and Katharine Park, *Wonders and the Order of Nature, 1150-1750* (New York: Zone Books; Cambridge, Mass.: Distributed by the MIT Press, 1998); *Merchants & Marvels: Commerce, Science, and Art in Early Modern Europe*, eds. Pamela H. Smith and Paula Findlen (New York: Routledge, 2002); Londa Schiebinger, *Plants and Empire: Colonial Bioprospecting in the Atlantic World* (Cambridge, MA: Harvard University Press, 2004); *Colonial Botany: Science, Commerce, and Politics in the Early Modern World*, eds. Claudia Swan and Londa Schiebinger (Philadelphia: University of Pennsylvania Press, 2005).

39. *The Constitutions of the Society of Jesus and their Complementary Norms: A Complete English Translation of the Official Latin Texts* (St. Louis: Institute of Jesuit Sources, 1996).

40. On the importance of "reverence" in the writings of Saint Ignatius see Howard J. Gray, S.J., "Ignatian Spirituality," in As Leaven in the World: Catholic Perspectives on Faith, Vocation, and the Intellectual Life, ed. Thomas M. Landy (Franklin, Wis.: Sheed & Ward, 2001); reprinted in *An Ignatian Spirituality Reader*, ed. George W. Traub (Chicago: Loyola Press, 2008). See also: *A Pilgrim's Journey: The Autobiography of Ignatius of Loyola*, introduction, translation and commentary by Joseph N. Tylenda (Wilmington, Del.: Michael Glazier, 1985); and David L. Fleming, *Draw Me into Your Friendship: A Literal Translation and a Contemporary Reading of The Spiritual Exercises* (St. Louis, Mo.: Institute of Jesuit Sources, 1996); and *The Constitutions of the Society of Jesus*, cited.

41. Paul Rule, "The Chinese Rites Controversy: A Long Lasting Controversy in Sino-Western Cultural History," Pacific Rim Report No. 32 (February 2004); www.pacificrim.usfca.edu/research/pacrimreport/pacrimreport32.html .

42. George Minamiki, *The Chinese Rites Controversy: From its Beginning to Modern Times* (Chicago: Loyola University Press, 1985); *The Chinese Rites Controversy: Its History and Meaning*, ed. D. E. Mungello (Nettetal: Steyler Verlag, 1994); Andrew C. Ross, *A Vision Betrayed: The Jesuits in Japan and China, 1542-1742* (Maryknoll, N.Y.: Orbis Books, 1994).

43. Sidney F. Smith, S.J., *The Suppression of the Society of Jesus*, ed. Joseph A. Munitiz (Leominster: Gracewing, [1903] 2004).

44. As the reference above to the ultra-right journal *La Civiltà Cattolica* suggests, the nineteenth-century Jesuits of the post-Napoleonic restoration differed significantly from those in the pre-Suppression Society. Fiercely Ultramontanist and anti-modernist, the restored Society might ironically be seen as being at odds with the order's own pre-Suppression culture. For portraits of the restored Jesuits both actual and fantastical, see John W. Padberg, *Colleges in Controversy; The Jesuit Schools in France from Revival to Suppression, 1815-1880* (Cambridge, MA: Harvard University Press, 1969); Geoffrey Cubitt, *The Jesuit Myth: Conspiracy Theory and Politics in Nineteenth-century France* (Oxford: Clarendon Press; New York: Oxford University Press, 1993); and David I. Kertzer, *The Kidnapping of Edgardo Mortara* (New York: Alfred Knopf, 1997).

45. Sacred Congregation for the Propagation of the Faith, *Acta Apostolicae Sedis* 32-24 (8 December 1939). See Beverly Joan Butcher, "Remembrance, emulation, imagination: The Chinese and Chinese American Catholic ancestor memorial service," Ph.D. Diss., University of Pennsylvania (1 January 1994).

46. Most brilliant and justly famous among these critics would be Blaise Pascal's *Provincial Letters* (1660): oregonstate.edu/instruct/phl302/texts/pascal/letters-contents.html. For the history see Dale K. Van Kley, *The Jansenists and the Expulsion of the Jesuits from France, 1757-1765* (New Haven, CT: Yale University Press, 1975); Van Kley, *The Religious Origins of the French Revolution: From Calvin to the Civil Constitution, 1569-1791* (New Haven, CT: Yale University Press, 1996).

47. Marvin R. O'Connell, *Critics on Trial: An Introduction to the Catholic Modernist Crisis* (Washington, D.C.: Catholic University of America Press, 1994). See also: Gabriel Daly, *Transcendence and Immanence: A Study in Catholic Modernism and Integralism* (Oxford: Clarendon Press; New York: Oxford University Press, 1980); David G. Schultenover, *A View from Rome: On the Eve of the Modernist Crisis* (New York: Fordham University Press, 1993); *Catholicism Contending with Modernity: Roman Catholic Modernism and Anti-modernism in Historical Context*, ed. Darrell Jodock (Cambridge, U.K.; New York: Cambridge University Press, 2000); David G. Schultenover, *The Reception of Pragmatism in France & the Rise of Roman Catholic Modernism, 1890-1914* (Washington, D.C.: Catholic University of America Press, 2009).

48. David G. Schultenover, *George Tyrrell: In Search of Catholicism* (Shepherdstown, WV: Patmos Press, 1981); Nicholas Sagovsky, *On God's Side: A Life of George Tyrrell* (New York: Oxford University Press, 1990).

49. George Tyrrell, *Medievalism; A Reply to Cardinal Mercier* (New York: Longmans, Green, and Co., 1908).

50. George Tyrrell, *Medievalism: A Reply to Cardinal Mercier* (Allen, TX: Christian Classics, 1994).

51. "Lester R. Kurtz, *The Politics of Heresy: The Modernist Crisis in Roman Catholicism* (Berkeley: University of California Press, 1986).

52. Henry Hogarth, *Henri Bremond; The Life and Work of a Devout Humanist* (London: S. P. C. K., 1950); André Blanchet, *Henri Bremond, 1865-1904*, preface by Henri Gouhier and postscript by Père Henri Holstein (Paris: Aubier Montaigne, 1975); Charles Chauvin, *Petite vie de Henri Bremond: 1865-1933* (Paris: Desclée de Brouwer, 2006).

53. Henri Bremond, *Histoire littéraire du sentiment religieux en France: depuis la fin des guerres de religion jusqu'à nos jours*, new expanded edition, under the direction of François Tremolières, 5 vols. (Grenoble: Jérôme Millon, 2006).

54. For a brief vivid account of the period, see Thomas F. O'Meara, O.P., "Raid on the Dominicans: The Repression of 1954," *America* 170 (1994): 8-16; and also Joseph Komanchak, "The Silencing of John Courtney Murray," *Cristianesimo nella Storia: Saggi in onore di Giuseppe Alberigo*, ed. A. Melloni, D. Menozzi, G. Ruggieri and M. Toschi (Bologna: Il Mulino, 1996) 657-702. John T. McGreevy gives a lively extended account in *Catholicism and American Freedom: A History* (New York: W.W. Norton, 2003). See also the forthcoming book by Robert Nugent, *Silence Speaks: Teilhard de Chardin, Yves Congar, John Courtney Murray, and Thomas Merton* (Mahwah, NJ: Paulist Press, 2011). For recent studies of the Nouvelle théologie movement, see Hans Boersma, *Nouvelle Théologie and Sacramental Ontology: A Return to Mystery* (New York: Oxford University Press, 2009); Jürgen Mettepenningen, *Nouvelle Théologie - New Theology: Inheritor of Modernism, Precursor of Vatican II* (New York: T&T Clark, 2010).

55. Schloesser, "Against Forgetting."

56. John W. O'Malley, *What Happened at Vatican II* (Cambridge, MA: Belknap Press of Harvard University Press, 2008). For Congar, see Joseph Komanchak, "A Hero of Vatican II: Yves Congar," *Commonweal* 122 (1 December 1995) 15-17.

57. Ursula King, *Spirit of Fire: The Life and Vision of Teilhard de Chardin* (Maryknoll, NY: Orbis Books, 1996).

58. For a chronology of these publications, see Schloesser, "Against Forgetting."

59. Nicholas Boyle, "On Earth, as in Heaven." *The Tablet* (9 July 2005). www.thetablet. co.uk/article/1123

60. *Gaudium et Spes* (*The Church in the Modern World*, 7 December 1965) ¶ 5. www.vatican.va/archive/hist_councils/ii_vatican_council/documents/vat-ii_ cons_19651207_gaudium-et-spes_en.html.

61. The bibliographical evidence for this is vast and rapidly expanding. Thankfully, a sizable amount has been collated in a recent collection of articles comprising the "*AHR Forum: Transnational Sexualities*," *The American Historical Review*, 114/5 (December 2009) 1250-1353. See also the endnote below on "biopolitics" and "biopower."

62. Although this lecture was given a year and a half before Cardinal Levada was interviewed by the Belgian newspaper *Mondiaal Nieuws* (published 14 February 2007), his observation is worth noting here: "the magisterium is usually far behind on the evolution of moral challenges." For English summary see *Mondiaal Nieuws*, "Cardinal William Levada: Neoliberalism is not Compatible with Catholic Social Teaching," at www.mo.be/index.%20php?id=61&tx_uwnews_pi2[art_id]=17590.

63. Reinhart Koselleck, *Futures Past: On the Semantics of Historical Time*, tr. Keith Tribe (Cambridge, MA: MIT Press, 1985).

64. On cultural trauma see Schloesser, *Jazz Age Catholicism*, especially 10, 330n31.

65. See especially Arthur G. Neal, *National Trauma and Collective Memory: Extraordinary Events in the American Experience*, 2nd ed. (Armonk, NY: 2005). This edition contains a newly added chapter on 11 September 2001 and its cultural effects.

66. The coverage has been archived: www.boston.com/globe/spotlight/abuse/.

67. The coverage has been archived: www.boston.com/news/specials/gay_marriage/.

68. The timeline has been archived: news.bbc.co.uk/2/hi/americas/4358877.stm.

69. Susan Dunn, *Sister Revolutions: French Lightning, American Light* (New York: Faber and Faber, 1999).

70. "Memorandum by MCC Staff on Erroneous Testimony on Catholic Teaching at April 28 Hearing in the Massachusetts Legislature on H. 3190, the Marriage Affirmation & Protection Amendment," 2 June 2003. www.macathconf.org/03_memo_ on_erroneous_testimony_4.htm.

71. The wording of *The Catholic Catechism* implicitly leaves room open for "just discrimination": "The number of men and women who have deep-seated homosexual tendencies is not negligible. This inclination, which is objectively disordered, constitutes for most of them a trial. They must be accepted with respect, compassion, and sensitivity. Every sign of unjust discrimination in their regard should be avoided." (¶ 2358) www.vatican.va/archive/catechism/p3s2c2a6.htm.

72. "Spain Legalizes Same-Sex Marriage," *The New York Times* (30 June 2005); "Spain Legalizes Same-Sex Marriage. Prime Minister Makes Unexpected Speech Backing Law Termed 'Unjust' by Church," *The Washington Post* (1 July 2005).

73. i.e., "Memorandum by MCC Staff," 2 June 2003: www.macathconf.org/03_memo_on_erroneous_testimony_4.htm.

74. Alan Ziajka, *Legacy & Promise: 150 Years of Jesuit Education at the University of San Francisco* (San Francisco: USF Office of Publications, 2005) 391-2.

75. See, for example, *The New York Times*: "Autopsy on the Schiavo Tragedy" (16 June 2005) www.nytimes.com/2005/06/16/opinion/16thu3.html.

76. Betty Clermont provides some historical perspective for these events in *The Neo-Catholics: Implementing Christian Nationalism in America* (Atlanta, GA: Clarity Press, 2009). It is only a first yet important step in sorting out what will undoubtedly be seen in the future as an enormously confusing decade

77. As I revise this in August 2010 with the perspective of five years, I would prefer to use the terms "biopower" and "biopolitics." They appeal to me more than "sexuality," "gender," "reproduction," and "bioethics" because they unify issues surrounding human interactions with "life" --- *bios* --- on the planetary as well as individual levels. Today's most urgent emerging "life" questions are "environmental" questions, i.e., about the very possibility of future life on earth. But even here, as Krista Tippett has recently observed, our emerging awareness transcends more limited categories like "sexuality" and "ecology": "It's been striking how, across the past few years, the environment has found its way inside my guests' reflections on every subject, as they say, under the sun. And we do need fresh vocabulary and expansive modes of reflection on this subject that, we've come to realize, is not just about ecology but the whole picture of human life and lifestyle." speakingoffaith. publicradio.org/programs/2010/moral-math/kristasjournal.shtml. Perhaps Pope Benedict XVI will indeed be remembered as a "green" Pope. See Woodeene Koenig-Bricker, *Ten Commandments for the Environment: Pope Benedict XVI Speaks Out for Creation and Justice* (Notre Dame, IN: Ave Maria Press, 2009).
For the origins of these "biopower" and "biopolitics," see Michel Foucault, "Right of Death and Power over Life," in Paul Rabinow, ed., *The Foucault Reader* (New York: Pantheon Books, 1988), 258-272; Foucault, "The Birth of Biopolitics," in *Ethics, Subjectivity and Truth: Essential Works of Foucault*, vol. 1, eds. P. Rabinow and J.D. Faubion (New York: New Press, 1997), 73-79; Foucault, Lecture 11 (17 March 1976) in *Society Must be Defended: Lectures at the Collège de France, 1975-76*, eds. M. Bertani, A. Fontana, F. Ewald, and D. Macey (New York: Picador, 2003), 239-264. For an instructive overview, see Paul Rabinow and Nikolas Rose, "Biopower Today," *BioSocieties* 1/ 2 (2006): 195-217. For a vision of the future, see Nikolas Rose, *The Politics of Life Itself: Biomedicine, Power, and Subjectivity in the Twenty-first Century* (Princeton: Princeton University Press, 2007). For the thought of Italian political theorist Roberto Esposito, see the special issue edited by Timothy Campbell and entitled "Bios, Immunity, Life: The Thought of Roberto Esposito," *Diacritics* 36/2 (Summer 2006); and Esposito, *Bíos: Biopolitics and Philosophy*, translated and with an introduction by Timothy Campbell (Minneapolis: University of Minnesota Press, 2008). I am grateful to Andrea Vicini, S.J., for directing me to Esposito's work.

78. Charles C. Mann, "The Coming Death Shortage," *Atlantic* (May 2005). www.the-atlantic.com/magazine/archive/2005/05/the-coming-death-shortage/4105/.

79. The Cardinal continued: "The idea of natural law presupposed a concept of 'nature' in which nature and reason overlap, since nature itself is rational. With the victory of the theory of evolution this view of nature has capsized: nowadays we think that nature as such is not rational. . . ." Cardinal Joseph Ratzinger, "That which Holds the World Together: The Prepolitical Moral Foundations of a Free State," a talk given at the Catholic Academy of Bavaria in January 2004, reprinted in his *Europe Today and Tomorrow: Addressing the Fundamental Issues* (San Francisco, CA: Ignatius Press, 2007), 75-76. Quoted in Aidan O'Neill, "Roman Catholicism and the Temptation of *Shari'a*," *Common* Knowledge 15/2 (Spring 2009): 269-315, at 272.

80. www.time.com/time/magazine/article/0,9171,752737,00.html.

81. For background on birth control in late-modern Catholic thought, see Leslie Woodcock Tentler, *Catholics and Contraception: An American History* (Ithaca: Cornell University Press, 2004); Claude Langlois, *Le crime d'Onan: le discours catholique sur la limitation des naissances, 1816-1930* (Paris: Belles lettres, 2005). For Catholicism and "The Social Problem," see Owen Chadwick, *The Secularization of the European Mind in the Nineteenth Century* (New York: Cambridge University Press, 1975); Roger Aubert et al., *The Church in the Industrial Age* (New York: Crossroad, 1981); and Aubert, *Catholic Social Teaching: An Historical Perspective*, ed. David A. Boileau (Milwaukee: Marquette University Press, 2003).

82. Elaine Tyler May, *Homeward Bound: American Families in the Cold War Era*, fully revised and updated 20th anniversary ed. with a new post 9/11 epilogue (New York, NY: Basic Books, 2008).

83. The bibliography on eugenics is large and growing. See for example: Daniel Kevles, *In the Name of Eugenics: Genetics and the Uses of Human Heredity* (New York: Knopf, 1985); Wendy Kline, *Building a Better Race: Gender, Sexuality, and Eugenics from the Turn of the Century to the Baby Boom* (Berkeley: University of California Press, 2001); Elof Axel Carlson, *The Unfit: A History of a Bad Idea* (Cold Spring Harbor, N.Y.: Cold Spring Harbor Laboratory Press, 2001); Nancy Ordover, *American Eugenics: Race, Queer Anatomy, and the Science of Nationalism* (Minneapolis: University of Minnesota Press, 2003); Edwin Black, *War Against the Weak: Eugenics and America's Campaign to Create a Master Race* (New York: Four Walls Eight Windows, 2003); Christine Rose, *Preaching Eugenics: Religious Leaders and the American Eugenics Movement* (New York: Oxford University Press, 2004).

84. www.eugenicsarchive.org/html/eugenics/static/themes/39.html.

85. Peggy Pasco, *What Comes Naturally: Miscegenation Law and the Making of Race in America* (New York: Oxford University Press, 2009).

86. Stefan Kühl, *The Nazi Connection: Eugenics, American Racism, and German National Socialism* (New York: Oxford University Press, 1994); Dagmar Herzog, *Sex after Fascism: Memory and Morality in Twentieth-century Germany* (Princeton, NJ: Princeton University Press, 2005).

87. "But there are many today who maintain that the increase in world population, or at least the population increase in some countries, must be radically curbed by every means possible and by any kind of intervention on the part of public authority. In view of this contention, the council urges everyone to guard against solutions, whether publicly or privately supported, or at times even imposed, which are contrary to the moral law.... Men should discreetly be informed, furthermore, of scientific advances in exploring methods whereby spouses can be helped in

regulating the number of their children and whose safeness has been well proven and whose harmony with the moral order has been ascertained." *Gaudium et spes*, ¶ 87. www.vatican.va/archive/hist_councils/ii_vatican_council/documents/vat-ii_cons_19651207_gaudium-et-spes_en.html.

88. However, shortly after this lecture was delivered, a volume was published in which moral theologian Lisa Sowle Cahill analyzes John Paul II's encyclical *Familiaris Consortio* (On the Role of the Christian Family in the Modern World, 22 November 1981) as a document within the tradition of "Catholic Social Teaching." See *Modern Catholic Social Teaching: Commentaries and Interpretations*, ed. Kenneth R. Himes, assoc. eds. Lisa Sowle Cahill et al. (Washington, D.C.: Georgetown University Press, 2005).

89. Just months following this lecture, this precise scenario played out when Boston College invited Secretary of State Condoleezza Rice to receive an honorary doctorate. See for example: "Invitation to Rice debated at BC. Honorary degree draws objections," *The Boston Globe* (3 May 2006) www.boston.com/news/local/massachusetts/articles/2006/05/03/invitation_to_rice_debated_at_bc_honorary_degree_draws_objections/ ; "Big Sham on Campus. Catholicism and academic freedom," *National Review Online* (10 May 2006) article.nationalreview.com/279485/big-sham-on-campus/jonah-goldberg ; and George Weigel's syndicated column, "The Boston College Follies. The Catholic difference" (7 July 2006) www.dioceseofmarquette.org/upcarticle.asp?upcID=821.

90. The quip originated in a telephone conversation between Garry Wills and William F. Buckley and ended up on the gossip page (77) of *National Review* (12 August 1961).

91. *Gaudium et spes*, ¶ 21. www.vatican.va/archive/hist_councils/ii_vatican_council/documents/vat-ii_cons_19651207_gaudium-et-spes_en.html.

Foundations for a National Ethical Discussion about Iraq

Most Rev. Robert W. McElroy

Auxiliary Bishop of San Francisco. Most Rev. Robert W. McElroy served as Lo Schiavo Chair in Catholic Studies and Social Thought at USF in 2008. He was appointed Auxiliary Bishop in 2010.

CATHOLIC SOCIAL CONCERNS LECTURE SERIES I February 1, 2008

N ext month we will begin the sixth year of our war in Iraq, establishing Iraq alongside Vietnam as the longest wars in American history. If this is a sobering milestone for Americans, it is a much more monumental and tragic one for the people of Iraq, who have seen their society roiled by constantly shifting waves of progress and disappointment over these past five years, which leave them no more confident of achieving a secure, stable and free Iraq today than they were two or three or four or five years ago. In those five years more than one hundred thousand Iraqi civilians and four thousand coalition soldiers have died.

The war lurches on, and yet the American national debate on Iraq abates. The United States (U.S.) has come to the conclusion that another year of fighting in Iraq is inevitable. Acquiescence is the order of the day, dictated either by a conviction that the surge is a sign of the broader success that is looming up ahead or the contrasting belief that a new administration will create a pathway to extricate the United States from an unending commitment that its military force structure, and ultimately its political will, cannot sustain.

It hardly seems the moment to begin a fundamental reexamination of the ethics of America's continued commitment to fight in Iraq. But this is precisely the moment when those religious, educational and cultural communities committed to wrestling with issues of war and peace in American society should undertake a new level of reflection and debate about the continuation of the American military effort in Iraq. For if the surge turns out to be, like many of its predecessor harbingers of success in Iraq, merely a respite in the cycle of hope and disappointment, which has characterized the Iraqi conflict, then there will be a renewed and volatile debate within the United States about America's moral obligations in Iraq. It is vital that this debate be framed not by the sound-bites and partisan warfare that masquerade as political discussion in America, but rather by an ethics that values every human life equally, that views war as a last resort, that recognizes the power of evil in the world and that respects both America's democratic impulse and the vastness and limits of American power.

This will require providing a framework and vocabulary for identifying the issues at stake in Iraq and the moral reasoning necessary to work through the complex and countervailing ethical imperatives, which will have to be weighed one against another in determining a future course of action for the

United States. For the Catholic community, contributing to this public, ethical debate on Iraq will require drawing upon the two counterpoised traditions of Catholic teaching on war and peace. The first of these traditions is the deep suspicion of any recourse to war, which has flowed from the pacifism of the early Church, up to the writings of the modern popes. The second of these traditions is assertion of the just-war tradition in which war can be legitimate and even obligatory, at times.

In early Christianity, pacifism dominated the theological and pastoral life of the Church. Writers could not comprehend how the Jesus who counseled true love of enemies could ever sanction the systematic taking of human life endemic to war. After all, how could the parable of the Good Samaritan, which required strenuous love of the stranger, ever be reconciled with the wholesale slaughter intrinsic to war? How indeed? This was the question that Saint Augustine confronted in the fifth century when, as bishop of Hippo in North Africa, he was the leader of a Christian culture facing the onslaught of the barbarians. Augustine read the same Gospels as the early Fathers of the Church who formed the pacifist tradition, but came to a radically different conclusion about the Gospels' reconcilability with war. As Paul Ramsey, the great Protestant theologian, has noted, Augustine turned the parable of the Good Samaritan on its head. What if the Good Samaritan had been coming down the road twenty minutes earlier, while the man by the side of the road was being beaten? What then would have been the obligation of the Samaritan filled with love for his neighbor? That obligation, Augustine concluded, would have been to intervene with force if necessary to drive off the robbers. So too, the use of force in war was necessary at times to defend the lives and fundamental human rights of peoples who were being victimized.

From this assertion that the call to love not only tolerates a recourse to war, but at times demands it, Augustine fashioned what came to be the just war teaching on the ethics of warfare that has been refined over fifteen centuries and now stands as the central ethical framework for evaluating the ethics of war in Western culture. Essentially, the just-war tradition consists of the *ius ad bellum* (the conditions that need to be present before a nation can morally resort to war) and the *ius in bello* (the limits placed upon actions even in a morally legitimate war).

Under the *ius ad bellum*, there are seven conditions that must be clearly and simultaneously fulfilled before a decision is made to go to war: First, there must be a just cause rooted in the defense of a nation or community against lasting, grave and certain attack; second, a nation must have a right intention in going to war, namely the intention to redress the grave wrong, which has been wrought or is threatened; third, war must be a last resort, i.e. all other realistic avenues for redress must have been exhausted before there is a decision to go to war; fourth, there must be serious prospects of success in a contemplated war; fifth, the war must be proportional; sixth, the war must not produce evils graver than the evil that will be eliminated; finally, a war must be declared by the competent national authority. The *ius in bello*, which governs conduct during war, traditionally treats solely questions of means. It consists of two requirements: the prohibition of the direct targeting of non-combatants and the requirement that every act of war should be weighed to insure that the evils unleashed by that act do not outweigh good achieved by the act.

Taken together, the elements of the *ius ad bellum* and the *ius in bello* are meant to embody three countervailing convictions about the moral realities of warfare: 1) War is an enormously evil element of human existence which is all too alluring for human societies; 2) in very limited circumstances, war constitutes a morally legitimate and even obligatory avenue for the defense of the most fundamental rights of nations and peoples; and 3) even when war is morally legitimate, it must be fought under strict constraints.

The just-war tradition has reflected the fundamental Catholic position on warfare for almost fifteen centuries, but, during the past fifty years, enormous changes in the nature of warfare have led the Church to dramatically refine its teaching on the moral legitimacy of war. The invention of strategic bombing has transformed the battlefield, leading to the chilling reality that whole nations are targets of modern weaponry, tactics and strategy. Weapons of mass destruction portend suffering unimaginable in scale and scope, and also the very real threat that, for the first time in its history, humanity possesses weapons capable of ending its own existence. Finally, the proliferation of such weapons necessitates the sobering calculation that the next recourse to war may easily involve nuclear powers in conflict with one another.

Against this backdrop, Catholic moral teaching has dramatically strengthened its presumption against war. From *Pacem in Terris'* assertion in 1962 that "it is hardly possible to imagine that in an atomic era, war could be used as an instrument of justice," to Paul VI's clarion call "No more war, war never again," to Benedict XVI's questioning whether "amidst the current destructiveness of war it is even licit to admit of the possibility of a just war," the popes of the modern era have narrowed the pathway for legitimate recourse to war. Specifically, Catholic teaching has strengthened the obligation on nations to exhaust every alternative to war; has called for increased scrutiny of the intentions of any nation that goes to war without the sanction of international authority; and has emphasized the moral obligation of all nations, especially those with the greatest armaments, to reduce stockpiles of nuclear, chemical and biological weapons with the hopes of ultimately eliminating them entirely. Given this development of doctrine in the Catholic teaching on war and peace, what perspective can Catholic theology bring to the discussion of American policy in Iraq? Specifically, what clarity and insight can Catholic teaching bring to the debate, which lies before us about whether America should continue its commitment to the war in Iraq or withdraw militarily?

The *Post Bellum*

Recent ecclesial, philosophical and international legal authorities have proposed that there exists a third element of the just war ethic which complements the *ius ad bellum* and the *ius in bello*: namely the *ius post bellum*. For many Catholic thinkers, ranging from Kenneth Himes to Louis Iasello to George Weigel, the answer to the above question about Iraq can be found in the *ius post bellum*, which is a significant development in the just-war tradition as it touches upon the obligations of nations that are victorious in war. This new doctrinal trajectory, which has occurred both within Catholic moral theology and international law, asserts that the questions of moral obligation after a war has ended have come to occupy such importance that any just war ethic must include, as a prominent feature, a specification of the moral obligations of victors toward vanquished nations.

The Church has envisioned the goal of this *ius post bellum* as broad and penetrating, namely the obligation "to achieve quickly and effectively the establishment of a just and lasting peace, which is the only admissible goal for the use of force." Concretely, architects of the *ius post bellum* propose four major elements for action by the victors in war. The first is action designed to guarantee the safety and security of the people of the defeated nation. This entails restoring order, reestablishing effective police functions, if they have been disrupted, and maintaining an equitable system of justice, which is not run to advance either local elites or the interests of the victor. The second obligation of victors is restoration, the initial reconstruction of civil society and the nation. This restorative obligation involves both material and social elements: The reconstruction of infrastructure necessary for the operation of the defeated nation's economy and national life, as well as the nurturing of the social and political institutions which are vital to the future functioning of the vanquished state and people. The third obligation of the victorious nation under is to design all of the elements of its occupation so that they contribute toward the earliest possible end of occupation consistent with the ongoing well being of the defeated nation. And the final element of the *ius post bellum* is a continuing provenance for the defeated nation, which includes, at minimum, a role in deterring other enemies from attacking the vanquished state even after occupation has ended.

This elaboration of the just-war tradition to include a specific *ius post bellum* is a productive refinement of the tradition. But does the *ius post bellum* constitute the appropriate framework for evaluating America's current military obligations in Iraq? Writers like Himes, Iasello and Weigel have concluded that it does, and these thinkers suggest that, when the United States conquered Baghdad in 2003, it inherited all of the obligations of a victorious party. Accordingly, those obligations form the lens through which the current debate on Iraq should be conducted.

But underlying this argument that the *ius post bellum* should be the starting point for analyzing America's current ethical obligations in Iraq is the tacit assertion that the war in Iraq ended in May of 2003. This ethical equivalent of flying a *Mission Accomplished* banner does such distortion to the realities of the past five years that it cannot serve as the foundation for an incisive national, ethical discussion about our obligations in Iraq. The Iraq war did not end in 2003. It did not end in 2004. It did not end in 2006. And it has not ended, even today. What ended in 2003 was the war that the United States wanted to fight. The war we find ourselves engaged in now is the war we did not want to fight, but it is the war we should have anticipated when we first entered Iraq: a war of religious, social and political complexity in which military victory is improbable, even by the greatest power the world has ever known. Victory is improbable because true victory must be political, social and religious in nature and, ultimately, can only emerge from the Iraqi people themselves.

The *ius post bellum* is a substantive and enormously helpful addition to the traditional delineation of the just-war tradition because it specifies the obligations of a victor to build a rightly ordered peace after war has ended. But it cannot be the starting point for America's reflection upon its continuing military commitment to the war in Iraq on two counts: This war is not over, and it is far from clear that America will be the victor.

Renewing the *Ius in Bello*

If the *ius post bellum* cannot provide a sound starting point for charting our nation's future course in Iraq, then what framework can serve as the foundation for a productive national debate on this searing issue? Such a framework will have to fulfill several specific requirements: First, it will have to recognize the fact that the United States is currently involved in a complex, deeply rooted and multi-front war; Second, a valid ethical framework must reflect an abiding commitment to the defense of human rights, especially the defense of human life and freedom; Third, this framework must testify to the suspicion toward war, which is at the heart of the Catholic ethical tradition, especially in the modern age. Fourth, such a framework must recognize the additional moral obligation that the U.S. now owes to the Iraqi people as a result of past American actions.

Such a moral framework lies latent within the just war tradition, but it is necessary to deepen that tradition in order to bring it to bear on Iraq. The just-war tradition demands, in the *ius ad bellum*, that a robust set of substantive conditions be fulfilled before legitimate recourse to war can be undertaken. These conditions touch upon questions of goals, intentionality, context, proportionality and societal and international approbation. Yet once a war is launched, the governing principles of the just-war tradition collapse to the two traditional elements of the *ius in bello*: noncombatant immunity and proportionality of individual acts. Both of these criteria concern means, not ends. Certainly it cannot be the intention of any moral tradition, which seeks to morally guide warfare, that once war is launched the only germane moral questions are those of means. Such a position is to assert that once a war is launched, it is placed on a moral autopilot, which assumes the deeper questions of war have been answered for a particular conflict once and for all.

But much of the horror and complexity of war lies in the fact that it is a dynamic reality, and the dynamism of the conditions on the ground in Iraq form the most vexing challenges posed to America's continuing military commitment there. For this reason, the current formulation of the *ius in bello* must be expanded to include both questions of goals and means, questions of proportionality and context. Specifically, the requirements of the *ius ad bellum* must be added to the *ius in bello* to signify that the moral legitimation of the resort to force in war is not a one-time event, but a legitimation that must be revisited periodically in any protracted conflict. Such an expanded *ius in bello* constitutes a comprehensive ethic of war termination to be utilized in assessing the moral obligations of nations who find themselves involved in a war with no sign of conclusion. As such, it provides the most compelling foundation for the current American debate on the war in Iraq because it asks the question: Does the American military intervention in Iraq today meet the substantive *and* the means tests posed by the just war tradition?

Just Cause

The first of those tests is that of just cause. Already, America is divided by a debate over whether the cause that lay behind the decision to invade Iraq was truly just. This debate is intensified by the fact that the just cause cited for the invasion of Iraq was in fact a jumble of differing causes that ranged from defending the world against Iraq's imminent threat of weapons of mass destruction, to the imperative to depose a despotic regime, to the desire to transform the Middle East into a democratic haven, to the necessity of drawing a line in the sand against international terrorism in Iraq. The current debate on the justice of the cause that supports remaining in Iraq cannot countenance such a jumbled just cause. Moreover, several of the justifications routinely offered for remaining in Iraq must be rejected out of hand as morally insufficient to constitute a just cause under the tradition's reasoning.

To say that America must remain in Iraq because withdrawal would weaken the United States in the eyes of the world at a dangerous moment in history does not qualify as a just cause. Reputational considerations cannot justify going to war or remaining at war in the just-war tradition.

To say that America must sustain a united Iraq as a counterweight to Iran and other hostile powers is not a just cause. War cannot be justly waged to prop up chess pieces in the international system.

To say that we must stay in Iraq because to leave is to dishonor the sacrifices of the courageous men and women who have died is not a just cause. The human costs of Iraq, those killed and wounded Americans, Iraqis and allies, constitute the most searing and tragic consequences of this war. But lives already lost or ruined cannot justify a cause that is not already just, and future lives cannot be put at risk in a war that is being waged for, what always was or has come to be, an insufficient cause.

To cite slogans, like democracy or freedom, in the midst of a protracted war is not a just cause. In this war, it is clear that the concrete realizations of the notions of democracy and freedom look different to Kurds, Shiites and Sunnis, and, very different still, to the Americans fighting there.

The only just cause, which can be invoked at the present moment to justify America's continuing military action in Iraq, lies in promoting the safety and well being of the Iraqi people who have suffered so much, especially in promoting their safety from the wholesale violence of sectarian fighting. In pointing to this specific cause as central to the moral legitimacy of combat in Iraq, an expanded *ius in bello* shares common cause with those evaluating America's continuing commitment to the war in Iraq through the prism of the *ius postbellum*. The defense of the human rights, security and freedom of the people of Iraq is a truly just cause, in just-war.

Right Intention

The just-war tradition is clear in its demand that a nation engaging in war must have, as its central intention, the service of the just cause that underlies their path to war. How, then, is one to assess the intention of the United States in Iraq today? In part, we are there to avoid the specter of defeat. In part we are there to project American power in the Middle East and to prevent a power vacuum from forming in the region. In part, we are there to nation-build. In part, we are still fighting in Iraq as a counterpoise to Iran. In part, we are there because oil makes the Middle East important. In part, we continue to be in Iraq to avoid a bloodbath.

If we stand back and compare our commitment to Iraq with our commitment to places like Darfur, can we assert that our commitment in Iraq reflects a humanitarian impulse to defend victims of violence and oppression more than it reflects the strategic interests of our nation? Just war analysis says that if our intentions speak as much to interest as they do to defending the rights of those who have been victimized, then making war is morally unacceptable.

It might seem that this criterion of right intention is an idealistic Kantian formula, concerned more with matters of conscience than real world ethics; but, in fact, this obligation is a hard-headed moral construct designed to safeguard against three grave consequences, which can easily flow from a lack of right intention. The first consequence is the tendency for powerful nations to instrumentalize other countries in war for their own ends. When one analyzes America's desire to fight in Iraq as a test case for democratizing the Middle East, or as a pivotal fight in the wider war against terror, or as critical to maintaining stability in the region, one discerns a commitment rooted more in American objectives, rather than a desire directed towards the safety and well being of the Iraqi people. Iraq became a means, rather than an end.

Similarly, America's mixed motivations give rise to a second harmful effect of an absent right intention: all parties to the conflict are forced to operate out of suspicions about U.S. goals and roles. Success in Iraq is critically dependent upon the willingness and ability of all major actors, Sunnis, Kurds, Shiites and Americans, to work in concert for a unified and equitable nation-state. This success has been undermined by the inability of the Iraqi people to rely upon America's commitment to the Iraqi people as truly central in the U.S. role as liberator-occupier-safeguard. At this juncture, perhaps more than ever before, it is essential that the various Iraqi factions trust the United States as a neutral guarantor of security. The influential role that American interest-based motivations have played and continue to play in determining U.S. conduct during the war makes this trust much harder to obtain.

The final consequence that the criterion of right intention helps to preclude is the tendency of nations to use a truly just cause as an excuse for waging an interest-based and interest-calibrated war. It should be extremely troubling to us that the professed just cause for our intervention in Iraq has shifted so many times during the past five years. Can we really assert that there is a central intention to our continuing military presence in Iraq today, much less that it is the just cause of protecting the Iraqi people rather than injury to U.S. standing and interests? It is difficult to escape the terrible conclusion that America's long intervention in Iraq is best characterized as ongoing war in search of a just cause, rather than as a just cause in search of redress through war.

Last Resort

The just-war tradition requires that war must be the last recourse of a nation seeking justice in the world. In a protracted war this entails two obligations: First, all parties must be constantly vigilant for any pathway to peace that might develop; second, all parties must be open to reducing the concrete aims of the war, even in a just cause. These obligations challenge the enormous inertia of war, which focuses on the realization of specific goals and often regards proposals to sacrifice any one of them as undermining the war effort. A *ius in bello* that considers both ends and means demands that every opportunity for peace should be pursued, and that alternative pathways to justice must be pursued even in a just war and even when such pathways might lead to the sacrifice of some just objectives.

There has been no such sustained search for peace by America in its intervention in Iraq. Alternatives to war were not exhausted before war began, and they are not being exhaustively pursued now. Options, such as a radical federalization of Iraq or an outright partition, are either critiqued unremittingly or rejected outright, largely, one suspects, because they contradict America's strategic vision for the region, which necessitates a unified Iraq. America must ardently pursue a constellation of alterative options for peace, and those options must include options that sacrifice substantive elements of its current war aims. A nation seeking true justice in the world should be known for its energy in pursuing alternative pathways to peace, not for its single-minded pursuit of the aims that led to war.

Approval by Competent Authority

The just-war tradition requires that a decision to use military force in war should have the approval of the competent governmental authority. An expanded *ius in bello* requires this approval at every stage of the war's duration. This raises an important constitutional question and a related moral question. The constitutional question arises from the fact that the Constitution gives Congress the power to declare war and the power to approve all war spending, but it gives to the President the authority to conduct wars. The history of the United States is replete with disputes about how these powers are to be exercised in time of warfare, and another round of separation of powers cases may well yet emerge from the war in Iraq.

But our focus here today is not the question of constitutionality, but of morality. As a moral concept and in just-war tradition, what does the mandate for the approval of competent authority mean in the midst of a protracted war? Certainly, it must mean that the decision to sustain war, one of the gravest decisions that any nation makes, should have a continuing level of approbation throughout society and the government. Certainly, it cannot mean that war may be waged by threat of veto and filibuster, the use of the parliamentary instruments of the minority, as the only bulwark continuing the approval of war by the competent authority. In both of the protracted, unresolved wars in American history, Korea and Vietnam, the presidents who began the wars refused to bring them to an end, even long after they had lost popular support and the support of Congress. Presidents will not end their own wars in failure; it is left to their successors. Constitutionally, this may be acceptable, but morally it is not. It is difficult to understand how one can make the moral case, with two-thirds of the American people and the majority of Congress in favor of ending the war in Iraq, that there still exists the moral approbation of competent authority, which the just-war tradition envisions, even if the president remains committed to the war.

Proportionality

The criterion of proportionality is traditionally tested by asking a narrow question: Will the good, likely to be achieved by a particular war, outweigh the harm? If advocates for American military action in Iraq were merely proposing that it is morally permissible for the U.S. to continue fighting in Iraq, then the criterion of proportionality would be confined to this important and intricate, but narrow question. But advocates of a continuing American military commitment to Iraq are not proposing that such a continuation is permissible; they are proposing that such a continuation is obligatory, obligatory to advance the order of justice in the world. In such a discussion, the question of proportionality is quite broad, because the nation seeking justice in the world confronts a commitment to a particular conflict not as an isolated choice, but as one in a constellation of choices about how to advance justice in the world. Thus proportionality is not a binary question but a comparative one. As it pertains to the issue of America's obligations to continue extensive combat operations in Iraq at the present moment, the question of proportionality is this: Does the expenditure of resources in Iraq, necessitated by an ongoing American military commitment, represent the best way that those resources can be utilized to advance the order of justice in the world?

The first step in answering this question lies in identifying what the United States will obtain by continuing its military commitment. The answer? It is not a free and stable Iraq. It is not peace. It is not any other certainty of outcome. Rather, the answer is the opportunity to see if sustained military action will promote better outcomes for the people of Iraq. That's it. There are reasonable arguments that continued military action might bring about stability in the country, which can allow Iraq's factionalized society to coalesce, or at least to come to a peaceful accommodation. There are equally reasonable arguments that America's continued military presence decreases the pressure for Iraq's conflicting factions to come to agreement about the nation's future. There are very strong arguments that an ongoing American combat presence is essential to preventing wholesale massacres after the United States leaves. There are also strong arguments that continued American military action only masks the cauldron of violent Iraqi factionalism, which will erupt whenever America ceases to station a hundred thousand fighting men and women to keep the lid on. Thus the objective that the United States will obtain by continuing its military commitment for the next several years is nothing more and nothing less than the opportunity to see if military action will bring about a better Iraq.

President Bush requested two hundred billion dollars in funding for the Iraq war in the 2008 federal budget. Is the expenditure of these funds on the war in Iraq the best way to advance justice in the world? How else might the resources, which will be consumed in Iraq during the next several years, be spent? The United Nations Food and Agricultural Organization estimates that twenty-four billion dollars per year to the poorest nations of the world would be enough additional official development assistance to halve world hunger in fifteen years. What good would this accomplish? Malnutrition is strongly associated with twelve million deaths of children under five in the developing world each year. One hundred fifty million children in developing nations suffer from protein-energy malnutrition. More than eight hundred million people are hungry and undernourished. Halving each of these numbers for the next twenty years would cost less than the cost of the Iraq war for the next two years. What calculus of justice would say that America's obligation to justice in the world is better fulfilled by fighting in Iraq rather than by fighting world hunger? What criterion of proportionality would say that the good to be achieved in Iraq outweighs a radical global drop in the malnutrition that kills millions of children a year?

Conclusion

Even as economic issues threaten to move public discussion of America's commitment to Iraq further offstage, the United States still faces a moment in which it will be forced to confront the question of Iraq policy once and for all. One essential ingredient for productive conversation about the painful options that confront America is a common ethical framework through which to evaluate America's conflicting moral priorities. An expanded *ius in bello*, containing a full-bodied moral analysis of the issues presented in this war, provides the most powerful foundation for a national dialogue that is substantive, incisive and respectful.

In my opinion, such an *ius in bello* reveals a genuine just cause for continuing widespread military operations in Iraq: safeguarding the future of the Iraqi people, especially from the specter of wholesale killings. If all that the just-war tradition required for waging war were a just cause, then the ethical legitimacy of remaining in Iraq would be secure. But just-war thinking has never been about any single element of moral analysis. American military commitment to war in Iraq falls short of meeting all of the other ethical requirements of the just-war tradition. Our mixed intentions do not constitute the clear right intention demanded by just-war thinking, and these mixed American intentions have greatly hobbled the war effort, especially in the minds of the Iraqi people. The just-war criterion of last resort demands that a nation constantly pursue all other non-combat means of achieving justice; the American intervention in Iraq is and has been marked by a profound inattention to alternative pathways. Where just-war thinking demands the approval of competent authority to wage war, the United States now wages a war, which neither Congress nor the American people wish to continue.

Finally, the United States faces the substantial claim to safeguard the future of the Iraqi people, but is that claim greater than other claims to America's power and treasure? Would, for example, a radical reduction in world hunger save more lives? This question is especially important given that the United States only gains the opportunity to determine if warfare can substantially advance the well being of the Iraqi people. If the best outcome is only a probability, can the U.S. morally justify spending hundreds of billions of dollars and, even more painfully, many American lives? The belief that America should begin a prudently planned military withdrawal from Iraq as soon as possible doesn't rest on an assertion that there is no just cause for remaining there. Rather, it rests upon the conviction of fifteen centuries of just-war thinking that a just cause alone is not sufficient for a decision to wage war. And it rests upon five years of experience, which teach us that the United States does not have the cultural insight, the moral authority, the strategy and tactics and the nation-building skills to guarantee a secure and stable future in Iraq.

Integral Human Development: The Challenge of Caritas in Veritate

Rev. James Stormes, S.J.

Lo Schiavo Chair in Catholic Studies and Social Thought at USF.

URBI ET ORBI LECTURE I November 9, 2009

Thisafternoon I would like to share some of the critical and hopeful points of view in Pope Benedict XVI's Encyclical letter (an encyclical being the highest form of Papal teaching), *Caritas in Veritate* (*Love in Truth*). I would like to do so by focusing on the vision of integral human development it posits. I hope to suggest what Benedict's message could mean for us as a University, both as an encouragement and as a challenge to us. I will start by giving the briefest outline of the tradition, the lineage if you will, that lies behind the Encyclical.

Church teaching has always included reflection on the social world in which the Church finds herself. In 1891, Pope Leo XIII wrote the Encyclical, *On the Condition of Labor*, which addressed the injustices and sufferings of the industrial revolution, and Leo's encyclical began a tradition of Papal, and other Church statements, which we now call Catholic social teaching. Catholic social teaching has been and continues to be addressed to Catholics, although more recently, the Church's teachings have also been addressed to all people of good will. The international dimensions of poverty became an important part of Catholic social teaching with the Second Vatican Council, and particularly with the 1967 Encyclical, *On the Progress of Peoples*, by Pope Paul VI. In *Love in Truth*, promulgated on June 29 of this year, Pope Benedict takes up the concerns raised by Pope Paul VI, describes the progress of the peoples (and lack of it) over the last 40 years, and adds his own analysis of the causes of and remedies for the suffering of humanity. Thus, a lot of what Benedict says restates the tradition, but there are several new emphases in the Encyclical, which I will underline. Pope Benedict's 87-page document ranges widely, moving back and forth from philosophical and theological principles to practical analyses, touching on issues from business models to bioethics, from immigration to media to the environment. Although we cannot summarize it all in today's talk, let me begin by looking at the title, *Love in Truth*.

One of the more interesting and insightful comments on *Love in Truth* comes from the University of Chicago historian, David Nirenbeg. He says, in a review in *The New Republic*, "The fundamental claim that runs through Benedict's Encyclical is that economic exchange requires love; and further, Benedict is asking a basic question about our markets and our societies: can the values they *require to function properly* be produced from within themselves, or must those values come from beyond themselves." Nirenbeg goes on to note, "Nobody is much interested in debating this crucial argument." This I think points to the radical nature of Benedict's contribution to Catholic social thinking, i.e., going to the root of Catholic social teaching, a contribution that I fear could be minimized or glossed over, if only because the word he is using, "caritas," if translated as "love," is overused, and, if translated as "charity," is seen as weak.

Benedict himself notes the term has often been misconstrued and distorted, but the Pope is clear that love is the heart of what it means to be human, as an individual and as a community. Love is not extraordinary saintly virtue, much less romantic feelings; it is the basic human dynamic, the principle and extraordinary force behind the ways we interact with each other, whether we know it or not. It is the heart of the authentic development of every person and society. This is true from the very origins of existence, which is the "astonishing experience of gift (34)" at all levels, whether we are talking about the universe we inherit or the life we are given by our parents or the share in God's own life graced upon us in Christ. Love, which is by definition a gift of self, is the energy and the basis for *relationship*, which Benedict considers the key to understanding our humanity.

This experience of gift, this gratuity, plays itself out in the interdependence that makes our lives possible. We are completely interdependent with others, whose gift to us is not something earned or won but given to us by our world. This is so from the air we breathe to the culture in which we function, from the history of which we are now a part to the practical realities of where our food, clothing and shelter come from. Recognizing this interdependence is part of what makes our humanity *integral*. We each make our small contribution to the mix, but to pretend that that contribution means that we have earned, and therefore own, in some sense, all that has made our lives possible is one of the great illusions of our time.

Love in relationship always moves the human person out of herself, beyond herself, always improving, stretching and transcending herself. It is this most basic characteristic of human life that Benedict calls *development*. Self-development comes about by participation in the development of the world in which we live; it is the human vocation. Thus, for Benedict, love and development are intimately linked because they are both at the heart of the human project, if you will. Love engaging this interdependent humanity in our journey of transcendence, a journey we make together: integral human development.

This emphasis on love at the heart of the Church's social doctrine is one of Benedict's stamps on Catholic social teaching. He integrates it with the concepts emphasized by others: justice, solidarity, liberation, but his focus on love, which began with his first Encyclical, *God Is Love*, is a new perspective.

Now, while we all nod in assent to and appreciation of this picture of a world with love at its core, we probably cannot help rolling our eyes when we hear it. Because this contradicts the view that self-interest is the basic human instinct and drive, a view that "passes through the hearts of each one of us," as the Jesuit

34th General Congregation said. That's who we are and there is nothing to be done about it. Our relationships are at best governed by *trust, yes, but verify*. We grow through self-improvement, and not through "other" improvement.

The fact that we have let ourselves believe this fallacy, and have built much of our lives and society around it, is part of the *truth* that Benedict wants us to understand.

The second reality that Benedict points to, *truth*, is, at least in part, the practical reality, the context for our loving human lives; it is the *locus* of charity [5]. It is the recognition and the reminder that love is *incarnational*. The only presence of God that we have is God as part of our flesh and blood human history. Only if our love is engaged with that reality will it avoid being "mere sentimentality."(2)

And the truth of our recent human history is not pretty.

The forty years since Paul VI's *On the Progress of Peoples* have been disappointing. While there has been economic growth since 1967 and billions of people have been lifted out of misery, particularly in China and India, Benedict points out that in much of the rest of the world "this growth is weighed down by malfunctions and dramatic problems, highlighted even further by the current crisis." (21) The scandal of inequality that Paul VI pointed to is now on the increase, showing that technical progress does not resolved the true issues of human advancement. (22)

The sad irony of this reality is that this is the age of globalization, the age in which the relationships among the human family are much clearer than they have ever been (33), it is played out daily in our media, both positively and negatively. Yet this clarity about our interrelations, our interdependence, has not yielded the kind of progress in human development that Paul VI hoped for. This insight is not only the view of Benedict and Catholic social teaching; many others see the poverty and inequality in our world as a scandal and offense against humanity. The debate is about the causes and appropriate responses.

Since, for Benedict, all human activity is love leading us to human development, the successes and failures of economic human activity are rooted in love or its lack, that is, they have a moral dimension. "The economic sphere is … part and parcel of human activity … and must be structured and governed in an ethical manner." [36] In particular, many "situations of underdevelopment are not due to chance or historical necessity, but are attributable to human responsibility." (17)

Again, this is not unique to Catholic social teaching. One thinks of Peter Singer's example comparing our moral responsibility for a nearby child drowning in a pond with that for a far away child dying of malnutrition. Part of the problem is that we do not see, at least as clearly, the child in Haiti or Ethiopia or India, and so we are not moved to act. Catholic social teaching calls us to see the impoverished and to see the world through their eyes. If we do not attempt to, learn to, see the world from the perspective of the marginalized, we cannot see the whole picture. Not seeing leads us astray with regard to our moral responsibility for each other. (47)

For me, an example of the power and the *uncomfortableness* of seeing the world through the eyes of the marginalized, is Michael Moore's recent movie, *Capitalism: A Love Story*. Obviously his is no more the whole story than is our own comfortable narrative, but sitting in a theater in Oakland with folks who looked, to me, like community organizers and the impoverished with whom they work, I can tell you that Moore's is a view of the world that many people see as more accurate than the Wall Street Journal. For Benedict, the *truth* in which *love* must play itself out includes the staggering and scandalous degree of inequality in human development, due, in part, to blindness to that reality, to a lack of realization and acceptance of our moral obligations towards each other.

But the Pope sees a deeper reason for this human failure, and he returns to it over and over again throughout the Encyclical: The key, for Benedict, is that we fool ourselves into thinking we are self-sufficient. (53) "Sometimes modern man is wrongly convinced that he is the sole author of himself, his life and society." (34) We see how we act in ways that contribute to our own development, but we forget, or refuse to see, the ways that our lives are completely dependent on one another. We misunderstand the gratuity with which we are surrounded and which gives us life. Let me be clear: This is not saying simply that we are greedy or selfish, or even fundamentally self-interested. For Benedict, we have a fundamental misunderstanding about ourselves, which has implications not only at the personal and social levels, but also at the structural level of our decision-making.

In particular, for Benedict, this erroneous sense of self-sufficiency underlies our love affair with technical solutions to problems. (68) We ask about the *How* of a solution instead of the *Why* of the situation. (70) To find technical solutions we limit our reading of the signs, our analysis, to those parts of reality that fit our expertise, ignoring, for example, the moral dimension of that reality, or the perspectives of the impoverished. Benedict gives a variety of examples, from economics, politics, society and culture, to show how pervasive and structural he sees this misunderstanding to be.

Our culture of materialism focuses on what we can control through technology, which then becomes the goal of our activities. Benedict's predecessor, John Paul II, used the term "superdevelopment" for the trap that we, of the wealthy world, find ourselves in: we are driven to get whatever is available instead of what is needed. *Having*, instead of *being* drives us.

While economics is a powerful set of technical tools, Benedict reminds us that the market itself is a relationship (35), not an equation, and the importance of human virtues, such as trust and honesty, in the economy have become obvious. "Development depends on seeing ourselves as a human family, not as a group of subjects who happen to live side by side." (53)

Politically, Benedict points out the power of ideologies, (14) again self-focused and often highly technical, to cut human beings off from each other and provide legitimacy for the most horrible crimes against humanity ever seen. And the fact that religion can and has become ideological and fundamentalist has driven many of our intelligent and caring brothers and sisters to see religion as a horror, not a grace.

Culturally, Benedict points to the tendency of globalization to impose, perhaps softly, but impose nonetheless, one particular culture and set of values on the rest of the world. On the other side, he critiques societies that are incapable or unwilling to learn anything from others. Again, both of these errors are rooted in a sense of self-sufficiency and technical control. (26, 59)

What each of these examples (and other examples that could be given) has in common is that they ultimately offend human dignity and limit human freedom. And, for Benedict, human freedom, indeed liberation, is at the heart of integral human development. (17)

These are some of the critiques made by Benedict in *Caritas In Veritate*; what of the hopes he presents? What would *truth lived in love* look like in the real world? As I briefly enumerate examples of Benedict's alternative vision, I will also try to show where others of good will share that vision. For as Benedict reminds us, the demands of love do not contradict those of reason. (30)

For Benedict, Christian humanism is the driving force, the authentic incentive, of human life. It is a focus on being, not having, a sense of the importance of the spiritual (in a broad sense), the soulful, the fully human, the true fruit of love, if you will. Materialism, both in the narrow sense of consumerism and in the broad philosophical sense, simply does not fulfill us. And, of course, we do not need to look far to find people of other traditions, religious and non-religious, who have discovered this and seek to share it with others. Ironic as it may seem, the *business* of spirituality, where entire sections of bookstores are dedicated to self-help and the spiritualities of exercise and sleep, cooking and fasting, and so on, points to the fact that many in our day agree with Benedict on this point and wish to create a society in which humanism replaces materialism as the driving value.

In spite of the critiques he underlines, Benedict sees globalization as a great opportunity, if it is recognized as a growing worldwide interdependence (33) by which humanity is increasingly interconnected, rather than increasingly alienated by anonymous impersonal forces (42). This fraternity (38) can, for example, make migration a source of wealth production and cultural exchange, instead of a problem. We can move towards steady employment for all, building up the networks of social capital indispensable to the functioning of the international market. (32) The focus on international aid could be on consolidating systems to improve the potential of marginalized economies; we can have redistribution of wealth, not redistribution of poverty (42). In short, we can have a "civilizing of the economy." (38) For Benedict and the tradition he inherits, the causes of underdevelopment are not primarily of the material order; rather, they lie in a lack of solidarity, a solidarity that includes deep reflection by wise people in search of a new humanism, (19) and the provision of social resources most of which are institutional (27) and cultural. (75)

Many economists, experts in development, now focus on the need for a more holistic approach. This approach includes integrating the role of political and social institutions in economic development; it also includes the importance of the local history of conflict, as well as using the tools of behavioral economics, which recognizes and tries to integrate "irrational" human decision-making, which previously would have been considered the realm of psychology.

The best example of what Benedict thinks happens when we let ourselves live love in truth in this civilized economy is that of business activities that "comprise a new composite reality ... an intermediate area ... between profit-based companies and non-profit organizations ... that does not exclude profit, but instead considers it a means for achieving human and social ends." (46) And he roots that idea not only in his description of love-generated activity but also in concrete experience: civil-economy models and economies of communion. Economies of communion refers to an actual functioning network of for-profit companies who utilize profit primarily for solidarity with those in need, as well as reinvestment and values education. Linked to the international Catholic lay movement of spirituality and service, *Focolare*, this network now includes 750 businesses in 65 countries, and it is growing. Many of those involved do not find it contradictory that a for-profit company focuses on solidarity and a wider view of stakeholders (40); instead, they find more incentive in operating this way than in ever-increasing income.

Finally, we've already mentioned Benedict's reminder that the market is fundamentally an encounter between persons. "Without internal forms of ... mutual trust, the market cannot ... fulfill its proper function." And indeed the role of trust and confidence, or its absence, has dominated much of the analysis of the financial breakdown of the last two years. Benedict argues that the market "cannot rely on itself" to guarantee the needed kinds of human relations, but must rely on moral energies beyond itself. (35) Or, as Alan Greenspan (among others) has learned, the market is not always self-correcting.

Turning briefly to the political realm, Benedict's recommendation in this area is perhaps the most often quoted part of the Encyclical: his call for "a true world political authority," an authority whose task is to "secure authentic human development inspired by the values of charity in truth." (67) The concreteness of this proposal and the strong reactions to it underline the real-world implications of Benedict's approach, which, as he notes, has been the consistent approach of Catholic social teaching since Blessed Pope John XXIII, in 1961. With all of its difficulties and failures, the continual commitment of the world community to the United Nations makes clear that this is not simply Benedict's dream but a concrete work in progress. In my own limited experience, there is nowhere that combines idealistic motivation with realistic political dialogue as much as the U.N. I find in it, and Benedict's challenge, a touch of hope.

Just a word about the positive possibilities in the cultural realm, as Benedict sees them: In his words: "Cooperation for development ... offers ... a wonderful opportunity for encounter [his key word] between cultures and peoples." The key is both to "rediscover oft forgotten virtues" and to strengthen the richness provided to all by a "multifaceted pluralism of cultural diversity." (59) At the heart of Benedict's description of the structures of human society is relationship. Given the painful recent history among a number of world cultures, and the much debated clash of civilizations, the effects of relationships not based on authentically human positive regard is clear. The fact that the solution to so many conflicts (in South Africa, in Northern Ireland, etc.) have been found, not so much in military victory, but in hard-won changes in intercultural understanding and agreement, suggests that relationship and dialogue based in love is indeed humanity's final hope.

To sum up: Benedict builds on the tradition of Catholic social teaching, and he adds two particular emphases: First, that love is the driving force in human life, and that integral human development is the living out of love in reality, in truth. Love is the living out of the interdependence that makes the common good of all the good of each, and love shows that solidarity is the surest road to freedom, and loves focuses our energy on those least well off in our society. Second, it is the lack of that connection and an overreliance on our self-sufficiency that has led us to treat each other badly, allowing brothers and sisters to live a life unworthy of our family.

Benedict isn't simply philosophizing or theologizing; he is advocating a holistic approach to strengthening our mutual effort towards integral human development. I would suggest the very style of the Encyclical, with its, sometimes frustrating, jumps from theory to practice and back again, exemplifies the holistic approach he advocates. The worldview presented by Benedict is both idealistic in the best sense, drawing us towards transcendence, and realistic, being carried out even now, if only in ways as small as a mustard seed. Getting it to grow is hard work. Indeed, integral human development is, in Benedict's own words, "an altogether new and creative challenge, one that is certainly vast and complex." (33)

Challenge to the University

Benedict's response to that complexity is, in part, what leads us to challenge ourselves as a university. I see three challenges: First, Benedict calls for "broadening the scope of reason and making it capable of knowing and directing these powerful new forces,"(33) requiring among other things, a "deeper reflection on the meaning of the economy and its goals." (32) This is the first challenge to us, to help understand these complexities, to analyze what Benedict sees as both the inconvenient truth of the failures of development as well the positive and creative options that are possible. I am reminded of my previous work ins advocacy in Washington, D.C., and the many times Catholic and other groups with whom we worked asked for the help of Jesuit Universities in developing the analysis that could guide and strengthen their policy work. Our network is a unique opportunity, which we do not always take advantage of.

Second, Benedict also challenges *how* we go about knowing and analyzing as a university, about the processes we engage in that guide the truths, if you will, that we will find. He finds the illusion of individualism and self-sufficiency in academia as well, a world he shares with us, and he specifically and directly warns us to avoid that danger: "The key to development is a mind capable of thinking ... and grasping the fully human meaning of human activities, within the context of the holistic meaning of the individual's being." (70) He calls not just for knowledge but for wisdom, and reminds us that Paul VI, 40 years ago, blamed underdevelopment on, among other things, "a lack of clear thinking capable of formulating a guiding synthesis, for which a clear vision of all economic, social, cultural and spiritual aspects is required." Perhaps touching even closer to university reality, Benedict continues, "The excessive segmentation of knowledge, the rejection of metaphysics by the human sciences, the difficulties encountered by dialogue between science and theology are damaging not only to the development of knowledge, but also to the development of peoples because these things make it harder to see the integral good of man in its various dimensions." (31)

Here at USF, we share that concern and have made a number of efforts to work together, learning to listen to each other across our disciplines and activities. But we know it is a challenging enterprise. We have all struggled with the tension between mastering our own disciplines and working in an interdisciplinary manner, especially in our research, which depend on the methodologies specific to our disciplines. About a month ago, at this years Western Conversations gathering, ten of us from USF were addressing just this issue with colleagues from other Jesuit universities. The need to develop better structures for working together came out of each one of our groups. And there was a creative reminder and recommendation from one of our speakers. She pointed out that this university shares in an intellectual tradition, the Catholic and Jesuit intellectual tradition, and that tradition can help guide us towards the common focus that we seek. I hope this conversation today is part of that process. Our own Catholic intellectual tradition, broadly understood as *finding God in all things*, as St. Ignatius of Loyola would say, provides a context for this work of a university, our university. In this way the challenge of love in truth is to be more who we are, a university, a community that seeks to integrate all that can be known into the mission of human development.

This challenge is not only about how we deal with each other within the university, complicated as that is. The other side of holistic development, and the knowledge that guides it, is that it includes *all* people. We must continue to reach out beyond ourselves, to make this university consciously and actively engaged in the social whole of which we are a part, in our neighborhood, in the city whose name we bear, as part of the set or family of Jesuit and Ignatian ministries that share our *charism*, our nation, which has such power and responsibility, and our world, our mother earth and the human race on which we depend so deeply and to whom we owe so much respect and care.

Third, and finally, we know that we see our world from a particular perspective, and we know that we have a choice about that perspective. The truth that drives our choice needs to be the same truth that motivates Benedict's Encyclical: too many people still cannot live truly human lives; the scandal of glaring inequalities still faces us; (22) hunger still reaps enormous numbers of victims; (27) and most importantly, many of these "situations of underdevelopment are not due to chance or historical necessity, but are attributable to human responsibility." (17) Paul VI, in *On the Progress of Peoples* said that the key task of educators is to teach their students to love, and in particular, to love those who live in misery. Our choice must be to see the world from the perspective of the impoverished, the marginalized. We seek to see the world through their eyes, to learn from them the realities that we cannot see, and to be guided by that knowledge, not only to solve those problems in a technical sense, as Benedict warns us, but to better face our own impoverishment and vulnerability, the truth about ourselves that only love can make whole.